A Different Way

A human approach to the divine

A Different Way

A human approach to the divine

Roger Payne

CHRISTIAN ALTERNATIVE

Winchester, UK
Washington, USA

First published by Christian Alternative Books, 2015
Christian Alternative Books is an imprint of John Hunt Publishing Ltd.,
Laurel House, Station Approach,
Alresford, Hants, SO24 9JH, UK
office1@jhpbooks.net
www.johnhuntpublishing.com
www.christian-alternative.com

For distributor details and how to order please visit the 'Ordering' section on our website.

ISBN: 978 1 78279 878 1
Library of Congress Control Number: 2014949686

A CIP catalogue record for this book is available from the British Library.

Design: Stuart Davies

Printed in the USA by Edwards Brothers Malloy

CONTENTS

This book is dedicated to my father

Joe Payne (1907-1973)

for whom service to others was his primary
motivation as a Christian

Acknowledgements

I am grateful to all those who in various ways have knowingly or unknowingly contributed to this book. I have made reference to the use of quotations and other material where possible but there are inevitably stories and narratives that are now so embedded in my own sermons and writings that it is no longer possible to identify them. I apologise to any who find material in this book which may have originated in their own writings and which has not been acknowledged.

This book has also been enriched by discussions with members of the Parish of Bushey and others either individually or in House Groups over the years and I am indebted to them. I am particularly grateful to Rev John Churcher, Methodist Minister and former Chair of the Progressive Christianity Network Britain (PCN Britain), who discussed with me a first draft of the book, and to Mike Groushko who gave me valuable advice on the publication process.

The quotations at the head of each chapter are mostly taken from *The Eternal Vision*, an anthology of spiritual quotations compiled by William Sykes. Biblical passages are from the New Revised Standard Version (NRSV) of the Bible unless otherwise stated.

I have not used inclusive language in this book because it invariably becomes clumsy but in most cases references should be to both male and female gender.

Preface

This book is based on the premise that we need to encourage more debate in our churches about the essentials of our faith, and that the starting point for those discussions should be the nature of the human condition.

There is an urgent need for more debate and discussion in our churches because the integrity and credibility of our faith is at risk. Our integrity is at risk because it is not clear that we understand what it is that we profess. Our credibility is at risk because we seem unable to communicate that profession. We need to engage more vigorously with each other about those things that we claim to be so important to us. In particular we need to engage more actively at the intellectual level and to be willing to examine the fundamentals of our faith more critically. Such conversation is rarely encouraged in our churches and in some places it is actively discouraged.

Such discussion must start with a human rather than a divine perspective. There are two reasons for this. First, it is as human beings that we are embodied as persons, it is as human beings that we engage with the world around us and it is as human beings that we form relationships with the rest of the created order. Second, it is as a human being that that which we understand as God was embodied in the form of Jesus of Nazareth, thereby placing humanity at the pinnacle of creation and giving humanity the responsibility for the stewardship of the created order. Despite this, humanity has not been seen positively within the tradition of the Christian Church and the humanity of Jesus has been given much less emphasis than his divinity.

The overall aim of this book is to enlarge our vision of God and to enlarge our understanding of what it might mean to respond to that vision. The title and substance of J B Phillips's 1952 book, *Your God is Too Small,* is a salutary reminder of the urgency of the task.

Introduction

An unexamined life is not worth living.
Socrates

The nature of the problem

The Christian Church is a conservative institution and many of its members are conservative in their attitude to change. This is not surprising as the church has been around for a long time and its changeless nature is for many one of its most attractive features. It provides a sanctuary in a world of turmoil; it provides constancy in a world of change; it provides certainty in a world of doubt. The difficulty is that sanctuary, constancy and certainty are not always in the best interests of individual Christians and of the Christian enterprise as a whole.

The church as a place of sanctuary has been an important part of its function. During times of persecution believers have been able to find sanctuary in monasteries, catacombs and secret places to preserve their way of life from those who would destroy it. Underground churches have sometimes emerged decades after they were thought to be extinct. The Chinese Church is one such example but there are others. The church is also a place of sanctuary for those who wish to take time out from the pressures and routine of daily life and to seek spiritual refreshment. Church people have always been encouraged to make regular retreats and to attend occasional 'quiet days' in the nurture of their spiritual health. Television series like *The Monastery*, *The Convent* and *The Retreat* have encouraged large numbers of other people to spend time in 'a place apart'.

But the church can also be a place of sanctuary for those seeking to separate themselves from the company of those who hold different views. They seek shelter from the plurality of religious discourse. They seek defence against those who practice a different form of churchmanship. They seek protection from what they see as the contamination of heresy. But the message of the Christian faith must be one of engagement with the world of faith in all its rich variety and diversity. To claim the whole truth and to reject alternatives out of hand is to close the door to that engagement.

The constancy of the church has also been seen as one of its strengths for it has preached a steady and continuous message over a period of two millennia. It has provided an anchor for the lives of millions of people who have otherwise been tossed about in the great sea of change. This is particularly true in countries which have suffered the most traumatic changes in recent times. The Russian Orthodox Church survived the rise and fall of the Soviet Union and gave the people hope during decades of oppression despite some unfortunate accommodations with the regime. The church has also resisted the forces of those who would direct it and mould it to their own ends. The Confessing Church in Nazi Germany arose in opposition to government-sponsored efforts to 'Nazify' the German Protestant church and many of its leaders paid the ultimate price for their heroic stand.

But the church has also fought against those who have sought alternative visions of what it means to be a Christian. Roman Catholic, Protestant and Reformed churches have all been guilty of demanding that people 'toe the line' and have mounted vicious campaigns against those they label as heretics. During the Thirty Years War millions were harassed, tortured and killed on all sides because they belonged to the 'wrong' branch of Christianity. The Medieval Cathars of southern France were wiped out because the Roman Catholic Church could not tolerate their divergent views. Even in our own time there are those who fight 'tooth and nail' to protect their version of 'the truth'. Christian fundamentalists are at least as intolerant as their forbears in defending their narrow views even if they do not go about killing people. And then there are those who fight against change because they are fearful of anything that challenges traditional norms. Those members of the Church of England who were against the ordination of women as priests and who fought a rearguard action against the consecration of women as bishops have some very weak arguments. The position of those who claim that homosexuality has no place in the church is indefensible.

Finally, certainty has given many people encouragement in times of doubt. As the pace of change increases and as traditional approaches are questioned, it is not surprising that many people want reassurance that their fundamental beliefs stand firm. As science and technology increasingly dominate our lives people want to know if there is any necessary conflict between science and religion. As militant atheists try to persuade us that religion is not only completely irrelevant but positively dangerous then it is worrying if we cannot find the right words to disarm them.

But unfortunately Christians have defended their faith by claiming implicitly or even explicitly that certainty is a virtue and that doubt is a sin. The hugely popular Alpha Course is based on the premise that the Christian faith provides answers. And in one sense it can; but in another sense it cannot. For Christian living is much more about questions than answers. It is about a journey in which we should be forever raising questions. If we think we have the answers then our journey is at an end and we have reached our goal. If we have reached our goal and others have reached a different goal then we are more than inclined to think that we are right and they are wrong. And that is a very arrogant and dangerous position to be in.

How did this book arise?

This book arose from a conviction that that there is an urgent need for more debate, discussion and conversation in our churches; that we need to engage more vigorously with our faith and with each other about those things that we claim to be so important to us. In particular we need to engage more actively with our faith at the intellectual level and to be willing to examine the fundamentals of our faith more critically. Such conversation is rarely encouraged in our churches and in some places it is actively discouraged and has led to a huge gap emerging between theologians and churchgoers. While theologians are free to explore the breadth and depth of the faith, those in the pews are left with a church life that is often grounded in understandings of much earlier generations and is constrained by dogma and tradition that no longer engages with people in the twenty-first century. Although many churches can be described as having a lively devotional life there are few which can be described as intellectually stimulating. The rank and file of the church deserve better.

The fact that few of the insights of nearly two centuries of biblical criticism have penetrated routine church teaching is but one example of the failure to do justice to the intellectual content of the faith. Biblical scholarship has clearly demonstrated that the richness of this wonderful book is destroyed if it is taken to be a work that can only be understood literally. The fact that so much of our liturgical practice is based on theological models that are no longer accepted is another failure. For example, the doctrine of sacrificial atonement, or the 'child abuse model' as some have described it, is now widely rejected as an acceptable model of the incarnation. Our unwillingness to engage with the insights of the social sciences is another barrier to the forward progress of the Christian enterprise. These failures are already so serious that our critics think they are engaging with mainstream faith when in reality they are attacking those with convictions at the extremes of the theological spectrum. Those who preach the infallibility of the Bible or the Church are giving the rest of us a bad name.

That is not to say that that our intellectual faculties are somehow superior to other faculties but it is to say that they have been sadly neglected in the life of our churches. The result has been that those both inside and outside the church are seriously ignorant of current theological reflection. We must be in a position to formulate our faith coherently so that people know exactly what we stand for. We must also be in a position to communicate that faith effectively to them. The mission of the church is seriously compromised if we cannot get our intellectual house in order. That does not mean that we must all conform to one orthodox view but it does mean that we must be individually prepared to stand up and be counted. We have for too long hidden behind propositions couched in language that is unintelligible to many churchgoers let alone those outside the church. We need to understand that language has severe limitations and that theological statements can be quite incomprehensible even to those who profess a faith. In his book, *Speaking Christian,* Marcus Borg goes further:

> Christian language has become a stumbling block in our time. Much of its basic vocabulary is seriously misunderstood by Christians and non-Christians alike. Big words like *salvation, God, Jesus* and *Bible* and collections of words *like the creeds, Lord's Prayer,* and *liturgies* have acquired meanings that are serious distortions of their biblical and traditional meanings (Borg, 2011:1).

He then goes on to explain how these distortions have come about. 'Salvation' is a good example. In common usage, the word is closely associated with 'going to heaven' in the afterlife. The biblical meaning of the word has much more to do with 'liberation from bondage' in this life. The point is that words themselves not only have severe limitations in the communication of the faith but that the meanings of these words change and become distorted. We need to examine them again.

But a gap not only exists between theologians and churchgoers but also between churchgoers and the wider world. There is an urgent need for us to relate our faith to the wider world and to issues of social justice and human dignity. These are not easy issues to confront but it is our duty to engage with them and for two reasons. Not only are these issues in urgent need of serious debate, but we cannot claim our humanity without engaging with them. Yet we continue to perpetuate a distinction between the sacred and the secular and seem unable or unwilling to integrate our relationship with the divine with our relationship to each other. Our liturgy also too often reinforces this distinction when we pray for the needs of the world as a kind of afterthought at the end of our intercessions. The needs of the world and our relationship to them are central. We have to understand that we are only truly ourselves in relationship and that the fullness of our humanity can only be expressed through those relationships. It is that full humanity that this book is written to celebrate.

To whom is the book addressed?

The book is addressed to three groups of people within our churches. It seeks to encourage those who are nervous of asking questions to speak out; to challenge those who are comfortable to be more critical about their faith; and to convince those who are confident of the truth to be more willing to admit that they do not always have the answers.

There are many people in our churches who are uncomfortable about their faith. They are reluctant to question it because they do not want to be accused of doubting its fundamental precepts or the way in which those precepts are expressed. They may feel insecure about a theology that they do not understand and which appears to them to lack credibility. They may feel unsure about an ecclesiology that seems to be inward looking and to ignore the real world of people and events. This book aims to give such people 'permission to speak'!

There are others in our churches who are quite comfortable

with their faith. They go to church but do not expect to be challenged. They give little thought to their faith and are quite content to drift. They are prepared to be involved but not beyond their 'comfort zone'. They certainly do not want to be exposed. This book aims to give such people a 'challenge to speak'.

Then there are those in our churches who are so sure of their ground that they will vigorously resist any attempt to question them. They know the answers even if they are unsure of the questions. They are conservative in outlook and claim that biblical revelation or church tradition contains the 'deposit of faith' and that all they have to do is to follow the lead. This book aims to give such people 'a charge to speak'.

The book is also addressed to those outside our churches who are sympathetic to the Christian faith but who as yet are unable to embrace it. It is to be hoped that they will realise that there are people within the Church who are seeking to recast the faith for the modern world in a way that perhaps makes more sense to them. Furthermore, that there are those who are prepared to 'go out on a limb' to do this. Those who do this often come from the liberal or progressive wing of the Church and are represented by such organisations as Modern Church and the Progressive Christianity Network. The websites of these organisations provide links to many other groups working to make the Christian faith credible in the modern world.

It would be naïve to suggest that any discussion will only be governed by intellectual faculties like abstract thought, rational analysis and problem solving. Emotional factors will also play a large part in any debate. As persons we have faculties for feeling and our different moods, temperaments and dispositions have a significant bearing on the way we respond. Volitional factors will also be involved. As persons we have a will which enables us to decide on courses of action and to commit to them. These three aspects of our psychological disposition – thinking, feeling and willing – are the faculties which together form us as persons and determine our response in debate. Despite what many may assume, there is neither evidence that our religious sentiment works independently of that psychological disposition, although it clearly has a bearing on it, nor, that the Holy Spirit somehow navigates his own way through our psyche.

But we respond differently and we do so because we are different people. Sadly the richness of this diversity is not always recognised in our churches. Church leaders tend to be unsettled by anyone who approaches issues at a slightly different angle. Their reluctance to encourage debate is understandable if it is for pastoral reasons but an unwillingness to offend sensibilities is not an adequate reason for caution. Any reluctance to encourage debate is certainly not understandable if it is for personal reasons or because of the fear of losing the authority and power of ecclesiastical position. There are currently too many leaders in our churches who stifle open and honest debate. We need a little more honesty, courage and humility.

In his seminal work, *The Individual and His Religion*, subtitled, *A classic study of the function of religious sentiment in the personality of the individual*, Gordon Allport argues that just as people can grow and mature in other areas of their lives – for example, people can become more emotionally mature as they get older (or not), can become more socially mature, in their ability to relate well to others (or not), can become more intellectually mature (or not), etc – so also can people become more mature in their religious development (or not). It is perhaps greater maturity that this book seeks to achieve (Allport, 1969).

How will the book achieve its purpose?

This is not an academic book although it arises from academic work. It is a book that arises from study and reflection but which seeks above all to be clear and faithful to its basic premises outlined below. It also arises from the experience of running courses and groups within the local church on a wide range of issues and with individuals representing a broad range of churchmanship. It is very possible that some of its foundations will appear weak and some of its arguments will appear to lack rigour but it is not against those criteria that it should be judged. It should be judged as an honest attempt to pursue an approach that has been sadly neglected.

It is also not intended to be a devotional book though it could certainly be used devotionally. It is a book that aims to give reflection and meditation a new perspective on the Christian enterprise and to give it something of an edge. It will inevitably upset people and appear at times to be unnecessarily contentious but that is not the intention. Its primary purpose is to challenge current ways of thinking. It is designed to be used by individuals and groups to help with discussion of those things that lie at the heart of our faith. It is presented in a number of short chapters that concentrate on some of the aspects of the human condition which seem to be most positive and productive to Christian flourishing.

These themes are not mutually exclusive and there is considerable overlap between them. Other themes could have been used but the themes chosen successfully preserve the thread of continuity that is so important to the whole enterprise. The thread of continuity is preserved because each of these themes can express in different ways a human approach to God. They each take a different angle in that approach and so give that human approach both depth and breadth. In a similar way, the artistic movement of the early twentieth century known as Cubism was an attempt by Picasso and others to give more depth to their work by representing objects from a number of different angles in the same space. God is love, and perhaps it is not too wide of the mark to say that God is integrity, virtue… too.

It will be clear that there is a marked absence of theological language in this book. This is part of the attempt to focus on the human rather than the divine and to use language which is familiar and in common usage rather than language which may be familiar but which generally needs clarification. The language of human discourse does not generally need to be defined but the language of theological discourse certainly does. The church too readily assumes that its language is accessible when in reality it is not.

The traditional themes of the Christian faith have not been abandoned in this book but some have certainly been put on one side. Personal salvation, for example, is at the centre of their faith for many people yet there is no mention of it in this book. That is because 'salvation' is a word like many others which has lost its original biblical meaning and urgently needs to be redefined. In any case the major themes of liberation and justice which are central to a biblical understanding of salvation are also central themes in the book.

There will be some who will have difficulty with the approach adopted in this book despite their willingness to 'give it a go'. They may find that the intellectual or emotional challenge takes them well beyond their 'comfort zone'. If that is the case then they can be reassured that they have already taken the most important step in their willingness to try something new and any further progress that they make is a bonus.

On what assumptions is it based?

The assumption which lies at the heart of the book is that any discussion of the Christian enterprise must start with the human and not the divine. The divine has had a good run for its money and has been notably unsuccessful in convincing a sceptical world of the credibility of the faith. The human has largely been ignored and yet is arguably the only place where we can start because that is ultimately all that we know. The humanity of Jesus has been sadly neglected. This book also assumes that contributions from the whole range of human knowledge and experience to the understanding of the Christian enterprise have so far been inadequately explored. This particularly applies to the social sciences – anthropology, sociology, psychology and the rest. It is also widely assumed that the religious sentiment works independently of our human faculties or, to put it another way, the Holy Spirit navigates its own way through our psyche. This is rejected.

The book also rejects literal readings of biblical texts or any suggestion that they are inerrant. It assumes that these texts were written over a long period by men and women who may or may not have been inspired. It assumes that these writings represent the richest source of revelation that we have about what we call God. It assumes that they provide us with at least a glimpse of the man Jesus. But they are not infallible. This book also rejects the notion of ultimate authority in the church and any suggestion that human beings can be infallible. Although it is accepted that authority structures are necessary within any human institution, the only authority that has lasting value is that of service and love.

This book will argue that Christianity is not ultimately about the assent to a creed but the living of a life. It is not what we believe that ultimately matters but how we put those beliefs into practice. In fact, 'belief' is a word that has been corrupted in the modern world. It was not originally something that people thought but something they did. The book also argues that asking questions is more productive than seeking answers and that honest doubt is much more constructive than uncompromising certainty. It is concerned with 'living the questions'.

Finally, this book is about making journeys not reaching destinations. Maya Angelou, the American author, was asked if she was a Christian. She turned the question back on the one inquiring of her: "Are you a Christian?" The person replied, "Why, yes, of course!" Angelou exclaimed, "Already?"

The imperative to ask questions

In his book, *The Human Face of God*, John Robinson, former Bishop of Woolwich, writes:

> I once saw scribbled on a church noticeboard proclaiming 'Christ is the answer', 'Yes, but what is the question?' What are the questions to which he would be that answer today? (Robinson, 1973:16).

In the introduction to his monumental work, *A History of Christianity:* Diarmaid MacCulloch, Professor in the History of the Church at Oxford University, writes:

> As well as telling stories, my book asks questions. It tries to avoid giving too many answers, since this habit has been one of the great vices of organised religion (MacCulloch, 2009:2).

Living the Questions is a course of study for groups wanting to explore Christianity in a new way, and is described as 'an open-minded alternative to studies that attempt to give participants all the answers'. Featuring thirty of today's leading religious voices, the course is based on a series of DVD programmes with associated written guides. It is outlined on the website www.livingthequestions.com.

In the book which accompanies the course, the authors write:

> Jesus was typical of the rabbis of his day. According to the canonical gospels, he rarely gave a straight answer to a question. Instead he responded with another question or told a story. For the most part, Jesus was not offering simple answers. Instead, he put his questioners in a position of having to think for themselves. Rather than offer his disciples answers to life's most perplexing problems, Jesus introduced them to deeper and deeper levels of ambiguity. Clearly Jesus

> knew what mystics and the wisest of spiritual guides have known all along: that answers can provide a false sense of security and confidence that can become barriers to an awareness of the divine (Felton & Procter-Murphy, 2012:3).

If this is true, then the followers of Jesus down the centuries have misunderstood, misrepresented and misused the character of his message. Individuals and institutions have repeatedly argued that Christianity provides answers and that doubt and uncertainty are not worthy of Christians. And each group has insisted that their answers are right and other answers are wrong. Some branches of the Christian Church have been uncompromising in their opposition to those with whom they disagree.

The Roman Catholic Church insists that the teaching of the Pope and the magisterium of the church are without error. And in earlier centuries it has been fully prepared to murder individuals and eliminate groups who have dared to disagree. The Spanish Inquisition tried and executed thousands for heresy. The Cathars of France were ruthlessly exterminated. Even today, individuals and groups are excommunicated or repressed if they take an independent line. Hans Kung, one the most impressive of Roman Catholic theologians, still suffers from intimidation.

But there are encouraging signs of change with the election of Pope Francis. In an interview before he became Pope, Jorge Mario Bergoglio said this:

> I don't have all the answers; I don't even have all the questions. I always think of new questions, and there are always new questions coming forward. But the answers have to be thought out according to the different situations, and you have to wait for them (Vallely, 2013:131).

The hierarchy of the Anglican Church is currently promoting the Anglican Communion Covenant. This document requires all members of the church to agree on a written statement of 'affirmations and commitments' on doctrine and belief. In the face of deep divisions within the church over gender and sexuality, this document is a desperate attempt to retain unity at all costs. The signs are that such a proposal will not have an easy ride for the Anglican Church which more than any other celebrates its diversity and has historically maintained that it is possible to have 'unity in diversity'.

Some Protestant Evangelical Churches insist that the Bible, or more accurately their interpretation of the Bible, is inerrant. It is not possible to argue with proponents of this view because for them revelation trumps reason at every turn. For the rest of us, revelation and reason go hand in hand. It is difficult to avoid the conclusion that the tenacity with which such groups hold these views results from a fear of what common sense and rational inquiry might reveal of this absurdity.

But even those Christians who inhabit the middle ground of churchmanship are wary of uncertainty and doubt and are uncomfortable or fearful of questioning traditional doctrinal propositions. This is reinforced by clergy who often seem unwilling or unable to handle dissent or alternative points of view and whose sermons rarely challenge their congregation to think. The result is that rank and file 'thinking' Christians keep quiet until or unless given 'permission to speak'.

The Alpha Course began in the late 1970s at Holy Trinity Brompton as a means of helping new Christians learn more about the Christian faith. In 1990, former barrister Nicky Gumbel realised the potential of the Alpha Course and adapted it to appeal to a wider audience. It spread fast and is now used throughout the world. It runs as a series of weekly meetings which each involve an informal meal, a talk and small group discussion and is outlined on the website www.alpha.org.

The Alpha Course has undoubtedly been very successful and has attracted many people who might otherwise have ignored

Christianity altogether. It has received wide support from church congregations and has been endorsed by senior church leaders. However, there are others who are increasingly uneasy about the content and process of the Alpha Course. It was developed by those on the conservative evangelical wing of the church and takes a 'high' view of the inspiration of biblical texts. In his book, *Alpha: Questions of Life*, Nicky Gumbel describes the Bible as '100 per cent inspired by God'. Quite apart from the difficulty of understanding what this phrase actually means, it is clear that those who have developed this course are close to claiming that the Bible is inerrant. As Gumbel also says, the Bible is '100 per cent the work of human being' which means that it is flawed as all human beings are flawed. It may contain inspirational passages but is not inspired overall (Gumbel, 1993).

This approach to the Bible is part of a wider assumption that there is only one 'grand narrative' to which all of us should assent and that those who do not express their faith in this particular way are not authentic Christians; this assumption that something as momentous as Christianity can be distilled in mere words in this way fails to admit to the limitations of language and the diversity of human understanding. A multitude of grand narratives have given depth and breadth to the overall pattern of Christianity throughout history and continue to do so geographically throughout the world. To suggest that the 'deposit of faith' is somehow complete and to deny that the richness of the enterprise continues to evolve in hitherto unknown ways is surely wrong. It may not be so neat and tidy for everyone to express their faith in a myriad of different ways but that is the reality and any attempt to push for the 'one size fits all' approach should be vigorously resisted.

The most serious objection to the Alpha Course is, however, the way in which it focuses on answers and not on questions. Although participants are encouraged to ask questions seeking clarification, they are not encouraged to ask questions that challenge the 'party line'. Those running the course have a clear narrative to pursue and anything which distracts from that narrative is unwelcome. Many have been disillusioned by this unwillingness or inability to engage with difficult and challenging questions. The simplistic assumption is that questions have answers and that problems have solutions when the reality is much more complex. The Alpha Course is therefore quite alien to the sentiments of this book.

The questions of Nicodemus

In the third chapter of the gospel according to John we read the story of Nicodemus' encounter with Jesus. Nicodemus was clearly a prominent member of the community in first-century Palestine. We are told that he was a Pharisee and a leader of the Jews. That probably means that he was a member of the Sanhedrin and so would be reluctant to meet Jesus in broad daylight. Perhaps he had been hovering around Jesus during the day and now sought the opportunity for a quiet word with Jesus away with from the crowds. So he chose to come to Jesus by night.

Here was a man thoroughly immersed in the history and traditions of the Jewish faith but who saw in Jesus something that intrigued him. Here was a man who was thoroughly familiar with the law and the prophets but who sensed that here there was something different about Jesus. Here was a man who recognised something of God in Jesus. Here was a man who was searching but who thought he knew what he had found.

He came to Jesus confident that he knew exactly who Jesus was. "I have heard your teaching and preaching. I have seen the miracles and healing. I have seen the signs and wonders. I know who you are." And Jesus replies. "No, sorry, you don't. You saw me supply wine for the wedding feast. You saw me cleanse the temple of those who were making a business there. And you think you can use this evidence to draw neat logical, conclusions about exactly who I am. Sorry, but it doesn't work that way." Nicodemus was confused.

He was a genuine seeker after truth but was conditioned by his background and circumstances to think and act in particular ways. He came to Jesus because he knew that Jesus knew the right answers. But unfortunately, Nicodemus did not know the right questions. Nicodemus wanted to know how to win the prize. What laws he had to follow. What rituals he had to perform. What would earn him God's favour. Jesus recognised Nicodemus' searching and answered the questions that Nicodemus did not know how to ask. Jesus told Nicodemus about being born again. And Nicodemus began to learn.

Jesus told Nicodemus a story of new birth. Initially this made no sense to Nicodemus but did prompt him to ask new and different questions. Jesus led Nicodemus on to an understanding that life with God cannot be earned. He showed him that life with God is not something that can be controlled, charted or calculated. He showed him that life with God involves vulnerability, risk and uncertainty. It involves putting ourselves in the hands of God and of our fellow human beings. We call it the journey of faith.

There are groups of Christians for whom the answers are all important. They think they have the right answers and everyone else is wrong. There are other groups of Christians for whom the questions are all important. They know that claiming to know the answers is not how faith works. They know that asking the right questions leads to an open mind but that claiming the right answers only leads to a mind that is closed.

The Christian life is of course about finding answers but it is also about asking questions. And if our faith is to be refreshed then it is to the questions that we must turn. Our faith is not refreshed if we sit comfortably with the answers. It is only refreshed if we are continually challenged by the questions. If we continue to 'live the questions'.

Early in his life Jesus stays behind when his parents return from Jerusalem. Then they started to look for him among their relatives and friends. When they did not find him, they returned to Jerusalem to search for him. After three days they found him in the temple, sitting among the teachers, listening to them and asking questions.

The Socratic Method and Critical Thinking

The saddest thing about current discourse on theological issues is that it so often conforms to the approach that is so common in contemporary debate. As Karen Armstrong points out in her book, *Twelve Steps to a Compassionate Life*, so much of modern debate has more in common with practice in ancient Athens in which:

> ...citizens argued competitively, to marshal arguments logically and effectively and to argue their case in order to win. They practised rhetorical ploys to undermine their opponents' position and had no qualms about discrediting them and their cause in order to marginalise their policies. The object was to defeat one's opponent: nobody was expected to change his mind, be converted to the other side, or to enter empathetically into the rival viewpoint (Armstrong, 2011:121).

The type of dialogue promoted by Socrates was quite different. His pupil Plato insisted that such dialogue:

> ...be conducted in a kindly, compassionate manner. It would not bring transcendent insight unless 'questions and answers are exchanged in good faith and without malice'. Nobody must be pushed into a position about which he felt uncomfortable. Each participant should 'make place for the other' in his mind, listening intently and sympathetically to the ideas

> of his partners in dialogue and allowing them to unsettle his own convictions. In return, they would permit their minds to be informed and changed by his contribution (Armstrong, 2011:122).

The aim of the Socratic dialogue was for both parties to become more enlightened in their search for truth. Since truth is what we all seek, this method has considerable potential as a way of debating the religious issues of our time. It is not unrealistic to expect the debates in the councils of the church to follow this pattern. It is certainly quite realistic to expect group discussion in our local churches to debate in this way. We urgently need to have this debate.

Although the Socratic Method is so often absent from debate in contemporary society, it has by no means been discarded. Critical Thinking is a process that owes its origins to the Socratic Method and is an important component of professional practice in many areas of the nation's life. According to the National Council for Excellence in Critical Thinking:

> Critical thinking is the intellectually disciplined process of actively and skilfully conceptualizing, applying, analysing, synthesizing, and/or evaluating information gathered from, or generated by, observation, experience, reflection, reasoning, or communication, as a guide to belief and action. In its exemplary form, it is based on universal intellectual values that transcend subject matter divisions: clarity, accuracy, precision, consistency, relevance, sound evidence, good reasons, depth, breadth, and fairness (www.criticalthinking.org).

In essence, Critical Thinking is a more disciplined and structured version of the Socratic Method which is more suitable for the professional environment. That does not mean that it is unsuitable for religious discourse but it must be applied with caution because the rational element in religion is only one part of the whole. However, the introduction of more objectivity into religious discourse would aid the quest which is at the heart of this book.

The Critical Religion Association is an organisation that has been formed to do just that. It brings together those in academia who are concerned with the application of critical thinking to religious discourse. Its work also percolates down to those working outside the academic community but with an interest in religious questions. The association website expands on some basic principles:

> We believe that the question of religion remains absolutely essential to our thinking about what it means to be human, and especially what it means to be human *in relationship*, in what we can now only call a post-secular twenty-first century. For us, religion must be examined with utmost rigour, not taking for granted pre-conceived notions or inherited traditions, but carefully examining the ideas of religion, with all their variegated histories, both in theory and in praxis, in order to uncover both the complexities and profundities that 'religions' have always embodied, as well as the new possibilities that the term 'religion' (or its substitutes) might now afford (www.criticalreligion.org).

Seeking the truth

The truth that we all seek cannot be adequately expressed in words and any attempt to do so is bound to fail. That does not mean that we should abandon attempts to formulate the truth but we must be aware of the limitations. Art, music, drama and the rest are equally capable of expressing aspects of the truth. Truth can be expressed in a multitude of different ways. Most importantly, we express the truth in the way we live. And our search for the truth will not produce just one answer that we might describe as definitive or absolute. There will be aspects of the truth that all of those engaged in this enterprise might express in similar ways but there will be other aspects of truth that are expressed very differently. Those who express themselves in similar ways will gather together and perhaps call themselves a church but one church may be very different from another.

There will be those who refute the suggestion that there are a multitude of ways in which truth may be expressed and that no single expression can represent the truth. Pope Benedict XVI was very concerned about the spread of what he called 'relativism'. But that is not surprising given the claims he makes for the authority of the teaching office of his church. For him, there is such a thing as absolute truth and it is expressed only in the way the magisterium expresses it. The same approach is adopted by conservative Protestant groups who expect members to subscribe to a written statement of doctrinal propositions. Those who are unwilling to 'sign on the dotted line' are marginalised or ejected. The leaders of such groups are desperately afraid that any compromise will undermine their authority. They ignore the fact that any formulation of words is at best only a guide and at worst, thoroughly misleading. Although some may be sympathetic to these propositions and the way in which they are expressed, others will find them quite alien to their understanding or expressed in ways that shed little light on any reality beneath.

There will be some who will dismiss the approach of this book as an example of relativism. They will claim that it encourages the notion that any one understanding is as good as another and that it denies any claim to absolute truth. There is some truth in this accusation because to claim that any particular human formulation of words is somehow the last word on a subject ignores the severe limitation of language. For the philosopher

Wittgenstein, language is simply a form of communication, and cannot have a status in its own right. All we can do is to use language as best we can to express what we believe to be true for us. If we import language from elsewhere even from our own tradition then we must interrogate it carefully before use.

The Need for a New Paradigm

Christianity is not about the divine becoming human so much as it is about the human becoming divine. That is a paradigm shift of the first order.
John Shelby Spong.

The concept of a *paradigm* in scientific discourse

The word *paradigm* first appeared in the English language in the fifteenth century and it meant 'pattern', 'example' or 'precedent' and it still bears this meaning today. However, in recent years it has more usually come to mean 'a way of looking at things', 'an interpretive framework' or 'a world view'. This newer meaning arises following the work of the historian of science, Thomas Kuhn (1922-1996). The Oxford English Dictionary Online summarises the modern usage of the word *paradigm* as 'a conceptual or methodological model underlying the theories and practices of a science or discipline at a particular time; (hence) a generally accepted world view.' The word is now part of general intellectual discourse and has been applied in many areas of knowledge. It has been widely used in science and is increasingly used in religion (www.oed.com).

The most important test of a scientific theory is that it is supported by experimental observations. In the 1950s it was claimed that these observations could be completely rational, objective and independent. They were not affected by any particular theoretical perspective. There were simply facts to be discovered. This *empiricism* was attacked in the 1960s by those who claimed that observations are always to some extent subjective and dependent on other factors. They always depend on the assumptions made by the observer, and on the way the observation is carried out. This attack on empiricism was taken further by Thomas Kuhn in his 1962 book, *The Structure of Scientific Revolutions*. Kuhn held that the thought and action of a scientific community are dominated by its *paradigms,* and that all attempts to assess theories through observation depend on the prevailing paradigm. The word *paradigm* describes the shared perspectives, assumptions and methods of the scientific community at a particular time and place (Kuhn, 2012).

Paradigm shifts can be well illustrated by reference to the world of Physics. Newtonian Mechanics was a perfectly satisfactory paradigm for most work in the physics of objects in motion until well into the twentieth century. It successfully accounted for the behaviour of motor cars and of rifle bullets. It was a way of looking at the world which produced results.

Moreover, it worked. However, following Einstein's work on Relativity in the early years of the twentieth century, it became clear that Newtonian Mechanics was unable to account for the way objects behave if they are very small and/or they are travelling at high speed, and that only a completely new approach could accommodate all the observations. There was therefore a paradigm shift from Newtonian Mechanics to Relativistic Mechanics within the scientific community. Experimental data was seen in new ways. New questions were posed and new answers sought. Newton's Laws were not discarded because they still worked in most routine situations but they were now seen within a wider context.

Sometimes old paradigms are perpetuated at the expense of the new. Ptolemaic Astronomy is a view of the universe based on a fixed earth around which the sphere of the fixed stars rotates every day carrying with it the spheres of the sun, moon, and planets. Ptolemy used geometric models to predict the positions of the sun, moon, and planets, using combinations of circular motion known as epicycles. As the number of observations increased, so did the complexity of epicyclic movement. And as discrepancies in observations increased, astronomers added more epicycles. It was only with the acceptance of the heliocentric or sun-centred theory of Copernicus in the sixteenth century that the geocentric or earth-centred theory of Ptolemy collapsed. This really was a revolution in scientific thought and well illustrates the notion of a paradigm shift.

There is not the space to give examples from other branches of science and the details of these paradigm shifts are not important for our purposes. What is important is that in the scientific world it has been found useful to identify these massive changes in perceptions as revolutions in scientific thinking. It is, of course, possible to argue with Karl Popper that Thomas Kuhn was wrong and that science does not progress in this way, but that would be to miss the point. The point is that changes of perception on this scale do happen and they do force us to look at a familiar world in a new way. And by looking at the world in this new way we find that every aspect of our previous approach to the data is challenged.

Historical paradigms in Christianity

One of most powerful writers of our time is the Swiss theologian Hans Kung (1928-). In his book *Christianity: Its Essence and History*, he argues that, 'it is possible, important and urgent to transfer the paradigm theory from the sphere of the natural sciences to that of religion and theology' (Kung, 1995:60).

He identifies five historical paradigms in Christianity – the Jewish apocalyptic paradigm of earliest Christianity; the Ecumenical Hellenistic paradigm of Christian antiquity; the Roman Catholic paradigm of the Middle Ages; the Protestant Evangelical paradigm of the Reformation; and the paradigm of modernity, oriented on reason and progress. But what were the characteristics of these paradigms?

The Jewish apocalyptic paradigm of earliest Christianity was based on the Jerusalem Church headed by James the brother of Jesus. Its characteristics included 'the eschatological horizon which the Jews who followed Jesus had in common with may Jews'. It also included the Jewish attitude to life, (including) the

'Mosaic ritual law, above all circumcision, Sabbath and festivals, (and) regulations about cleanness and food' (Kung 1995:77). The community is thought to have dispersed after the execution of James and before the outbreak of the Jewish-Roman war in 66 CE. Certainly, the complete destruction of Jerusalem in 135 CE and the expulsion of all Jews brought an end to the Jewish Christian community of Jerusalem and its dominant position in early Christianity. The overriding characteristic of this paradigm therefore is that during this period Christianity was seen through the lens of Judaism.

The Ecumenical Hellenistic paradigm of Christian antiquity arose in a shift from Jewish Christianity to Gentile Christianity as a result of the work of Paul and other Hellenistic Jewish Christians who settled in Antioch. Hellenistic civilisation arose from the spread of Greek language and culture into the Roman world following the conquests of Alexander the Great. Many people were absorbed into this culture despite the fact that they were not ethnically Greek and many communities arose that we have come to call Hellenistic. Antioch was one such community and had become a major city of the Roman Empire with a cosmopolitan population, the majority of whom spoke Greek. It was an important centre of international trade and it controlled the land routes to other important centres of the empire. It was here that the Hellenistic Jewish Christians first preached to the Gentiles and where the mixed community of Jews and Gentiles were first called Christians.

The person of Paul was fundamental to the paradigm shift. Although he was born and brought up as a Jew and had been strictly trained in the Pharisaic tradition, he was also imbued with the vibrant spirit of the Hellenistic age. Paul's message was that Gentiles could have unconditional access to God through the life, death and resurrection of Jesus Christ without having to submit to the demands of the Jewish law. As Paul spread this message passionately throughout the empire so Christianity broke away from the constraints of a small Jewish sect into the universal Christian religion that it soon became. In due course, 'there was an authentic inculturation of the Christian message in the world of Hellenistic culture' (Kung 1995:114). In other words, not only did this new religion make an impact on this culture but the influence of this culture made an impact on the evolution of its teachings.

The Roman Catholic paradigm of the Middle Ages arises as the centre of gravity of the Christian Church moves to Rome with the Pope at its head. Over the centuries tensions had arisen between the Greek speaking Eastern Church based in Constantinople and the Latin speaking Western Church based in Rome and a split becomes inevitable. Leadership of the Western Church is assumed by the Pope who claims apostolic succession from the Apostle Peter. He gains increasing power and control over peoples and events despite clashes with the civil power. The institution of the Roman Catholic Church becomes the focal point for that turbulent period which we call the Middle Ages.

There is also a theological shift taking place between the theoretical and philosophical concerns of the Eastern Church and the more practical and pastoral interests of the Western Church. This shift comes to its climax in the work of Augustine (354-430) who laid the foundations for a new theological paradigm. He was closely involved with the great controversies of his time and established new theological frameworks which were forged in the great upheavals of the decline of the Roman Empire. It is not necessary to describe Augustine's contribution in detail, merely to point out that one man can be the trigger for great change.

One man was also responsible for triggering the paradigm shift to the Protestant Evangelical Paradigm of The Reformation and that man was Martin Luther (1483-1546). By the beginning of the sixteenth century the Roman Catholic Church was in crisis. The institution had become a monster with exaggerated power and blatant corruption at its heart and was ripe for fundamental change. The papacy was under threat from within and without as different factions fought for control; its civil power disintegrated with the rise of the nation states. The lower echelons of the church were in disarray and the people were left to flounder in a mire of magic and superstition.

Luther's message was grounded in the demand that the church and its theology return to the gospel of Jesus Christ as originally attested in Holy Scripture and in particular in the writings of Paul. He believed that the Roman Catholic Church had so distorted and abused the gospel that only wholesale reform would do. Kung puts it this way: 'Against all the traditions, laws and authorities... Luther sets the primacy of scripture (*sola scriptura*). Against all the saints and mediators... Luther sets the primacy of Jesus Christ (*sola Christus*). Against all 'works', Luther sets the primacy of 'grace' (*sola gratia*)' (Kung 1995:537). Despite what appears to be a profound theological shift, Luther's aim was not so much the reformulation of doctrine as the renewal of the church.

For Hans Kung, the Paradigm of Modernity arose not from within but from outside Christianity. 'Up to the seventeenth century, Western culture, whether Catholic or Protestant, had been essentially shaped and pervaded by Christianity. But now an intellectual life was developing independently of the church and increasingly against it' (Kung 1995:675). This new intellectual life was based on the authority of human reason and we call it the Enlightenment. Although this new movement sometimes opposed the church, its proponents were not necessarily atheists. What had changed was the perspective from which questions of ultimate truth were addressed. No longer were these questions instinctively answered by reference to the authority of the Church or the Bible but by reference to human reason.

Not surprisingly, this new movement was resisted by many religious individuals and institutions that saw it as a threat to the authority of scripture and tradition. But it rapidly acquired a momentum which propelled it inexorably forward like a breath of fresh air generating new understandings of freedom, toleration and progress in its wake. No longer were political, social, economic and cultural processes dictated by religious, theological and ecclesiastical demands but quite the reverse. People started to take control of their own destiny. They believed that they had 'come of age'.

The impact of all this on both scripture and tradition was considerable. One of the defining movements of the new paradigm was the emergence of historical biblical criticism and the quest for the historical Jesus. Both movements sought to subject biblical texts to the kind of scrutiny that would reveal its true nature. In particular, which parts were historical and which needed to be understood in a different way. Although there were, and still are, those who insist on a literal reading of the scriptures, the consensus is that this wonderful book contains truths of many different kinds. For a whole host of reasons it became untenable to treat the Bible as inerrant and to read it literally.

Although many contributed to the new paradigm shift, it is Friedrich Schleiermacher (1768-1834) who can be described as the paradigmatic theologian of modernity. For here was a truly modern man who was comfortable with modern art, music and literature and who embraced modern science and philosophy. He was also a religious man. But for him, God was not a supernatural being but the 'ground of all being'. For him, religion was 'the feeling of ultimate dependence' on that God. But, according to Kung, 'this feeling is not to be understood in a restricted psychological sense as Romantic enthusiastic emotion, but in a comprehensive, existential way as a sense of being encountered at the centre, as immediate religious self-awareness' (Kung 1995:699).

The Paradigm of Modernity came to an end in the early years of the twentieth century when so much was shattered by the First

World War. But even before these cataclysmic events which modernity was unable to prevent it had become clear that the foundations of this paradigm were inadequate. Reason is only one of a multitude of human faculties. As Kung puts it, 'man does not live by reason alone. And the human spirit can do more than calculate and measure, analyse and rationalize'. And progress cannot continue unchecked. 'Subdue the earth in the biblical account of creation means the consciously responsible use and cherishing of nature and not unscrupulous exploitation and progressive destruction'(Kung 1995:767-768).

In his book, *Theology for the Third Millennium*, Kung describes the collapse of the paradigm of modernity and the emergence of a new paradigm which, for want of a better word, he describes as 'postmodern'. Although this new paradigm is difficult to define, it is radically different. It embraces the world as it is in a way that previous paradigms have never done, but at the same time holds on to eternal truths that have stood the test of time. It is a paradigm of both continuity and change. For Kung, the 'shape' of the theology of this new paradigm would be:

> 'Catholic', constantly labouring on behalf of the 'whole', the 'universal' Church – *and* at the same time 'Protestant', strictly intent on Scripture, on the Gospel; 'traditional', always responsible in the face of history – *and* at the same time 'contemporary', passionately addressing the issues of the present; 'Christocentric', decisively and distinctively Christian – *and* still 'ecumenical', oriented towards the 'ecumene', the whole 'inhabited globe', all Christian churches, all religions, all regions; theoretical-scholarly, occupied with teaching and truth – *and* at the same time practical-pastoral, labouring on behalf of life, renewal, and reform.' (Kung, 1988:206).

A new paradigm for Christianity

One form that such a theology might take is outlined by the American theologian Marcus Borg in his book, *The Heart of Christianity*. In this book, Borg identifies what he sees as a new paradigm of Christianity which is emerging to challenge the old. This paradigm change is 'not about a few items of Christian theology or behaviour, but between two comprehensive ways of seeing Christianity as a whole (Borg, 2003:7).

The earlier paradigm sees Christianity as grounded in divine authority. For Protestants, that authority is primarily in the Bible, with large numbers of people subscribing to literal and inerrant understandings of biblical texts. For Roman Catholics, authority is in both the Bible, and in the Church which is expressed in the teaching office of the church, and in the notion of apostolic succession, or in papal authority. For both groups, 'the earlier paradigm sees the Bible as a divine product… it is the unique revelation of God' (Borg, 2003:7).

This paradigm is also reflected in the language and the liturgy of the church. It is reflected in the words we use to describe the Father, the Son and the Holy Spirit. We speak of God in anthropomorphic terms and yet as 'wholly other', and cannot cope with the tension between transcendence and immanence. We describe Jesus as fully human and fully divine, but cannot cope with the conflict between our understandings of humanity and divinity. We conceive of the Holy Spirit as some external agent that can be called upon to perform at our behest, not as something which permeates everything in human relationships which builds rather than destroys. Our attempts at articulating the essence of Trinitarian faith are weak.

This paradigm is also reflected in the way we expect people to respond and behave. We give the impression that faith is about belief in a set of propositions rather than commitment to a way of life. We demand acceptance of particular interpretations of the birth, death and resurrection of Jesus which often rely on literal rather than metaphorical understandings of biblical texts. We give pride of place to *logos* rather than *mythos*. We are frightened of debate and see certainty as more worthy than doubt.

This paradigm rejects alternative ways to God based on misunderstandings of John 14:6, 'Jesus said to him, "I am the way, and the truth, and the life. No one comes to the Father except through me."' We are often unwilling to accept that other denominations, let alone other religions, might also have some elements of the truth. There are still those who believe in the reality of hell as a place to which 'unbelievers' will be consigned. We still encourage belief in heaven as a place where we retain our personal identity but inhabit a spiritual rather than a material body.

The emerging paradigm is quite different, particularly in its attitude to the Bible. It sees the Bible not as a divine product with divine authority but as a human response to God. It is not 'top down' but 'bottom up'. Borg describes three ways of 'seeing' biblical texts – 'historical, metaphorical and sacramental'. He writes:

> For the emerging paradigm, the Bible is the historical product of two ancient communities, ancient Israel and the early Christian movement. The Bible was not written to us or for us, but for the ancient communities that produced it. A historical approach emphasises the illuminating power of interpreting these ancient documents in their ancient historical contexts.
>
> The emerging paradigm sees the Bible metaphorically, by which I mean its "more-than-literal", "more-than-factual" meaning. It is not much concerned with the historical factuality of the Bible's stories, but much more with their meanings. It is not bothered by the possibility that the stories of Jesus' birth and resurrection are metaphorical rather than literal factual accounts. It asks, "Whether it happened this

> way or not, what is this story saying? What meaning does it have for us?"
>
> The emerging paradigm sees the Bible sacramentally, by which I mean the Bible's ability to mediate the sacred. A sacrament is something visible and physical whereby the Spirit becomes present to us. A sacrament is a means of grace, a vehicle or vessel for the Spirit.
>
> The emerging paradigm sees the Christian life as a life of relationship and transformation. Being a Christian is not about meeting requirements for a future reward in an afterlife, and not very much about believing. Rather, the Christian life is about a relationship with God that transforms life in the present. To be a Christian does not mean believing in Christianity, but a relationship with God lived within the Christian tradition as a metaphor and sacrament of the sacred (Borg 2003:13-14).

These earlier and emerging paradigms are very different but the issue is not whether they are right or wrong. For some, the earlier paradigm has served them well and within it they have felt able to grow. For them, the emerging paradigm is an alien land with which they do not feel quite so comfortable. For others, the earlier paradigm no longer works. For them, the emerging paradigm provides a much more satisfactory framework. Although the message of this book is that a paradigm change is inevitable, the exact nature of that change is difficult to predict. However, the claim of this book is that an essential element of that change must be a new emphasis on human flourishing.

God as Love

You cannot believe in God until you believe in yourself. Swami Vivekananda

Children's Letters to God

Children's Letters to God is a wonderful little book. It is full of short hand-written letters to God. It is full of gems. 'Dear God, My father can never get a fire started. Could you make a burning bush in our back yard?' or 'Dear God, OK, I kept my half of the deal. Where's the bike?' and then 'Dear God, It must be hard to love everybody in the world. I've only one little brother and that's hard enough' (Marshall & Hample, 1980).

We laugh at the innocence of these letters. We enjoy the freedom from inhibition and the absence of cliché. But we rarely appreciate how profound they actually are. For these are first attempts to grapple with truth. They are fresh and untainted. But they are sometimes incredibly perceptive. The writer of the last letter has an instinctive feel for what might be meant by 'love'.

As adults, we sometimes behave as if our purpose in life is to compete with one another, or to dispute with one another, or even to quarrel. We get caught up in the struggle to win the argument and to come first. But we know deep down that our real purpose must be something quite different. Our faith teaches us that from the moment we are born until the moment we die, our real purpose in life is to learn how to love. This is not something that we learn in a day, in a month or in a year. It is something that grows as every other aspect of our personhood grows.

But as that love grows so its shape changes. If you are three or four years old then the shape of your love is that of a three- or four-year-old. You throw your arms around people hugging and kissing them. You are quite uninhibited in your actions. Your love just gushes out quite indiscriminately. If you are a few years older you look with embarrassment on this behaviour for the shape of your love has now changed. Your love is now directed towards a group of close friends. It is equally intense but its shape is very different.

If you are now a teenager then that love changes yet again. Your love is directed at particular people. In the turmoil of adolescence you fall in and out of love with them on a weekly basis. Your love is equally intense but its shape is different. You begin to learn that love makes you vulnerable. That it involves joy as well as suffering. That love is not always easy. That love can be hard.

Then as you grow older that love changes shape again. It may become directed at one person in particular and you get married. Later on you may have children and that love changes again. Later still, grandchildren may come along. Finally, that love changes again as age and infirmity take their toll and the family move away. Perhaps you now love someone who does not even recognise you and cannot return that love.

Sometimes love takes a different course. Love is expressed within the wider family circle and between friends. Love is expressed in dedication to the care and compassion for people in need. Love is expressed in dedication to a humanitarian cause or a movement for change.

What all these ways of loving have in common is their capacity for selfless giving. But despite the best of intentions we so often fall short. But we know that that is where we should be. We know that that is the kind of person we should be; the kind of person that was so supremely demonstrated in the life of Jesus; the personhood that was his supreme legacy to us. It is the reason that we can say with confidence that God is love. Learning to love others as God loves us is the greatest challenge that we face. It is the core of what it means to be a Christian. It is therefore the core of what it means to be human.

As Martin Buber the philosopher puts it:

> Existence will remain meaningless for you if you yourself do not penetrate into it with active love and if you do not in this way discover its meaning for yourself. Everything is waiting to be hallowed by you; it is waiting for this meaning to be disclosed and to be realised by you… Meet the world with the fullness of your being and you shall meet God. If you wish to believe, love! (Sykes, 1992:152).

The primacy of love

> "Teacher, which commandment in the law is the greatest?" He said to him, "You shall love the Lord your God with all your heart, and with all your soul, and with all your mind. This is the greatest and first commandment. And a second is like it: You shall love your neighbour as yourself. On these two commandments hang all the law and the prophets." (Matt 22: 36-40).

We cannot be sure that these are the words of Jesus; first, because of the uncertainties inherent in transmission of the oral tradition over the decades between the event and the writings of the first gospel. Secondly, because of the inevitability that each gospel writer would have moulded the texts to convey their own particular 'take' on the story; having said that, however, we can be confident of these words for two reasons; first, because they are fully consistent with what we do know of the message of Jesus from other parts of the New Testament. Second, because the differences between the gospels' accounts of this theme are remarkably small. We can conclude that even if these are not actually the words of Jesus, they certainly convey what he would have wanted to say. The fact that these words stand out so clearly and unambiguously in the gospel accounts adds weight to their impact. For in these words we have the essence of what it means to be a Christian.

But 'love' is not an easy word to handle. Not only does the word have a number of quite distinct meanings but also it has become corrupted in its common usage. In our contemporary culture the word is too often associated only with feelings and the affective or emotional aspect of our personality. In the biblical context the word is associated with feelings, yes, but also with the intellect, with the will and with action. It is associated with every aspect of our being. It would be possible at this point to digress into a detailed analysis of the word love and its roots but that would be to divert attention from its most important aspect. If the disposition that we call love does not lead to action then it is meaningless as a cornerstone of the Christian faith.

And it is not difficult to find accounts of 'love in action' in the Christian tradition. There are many examples of individuals and groups for whom 'love in action' has been at the centre of their lives. The ten carvings of twentieth-century Christian martyrs above the west door of Westminster Abbey serve to remind us of people like Maximilian Kolbe, Martin Luther King and Oscar Romero who gave their lives in the service of others. But it is not just Christians who have demonstrated 'love in action'. Mahatma Gandhi, the Indian leader is an example from the past. Camila Batmanghelidjh, the founder of Kids Company is an example from the present. The point is that although 'love in action' may be the central precept for Christians, it is shared by many who are not Christians.

But that does not mean that 'love in action' has been at the centre of the corporate life of the church. The church has been so preoccupied with itself that it has been unable to pursue its primary objectives. It has accumulated wealth and power well beyond what it needs to fulfil its mission. It has built ecclesiastical and organisational structures that obscure the essential elements of the faith. It has promoted the assent of propositions as the necessary 'litmus test' of faith so that 'love in action' takes second place. It has also promoted a separation between the love of God and the love of neighbour, so that inevitably the love of neighbour takes second place. I am sure that this is not what Jesus intended.

The gospel writers certainly believed in God as a transcendent being. It was therefore natural for them to see a distinction between the love of God and the love of neighbour. However, in the modern world there are many for whom this understanding of God has served its purpose and needs to be recast. If God is understood as the centre of 'being' rather than as a separate 'Being' then the love of God and the love of neighbour merge. Then, to love God is to love our neighbour; to love our neighbour is to love God. We therefore need to examine what we might mean by God.

The nature of God

Any attempt to describe God in words, or pictures, or in any other way for that matter, is bound to fail. Yet there is a very long history of attempts to do this because there is such an irresistible urge in western culture to describe the indescribable. This can blind us to the fact that in just asking the question we may be leading ourselves astray. For to pose the question implies that there is an answer however inadequate that answer may be. If, however, we accept that there may be many answers to the question 'Who (or what) is God?' and that each answer may express a partial truth then we may make more progress.

Two particular ways of describing God have been very important in the tradition – transcendence and immanence. A transcendent God is one who is 'wholly other' and above and beyond the world of time and space. The biblical God is primarily transcendent and this image has been dominant in the Christian tradition. But some modern theology has put more emphasis on divine immanence. An immanent God is 'indwelling'. Here, the symbol of 'depth' is used rather than 'height' to suggest that God is the principle which expresses itself within the world rather than an external power separate and independent from it. There have been those, most notably the Deists, who have separated the reality of God so much from the reality of the world that although responsible for creation, God plays no part in sustaining it. At the other extreme, Pantheists believe in one single reality and so claim that God and the world are identical. Between these two extremes there exists a continuum with many shades of opinion.

The important point, however, is that although none of these positions can convey all the truth, all of these positions can convey some of the truth. And the criteria that we should apply in assessing the quality of these positions cannot be the extent to which they come near to expressing the truth, for that is impossible to know, but the extent to which they lead to consequences which are consistent with what has been revealed to us through scripture and tradition and with what we believe we know from reason and experience. Traditionally this reflection has led to an emphasis on the transcendence of God. Increasingly, however, this image of an 'other-worldly' God has ceased to be convincing.

John Robinson (1919-1983) and *Honest to God*

One of the first people to publically challenge this image of an 'other-worldly' God in modern times was John Robinson in his book *Honest to God* first published in 1963 and at a time of intense debate about theological issues. He called for 'far more than a restating of traditional orthodoxy in modern terms'. Instead he called for 'a much more radical recasting… in the process of which the most fundamental categories of our theology must go into the melting (pot).' He identified 'an increasing gulf between the traditional orthodox supernaturalism in which our faith has been framed and the categories which the (many people) find meaningful today' (Robinson, 1963:7). In the years since the publication of this book, this gap has widened as people abandon institutional religion and seek their spirituality elsewhere. The task is therefore now urgent.

It is not easy to discard the image of God as 'the old man in the sky'. The Bible is full of spatial images which reinforce the notion that God is somehow 'above the bright blue sky'. It speaks of Jesus 'ascending' to God and 'descending' from God. And, although we have generally accepted that these are metaphorical and not literal descriptions, we still hold on to an image of God 'out there'. We are nervous of discarding such images because they reassuringly locate God as if he existed in time and space. Yet we know that such images are unsatisfactory because God is beyond time and space. The image of God 'out there' is so much part of our belief that God is 'wholly other' that it is difficult to displace. We will need to be convinced by and comfortable with any alternative.

In traditional Christianity it has been assumed that the notion of a transcendent God implies a supernatural God. This is an objective being who is above and beyond the world and exists over and against his creation. But supernatural transcendence is not only increasingly rejected by those who take the scientific world view seriously but it is also not the only way in which it is possible to understanding transcendence. It is possible to conceive of a transcendence that is present in the natural world and to see God in a completely new way. This is not to identify God with the natural world but to identify God with all that gives meaning and direction in nature. This is not an easy step to take for religious people who want to see God as separate from nature. This is also not easy for those with a scientific world view who too readily identify nature with materialism and mechanism.

Paul Tillich (1886-1965) and *The Shaking of the Foundations*

In considering this radical change of perception, John Robinson describes the inspiration he received from Paul Tillich's collection of sermons, *The Shaking of the Foundations,* published in England in 1949, and in particular one called *The Depth of Existence*:

> It opened my eyes to the transformation that seemed to come over so much of traditional religious symbolism when it was transposed from heights to depths. God, Tillich was saying, is not a projection 'out there', an Other beyond the skies, of whose existence we have to convince ourselves, but the Ground of our very being (Robinson, 1963:21).

It is important to quote directly from Tillich:

> The name of this infinite and inexhaustible depth and ground of all being is *God.* That depth is what the word *God* means. And if that word has not much meaning for you, translate it, and speak of the depths of your life, of the source of your being, of your ultimate concern, of what you take seriously without any reservation. Perhaps, in order to do so, you must forget everything traditional that you have learned about God, perhaps even that word itself. For if you know that God means depth, you know much about him. You cannot then call yourself an atheist or unbeliever. For you cannot think or say: Life has no depth! Life is shallow. Being itself is surface only. If you could say this in complete seriousness, you would be an atheist; but otherwise you are not. He who knows about depth knows about God (Tillich, 1964:63).

Robinson suggests that the difference between these two ways of thinking can best be expressed by considering what we mean by a personal God. The theists understand God as 'a supreme person, a self-existent subject of infinite goodness and power, who enters into a relationship with us comparable with that of one personality with another'. The other way of describing God does not discard the personal but places it in a different context. God is no longer the ultimate person but the ultimate in personality. 'To say that God is personal is to say that reality at its very deepest level is personal, that personality is of ultimate significance in the constitution of the universe, that in personal relationships we touch the final meaning of existence as nowhere else' (Robinson, 1963:48). But whence faith?

To believe in God as love means to believe that in pure personal relationship we encounter, not merely what ought to be, but what is, the deepest, veriest truth about the structure of reality. This in the face of all the evidence, is a tremendous act of faith. But it is not the feat of persuading oneself of the existence of a super-being beyond this world endowed with personal qualities. Belief in God is the trust, the well-nigh incredible trust, that to give ourselves to the uttermost in love is not to be confounded but to be accepted, that love is the ground of our being, to which we ultimately come home (Robinson, 1963:49).

Honest to God made a huge impact at the time of publication. For some, the book was heretical. For many, it was 'a breath of fresh air'. For others, it did not go far enough. It had removed a vital ingredient in our image of God but had failed to provide a viable alternative. The traditional notion of transcendence was replaced by something much less tangible. It was difficult to conceive of a personal relationship with a God who was 'the ground of our being'. John Robinson himself was marginalised by the hierarchy of the church and his early death prevented him from writing a necessary sequel to this ground-breaking book.

Don Cupitt (1934-) and *Taking Leave of God*

The next watershed in the debate came with the publication of, *Taking Leave of God,* by Don Cupitt, first published in 1980. For him, Robinson and others had 'somewhat confused the issue'. He goes on:

> The task is to overthrow religiously bankrupt, because falsely objectified, dogmatism and to put specifically religious categories at the centre. The task is *not* to move from an objective and god-centred theology to a man-centred theology, as has too often happened. It is not primarily a matter of putting man and human psychology at the centre, but rather of putting the religious and the demand for its subjective appropriation by us at the centre (Cupitt, 2001:47).

Cupitt argues that to be religious is not to assent to a set of theological propositions about an objective God but to strive within ourselves towards an ideal that is God. We 'gain sovereignty by self-surrender, riches through poverty, strength through weakness, and an immortal, universal and disinterested self by dying to the self'. He goes on,

> The main interest of religion is in the conquest of evil by the transformation of the self. We seek to escape from a self that is mean, narrow, darkened acquisitive, trapped in the world and terrified of death, and we seek to become autonomous, free, creative, universally-loving and disinterested spirit that has gained release from bondage to sin and to death (Cupitt, 2001:178).

John Shelby Spong (1931-) and *A New Christianity for a New World*

One of the most worthy successors to Tillich, Robinson and Cupitt is John Shelby Spong, Episcopal Bishop of Newark until his retirement in 2000. Indeed Jack Spong writes of the debt he owes to all these theologians. He is now well into his 80s and is still writing and travelling widely. In his 2001 book, *A New Christianity for a New World* he states clearly that he does not believe in a supernatural God. For him, God is not 'a being':

> I speak rather of the God I experience as the ground and source of all being and therefore the presence that calls me to step beyond every boundary, inside which I vainly seek dependent security, into the fullness of life with all its exhilarating insecurities (Spong, 2002:59).

Spong argues that it is simply not possible for us to describe God adequately in words. It is not just that words in themselves are limited but that the words we choose are bound to reflect our own nature and experience. In other words we cannot help but describe God in human terms. We cannot help but describe his attributes as extensions of our own. We cannot help but construct doctrines, creeds and traditions that have built in inadequacy. We cannot help but respond in infantile ways. We have unwittingly constructed God in our own image. As Spong points out, 'If horses had gods would they not look like horses' (Spong, 2002:61).

So if theism is to be rejected, what is to be put in its place? Spong spells it out in this way:

> God is the ultimate source of life. One worships this God by living fully, by sharing deeply. God is the ultimate source of love. One worships this God by loving wastefully, by spreading love frivolously, by giving love away without counting the cost. God is Being (not a being), the reality underlying everything that is. To worship this God you must be willing to risk all, abandoning your defences and your self-imposed or culturally constructed security systems (Spong, 2002:70-72).

The last word goes to Jack Spong for he captures so eloquently what this new understanding of God might mean:

> The death of theism calls us into responsibility. It provides us

> with the opportunity to step boldly into the fullness of life. It is an invitation to give up the pitiful human quest for security, which we all at some level know does not exist except in our pretence, and to experience the power found in the acceptance of the fact that radical insecurity is the very mark of our humanity. It enables us to grasp this humanity without denial and to enter the fullness of life with a mature new confidence. This enhanced humanity in turn opens us to a new awareness that we are not alone. It is not that our loneliness is overcome by a parental God in the sky waiting to come to our aid. Rather, it is that we experience ourselves as part of that which is eternal. There is a reality we call God that is the source of the life we live, the power of the love we share, the Ground of Being that calls us to be all that we can be. I live today in the conviction that I am not separate from this God. I participate in that which is eternal, infinite, and beyond all boundaries. My being is expanded by this experience. Otherness confronts me. Transcendence calls me. God embraces me (Spong, 2002:74).

It is difficult to explain in a few words or in short extracts what these theologians are attempting to convey but it is possible to give something of the flavour of their work and to show that there is a common theme. That common theme has to do with a change in perception and a new paradigm. They argue that we need to see God as a subjective not an objective reality.

We now come back to where we started. But some of us can now tentatively remove the distinction between God, our neighbours and ourselves in an all-embracing command to love. But there will be others of us who wish to retain the distinction because they hold to the traditional image of God. If so, then some other way must be found to give 'love in action' the priority it deserves. For in traditional church teaching, 'love of God' comes first and 'love of neighbour' comes second. This is reflected in the way in which the concern for social justice and human dignity are seen to be things that, although not optional extras, do not carry quite the same weight. But it is difficult to understand what 'love of God' can mean if it does not refer to these concerns. So, unless these two commands can somehow be integrated, merged or understood together then it is difficult to see how 'love in action' will have the force it needs. It is difficult to avoid the conclusion that 'love in action' should be the real 'litmus test' of Christian fidelity.

After the riots

In August 2011 the towns and cities of the United Kingdom were in convulsion. From a small but tragic incident in one part of the capital, the violence and disorder spread throughout the land. Violence, arson and looting were perpetrated on a huge scale. People and property were attacked and abused indiscriminately. It was terrifying for those involved.

The gospel according to Matthew contains a strange story. Jesus is outside Jewish territory for the first time. He is looking for peace and quiet and travels north beyond Galilee to Tyre and Sidon. There he meets a woman whose daughter is ill and who has been told that the girl is possessed. She pleads with Jesus for help. The woman is not only a gentile, but comes from old Canaanite stock, the ancestral enemies of the Jews. So it would have been no surprise to anyone if Jesus had acted instinctively and ignored her plea. Indeed that appears to have been what he did when she first approaches him. But that is the beginning not the end of the story. Despite the strangeness of this story it finally points to the compassion of Jesus that we know to be at its heart; compassion for someone who was outside but who desperately needed to be brought in; someone who had been brought low; someone who needed to be raised up (Matthew 15: 21-28).

During the riots we saw so much that pulled people down. Mindless violence, vicious assaults on people, sustained attacks on property, an absence of personal responsibility, a flagrant disregard for others. Countless politicians and commentators were interviewed and offered their thoughts. But few expressed themselves so simply and so clearly as a young man who was interviewed on the television programme, *Newsnight*. David Gustave worked with young people in Peckham and made the following observation. 'I am going to sound very altruistic but I sometimes think that some of the words that are missing in all this are love, care and compassion'. Although he did not apportion blame, he went on to say that he thought that the adult world had singularly failed to inculcate into these youngsters the kinds of values that would have made their behaviour unthinkable.

The following day Haroon Jahan was killed with two friends by a hit-and-run driver in the Winson Green area of Birmingham. Later his father Tariq spoke eloquently and passionately about the need for peace and an end to the violence. Singlehandedly he may well have prevented a downward spiral into racial violence which was simmering just below the surface in that area of the city. His was an act of courage, selflessness and compassion of a high order. And subsequent actions by others have shown that we live in communities that generally aspire to the heights rather than the depths of our human condition. Witness the financial and practical support that flowed in to those who had lost homes and businesses.

Compassion may be a Christian virtue but it is something shared by many who claim no allegiance to religion. Bertrand Russell, the atheistic philosopher, was almost apologetic when he wrote:

> The root of the matter is a very simple and old fashioned thing, a thing so simple that I am almost ashamed to mention it, for fear of the derisive smile with which wise cynics will greet my words. The thing I mean – please forgive me for

> mentioning it – is love, Christian love, or compassion. If you feel like this, you have a motive for existence, a guide to action, a reason for courage, an imperative for intellectual honesty (Russell, 2009: 626).

Those who respond to the needs of individuals and communities with love and compassion in times of crisis demonstrate what 'love in action' really means and come closer than any of us to an understanding of what it might mean to say that 'God is love'.

Jesus as Human

Jesus did not come into the world to make life easy; he came to make men great.
Anon.

Introduction

It is the claim of this book that the only possible starting point for our study of Jesus must be his humanity. As John Robinson puts it in his book, *The Human Face of God*:

The real world is the starting-point: the rest is interpretation, in terms of the imagination or the intellect. This means that we have to start any Christology today from this end – from the worldly rather than the heavenly, the human rather than the divine (Robinson, 1973: 32).

The significance of the shepherds

The story is told of a European king who was acting strangely. He kept disappearing and walking in disguise amongst his people. Members of his court were concerned for his safety and asked him to stop doing it. But he answered, 'I cannot rule my people unless I know how they live.'

In the gospel according to Luke we read the story of the shepherds and the author tells us that they were 'watching over their flocks at night' just outside Bethlehem. Angels appeared to them and they were terrified. But they were soon reassured when the angels announced the birth of Jesus. The shepherds hurried to the manger to see Jesus whom they recognised. They were amazed and spread the good news to others. It is a familiar story but perhaps so familiar that we can be in danger of missing its point (Luke 2:8-20).

Shepherds were despised by the orthodox Jews of early first-century Palestine. They were quite unable to keep the ceremonial law which was so important to Judaism at that time. They could not observe all the detailed rules and regulations and the meticulous hand-washings that they were required to perform. It was simply not practical. Their flocks made constant demands on them. They could not take the risk of leaving them to perform these duties. So the orthodox Jews looked down on them. The shepherds were on the margins of society. Why then are they given so much prominence in the gospels? Why do they have so much significance for us?

The shepherds are important because they draw us towards the humanity of Jesus. The astonishing thing about the incarnation is that Jesus was a real man. Jesus was born fully human. He lived a fully human life. And he died a fully human death. He went through childhood, adolescence and adulthood in the same way as we all do. He experienced joy and sorrow, laughter and tears as we all do. He experienced the heights and depths that we all go through in our journey. It is tempting to think that Jesus was somehow spared some of the extremes of human experience. That cannot be. It is only because he became fully one with us that he was and is able to do so much for us. Jesus was fully human.

But in embracing that humanity Jesus also embraced the material world. When God created the world, 'he saw all that he had made and it was very good.' Jesus would not have fully embraced humanity if that was not so. But there is still a feeling amongst a lot of people there is something rather ugly and sordid about the material world. We inherit this view from the ancient Greeks, some of whom believed that matter was evil. And we have carried this burden ever since. A former teacher of mine called it 'Platonic drag'. We really must get it out of our system.

What then of the shepherds? The shepherds are prominent in the Christmas story because Jesus is identified totally with them, the ordinary people of that time. They also identified with him. He is not like other kings living apart from his subjects and ignorant of the way they live. He has no need of a disguise like the king in the story. He lived openly amongst us. He knows the life we live because he lived it.

The historical Jesus

Jesus was an historical figure and the evidence that we have paints the following picture. He was born in an obscure village in Palestine at the start of the Common Era and was the son of orthodox Jewish parents. He worked as a carpenter for the first years of his life and thereafter became an itinerant preacher. He gathered many followers and attracted large crowds. He challenged the Jewish authorities who conspired against him, and was tried and convicted as public opinion was turned against him. He died after crucifixion but was claimed to have risen from the dead. He has since become the most prominent figure in history.

Few would dispute this basic outline of the life of Jesus, but the record of the words and actions of Jesus is much more contentious and for some time has been challenged by biblical scholars. For those who claim that the Bible is inerrant, there is no problem because, for them, every word and action attributed to Jesus is authentic. For those who make no such claim, these words and actions must be critically examined. The search for the historicity of Jesus was a series of movements which began in the nineteenth century and which continue to this day. This search was pioneered by the German theologian, David Friedrich Strauss (1808-1874). His book, *The Life of Jesus, Critically Examined,* published in 1835, caused a sensation.

All these movements were attempts to discover the Jesus of history using the tools of biblical scholarship and from the beginning these ideas were contentious. Some scholars claimed that such a quest was not appropriate since Jesus was not an ordinary man and that any conclusions were bound to be misleading. Others believed that it was important to establish the historicity of Jesus as accurately as possible in order to understand the Jesus of faith. One of the most prominent of these scholars was Albert Schweitzer (1875-1965), the title of whose book became the name of the series of movement which it describes – *The Quest for the Historical Jesus*. Schweitzer himself believed that the life of Jesus could only be understood in the context of his understanding of eschatology – the last days (Schweitzer, 2000). Others argued that Jesus was a sapiential teacher of wisdom rather than an apocalyptic prophet of eschatology. The debate continued throughout the nineteenth and twentieth centuries.

The latest stage in this quest began with the formation of The Jesus Seminar by Robert Funk in 1985. One of the most active groups in biblical criticism, the seminar members vote to decide their collective view of the historicity of Jesus, specifically what he may or may not have said and done as a historical figure. In the book *The Five Gospels*, Robert Funk summarises what he describes as the seven pillars of biblical criticism. These are the underlying assumptions agreed by members of the seminar as they undertake their work. The first pillar is the distinction that should be made between the Jesus of history and the Christ of faith. This is the distinction between viewing Jesus through the lens of historical criticism and viewing Jesus through traditional creedal formulations. The second pillar is the recognition that the synoptic gospels – Matthew, Mark and Luke – are closer to the historical Jesus than John. The third pillar is the agreement that Mark was written prior to and formed the basis for both Matthew and Luke. The fourth pillar is that there existed a document of the sayings of Jesus called 'Q' – 'quelle' in German, meaning 'source' – which also formed a basis for both Matthew and Luke. The fifth pillar was a rejection of Schweitzer's claim for the eschatological focus in the life of Jesus. The sixth pillar was a recognition of the fundamental distinction between the oral and written tradition. The seventh pillar is the assumption that:

> the gospels are a narrative in which the memory of Jesus is embellished by mythical elements that express the church's faith in him and by plausible fiction that enhance the telling of the gospel story for first century listeners who knew about divine men and miracle working at first hand (Funk, 1993:5).

The Jesus Seminar adds a final 'general rule of evidence', 'beware of finding a Jesus entirely congenial to you'. It needs to be pointed out that the fifth gospel is the *Gospel of Thomas* regarded by members of the seminar as claiming some authenticity.

The Five Gospels is the collective report of members of the Jesus Seminar working closely together for six years on a common question: What did Jesus really say? Together and singly, they first of all compiled a list of all words attributed to Jesus in the surviving ancient texts. They then examined those words in the several ancient languages in which they have been preserved. They produced a translation of all the gospels, known as the *Scholars Version*. And, finally, they studied, debated, and voted on each of the sayings of Jesus in the list. In the book, all the 1500 sayings attributed to Jesus have been colour-coded according to the results of the voting. The coding is red for those words most probably spoken by the historical Jesus. Pink, a weaker form of red, was used for those words the scholars felt less certain could be traced back to Jesus or which they are certain were modified in transmission. The scholars left in bold black those words that were put in Jesus' mouth by his later followers or enemies and are unauthentic. They used grey, as an intermediate level between pink and black, to categorise those words that Jesus did not say but which may reflect his ideas. Their overall conclusions were that only some 20% of the recorded words of Jesus in the Gospels were authentic and that in John's Gospel that figure fell to zero! Similarly, the book, *The Acts of Jesus* addresses the question: What did Jesus actually do?

The work of The Jesus Seminar has been sharply criticised by many scholars not least by Tom Wright, former Bishop of Durham. His detailed criticisms are substantive and need to be addressed in any assessment of the value of this project. However, it is at least arguable that the importance of this project lies less in the way in which it was executed than in the way it was conceived. From its inception it injected new momentum into biblical scholarship and in due course made that scholarship more accessible to lay men and women in the churches. For too long ordinary Christians have been led to believe that all the words attributed to Jesus are authentic. This is not always because they have been explicitly told so but because it has often been implicitly assumed to be the case. Despite decades of biblical scholarship the words of the Bible have been taken at face value, and questions about the authenticity of the recorded words and actions of Jesus have simply never been addressed. This has happened because there has been so much preoccupation with the divinity of Jesus that his humanity has been largely ignored. Or to put it another way, the Christ of faith has been emphasised at the expense of the Jesus of history. It has been forgotten that the one illuminates the other!

The discussion about the nature of God in the previous chapter has considerable bearing on the status of Jesus, and any rejection of a theistic God has serious implications for our understanding of Jesus. Jack Spong puts it this way:

> Why must we tell the Christ-story apart from the theistic concept of God? Quite simply, we must do so because the residual theism of the past is today strangling the very life out of Christianity. The theistic God-content, that has been so tightly wound around Jesus of Nazareth from a very early date, makes it all but impossible to see Jesus as having any meaning at all. So unless we loosen the hold that theism has

> on Christ, the death of theism will surely mean the death of Christianity.
>
> If the supernatural being who lives above the sky, invading life periodically to accomplish a divine purpose, has fallen into disrepute and is no longer a possibility for the belief systems of modern men and women, then surely we must acknowledge that what Jesus understood as the incarnation of this theistic deity is equally without a future. The Jesus of the supernatural entry into life through the miracle of the virgin birth; the Jesus of the supernatural exit from this world through the miracle of the cosmic ascension; the Jesus who in his earthly existence did such God like things as walking on water, stilling the storm, healing the sick, raising the dead, and feeding the multitude with but five loaves –this Jesus is little more than an earthly portrait of the theistic God in human form. If theism is dying today, a casualty of advancing knowledge, then the understanding of Jesus as the incarnation of this theistic deity is also mortally wounded. But is that all there is to Jesus? (Spong, 2002:81).

Spong argues that these theistic elements were not part of the original story of Jesus and that they only became integrated with that story as it was transmitted orally and in writing in the early years of the Christian Church. His evidence is that the early texts from which the gospels were written, and the Letters of Paul which also predate the gospels, contain few explicit or even implicit references to the supernatural. Even in the Gospel of Mark, which is generally regarded as the first of the written gospels, supernatural elements are not prominent and some important incidents are missing. For example, there are no miraculous birth stories in Mark. In the Gospels of Matthew and Luke however the use of theistic language increases dramatically. All of which suggests that there was a developing tradition in which theistic language was progressively introduced to account for the special qualities that Jesus demonstrated. If we can unravel this tradition then it should be possible to uncover the nature of that special quality and to re-caste it in a different way.

That special quality in Jesus which was increasingly given the status of divinity was actually his humanity. Our preoccupation with divinity has obscured humanity and given both divinity and humanity a separate and distinct status so that we are now asked to accept that Jesus was both fully divine and fully human. The contortions that are necessary to accommodate this duality are impossible to perform with any integrity and we are left with a thoroughly unsatisfactory result. It is, of course, possible to say that these things are beyond our knowledge and that only God knows how this apparent contradiction can be resolved. But that brings us back to a theistic God and will not do. If, on the other hand, divinity is approached through humanity then the dilemma disappears and we are left with a theology which takes seriously both humanity and divinity without the need for a theistic God. This is to assert that the qualities which Jesus exhibited were actually those that arise in the fullness of humanity. To follow Jesus is to work towards the perfection of the human person that he personifies and which we can also call the mystery of God.

John Dominic Crossan was one of the most prominent scholars in the formation of the Jesus Seminar and his book, *The Historical Jesus: The Life of a Mediterranean Jewish Peasant*, has been one of the most influential books in the debate. The book is introduced on the flyleaf as follows:

> The conventional wisdom of critical historical scholarship has long held that too little is known about the historical Jesus to say definitively much more than that he lived and had a tremendous impact on his followers. "There were always historians who said it could not be done because of historical problems" writes Crossan. "There were always theologians

> who said it should not be done because of theological objections. And there were always scholars who said the former when they meant the later."... Crossan emphatically sweeps these notions aside. He demonstrates that Jesus is actually one of the best documented figures in ancient history; the challenge is the complexity of the sources. (Crossan, 1991).

In the first chapter of his book, Crossan outlines the difficulties of reconstructing the historical Jesus in the face of so many filters and constrictions:

> The first century of the Common Era is obscured from our contemporary view by three giant filters. The past is recorded almost exclusively in the voices of elites and males, in the viewpoints of the wealthy and the powerful, in the visions of the literate and the educated. That already constricted report is available sometimes through the deliberate decision of later dominations but also through the vagaries of chance and luck, fate and accident. Either way, further constrictions (Crossan, 1991:3).

He then asks, 'How then is it possible for us to imagine the face of a Mediterranean Jewish peasant through those triple filters and across the gulf of those millennia?' He answers:

> Three major sources help at least somewhat to counter those three filters just mentioned. First, on the macroscopic level, there are anthropological and sociological studies and models, especially those using trans-temporal and cross-cultural disciplines. Next, on the mesocosmic level, and more local level, there are archaeological digs and discoveries. Finally, on the microscopic level, there are papyrus documents and archives, documentary texts predominantly from Egypt in which ordinary peasants have preserved an individual voice and a

> personal presence normally denied them by their illiteracy and their poverty (Crossan, 1991:4).

Crossan then goes on to tackle these challenges and following a detailed examination of his sources provides a picture of the historical Jesus. In his final chapter he offers some observations on his project:

> This book, then, is a scholarly reconstruction of the historical Jesus. And if one were to accept its formal methods and even their material investments, one could surely offer divergent interpretative conclusions about the reconstructable historical Jesus. But one cannot dismiss it or the search for the historical Jesus as *mere* reconstruction, as if reconstruction invalidated somehow the entire project. Because there is *only* reconstruction. For a believing Christian both the life of the Word of God and the text of the Word of God are like a graded process of historical reconstruction, be it red, pink, grey, black... If you cannot believe in something produced by reconstruction, you may have nothing left to believe in (Crossan, 1991:426).

One of the most important aspects of Crossan's book is the way he uses the sources available to him. Not only does he draw on the widest range of extra-biblical sources like the *Gospel of Thomas*, but he also draws on the insights of the widest range of academic disciplines like anthropology to illuminate his task. This reinforces the point that we really cannot ignore the human enterprise in our search for the divine truth.

Jesus as fully man

If we are to tackle the orthodox claim that Jesus was both human and divine then we must look more closely at the extent to which Jesus was a man.

In *The Human Face of God*, John Robinson examines the person of Christ. In the chapter, *A Man*, he states clearly that 'if Jesus is to be our man, he must be one of us…, completely part of the world…, in other words, a man in every sense of the word'. As he also makes clear, this has had 'to be insisted on again and again in the history of doctrine'. He goes on:

> It is a constant astonishment that the *first* serious heresy that the church had to face was that of Docetism, that is to say, that Jesus merely *appeared* to be human. Whatever else one would have expected men to doubt, one would never have expected men to doubt the evidence of their own eyes and the memory of one who, whatever *more* he was, was so obviously one of themselves, a man among men (Robinson, 1973: 36).

The very early Christians had no difficulty in accepting Jesus as fully human but within a few years uncertainty arose as controversy spread over the difficulty of reconciling the human and divine nature of Christ. Although Docetism was roundly condemned as a heresy in the early councils of the church, doubts about the full humanity of Jesus lived on and continue to exert an influence now. The implications of this are serious.

For Robinson, doubts about the humanity of Jesus:

> are much more destructive of the gospel than doubts about his divinity. For this is to undermine it from the start. It cannot even begin to be good news – let alone where it ends (Robinson, 1973: 38).

Or as John Knox writes in *The Death of Christ*:

> Unless it be agreed that he was truly man, it does not greatly matter what else can be said of him (Knox, 1959: 39).

But, in accepting the full humanity of Jesus we have to accept the implications. If Jesus was fully man, as we understand it at the beginning of the twenty-first century, then his manhood was determined by both his genetic and environmental history and circumstances, and his personhood was defined by his psychological and sociological dispositions. He could only have been fully man if he really was one of us.

Previous generations have found it difficult to accept that Jesus was genuinely shaped by the world around him and was not just 'passing through'. In *The Humanity and Divinity of Christ,* John Knox writes:

> An affirmation of Jesus' manhood is an assertion that he was born out of, and into, humanity in the same sense every man is; that he was a son of Abraham, just as every man participates in his own race or nation or culture; and, more important, that he was a son of Adam, as all men are, regardless of what their culture, nation or race may be. There is no other conceivable way of being a man (Knox, 1968:44).

In accepting the full humanity of Jesus we also have to accept that we sometimes recoil from full identity with him, and feel:

> a psychological necessity to set a break between Jesus' humanity and our own. We cannot stand the identity of the same flesh and blood, the continuity of genes and sperm and plasm. We want solidarity with us, but from the outside: identification rather than identity (Robinson, 1973:48).

In *The Death of Christ,* John Knox writes:

> For all his goodness and greatness, the wonder of his manhood, the qualities of mind and spirit which lift him so far above us, he was still a human being like ourselves. Not

> only should we not want it otherwise; we ought not to be able to bear it otherwise. Jesus was a man like ourselves; Jesus' nature was our common human nature. To say this is not to make a grudging concession to secular reason; it is to make a vital affirmation of Christian faith (Knox, 1959:125).

Jesus as perfect man

Even if we agree that Jesus was fully man we have to tackle the question of whether he was in some sense the 'perfect' man:

> It has tended to be taken as axiomatic in Christian thinking and devotion that Jesus was complete and perfect in every respect. He must have had everything, he must have been everything – or he could not have been the Christ. And this has been a powerful influence in the separation of him from ordinary humanity. He has been set on a pedestal by himself, an immaculate paragon, of whom it was impossible to think that he should fall short in anything. And as such he quickly becomes unique not because he is normal but because he is abnormal. What we want to say of him as *the* man paradoxically undercuts his humanity. And this is a powerful factor today in making him for many an unreal figure with the static perfection of flawless porcelain, rather than a man of flesh and blood (Robinson, 1973:68).

But a man of flesh and blood he must have been which means that he must have been subject to the same pressures and temptations as we all are and to have responded as we all do. But the particulars of our response will always depend on our individual dispositions so that there are a multitude of ways in which men can approach the best that men can be. So Jesus becomes one man among many who aspire to that ideal and is only distinguished by the superior extent of his achievement. We can separate Jesus in degree but not in kind from other men if he is to retain his humanity. The notion of the perfect man is therefore a nonsense.

Jesus as more than man

Christians wish to affirm that Jesus shows us not only man but God. So, having wrestled with the question of the extent to which Jesus is man, we must confront the question of the extent to which Jesus was God. The difficulty is that in ascribing divinity to Jesus we do not wish to compromise his humanity but that, sadly, is what has happened. The tradition has been established that Christ was not a human person but a divine person who assumed human nature without assuming human personality. There is therefore a bias in favour of divinity over and against humanity. This will not do.

Without going further into the debate about this issue that has raged over the centuries, it is clear that much of the difficulty arises because of the language that we use. It is assumed that it is possible to convey the whole truth by the use of words and that one language will do for both the human and divine. The fact we may need to use two different languages to convey that truth seems to have been missed. In *The Human Face of God,* John Robinson argues that if we focus on two languages rather than two natures then we may make some progress:

> The formula that we presuppose is not of one superhuman person with two natures, divine and human, but of one human person of whom we must use two languages, man-language and God-language. Jesus is wholly and completely a man, but a man who 'speaks true' not simply of humanity but of God. He is not a man plus, a man fitted, as it were, with a second engine – which would mean that he was not a man in any genuine sense. He is a man who in all that he says and does as a man is the personal representative of God: he stands in God's place, he is God to us and for us (Robinson, 1973:113).

This means that we must describe the Incarnation and all other aspects of Christian theology from two different perspectives:

> (We must) see the natural and the supernatural not as two layers of being that have to be joined together, so much as two sets of language, man-language and God-language, in which it is possible to speak of a single cosmic process. In other words, what we are talking about is not two storeys but two stories. The one is natural, scientific, descriptive. The other is supernatural, mythological and interpretative. The former views the course of events in the categories of evolutionary cosmology, the latter in terms of 'moments' like Creation, the Fall, the Incarnation, the Parousia (Second Coming) (Robinson, 1973:116).

Jesus as the decisive revelation of God

In his book, *Speaking Christian*, Marcus Borg adopts these two stories but in a different way. He distinguishes between the pre-Easter Jesus and the post-Easter Jesus:

> The pre-Easter Jesus refers to Jesus as a historical figure of the past, a Galilean Jew, born around 4 BCE and crucified around 30 CE. A flesh-and-blood human being like us, he was a particular height and weight, had to eat and drink, and was mortal. He had a beginning and an ending. This Jesus doesn't exist anymore. He is dead and gone. To say this does not deny Easter... Easter and the resurrection are not about the restoration of Jesus to his previous state. The post-Easter Jesus refers to what Jesus became after his death in Christian experience, reflection and tradition (Borg, 2011: 86-7).

Easter is grounded in the experience of the early followers of Jesus and it is clear that thereafter they experienced Jesus in a radically new way. The Gospels tell us of how the appearances of

Jesus led to a conviction that he was not simply a dead figure of the past but a living reality in the present. And this was a divine reality not a human one.

As time passes, the life and teaching of the pre-Easter Jesus is recorded in the gospels and elsewhere through the memories of those who were present at the time and through oral transmission of those who came after. At the same time, the experience and witness of the post-Easter Jesus emerges into a developing tradition amongst his followers in the decades after his death as the gospels and other writings testify.

The genuine epistles of Paul written some twenty years after the death of Jesus are the earliest record that we have. The latest writings in the New Testament are from the early to mid-second century. In these developing traditions Jesus is given titles like 'Messiah', 'Lord', 'Son God', 'Light of the World' and so on, all of which are the testimony of his followers of who Jesus had become for them in their experience, life and thought.

For Borg, 'the distinction between the pre-Easter Jesus and the post-Easter Jesus matters greatly'.

> To put it negatively, failing to see the distinction creates confusion. To put it positively, seeing the distinction is greatly illuminating. When we do not make the distinction, the result is a hybrid Jesus. Everything that is said about the post-Easter Jesus is projected back into the pre-Easter Jesus. The result is that even as a human being, he was divine – he could walk on water, feed a multitude with a few loaves and fishes, change water into wine, and so on. But all of this makes the pre-Easter Jesus more than human – and thus not really human (M. Borg, 2011:89-90).

The result is the heresy of Docetism – that Jesus only appeared to be human, but was really God:

> But to think of the pre-Easter Jesus as divine actually diminishes him. If he was divine and had the power of God, then what he did wasn't all that remarkable. He could have done so much more. But the classic Christian affirmation about the pre-Easter Jesus is not that he was God, but he was the decisive revelation of God. This is the cumulative meaning of the exalted language that Christians use for Jesus: in him, we see what can be seen of God in a human life (M. Borg, 2011:90).

Clearly, some of God's qualities cannot be seen in any human life, even the life of Jesus. It would not make much sense to describe any human being as omnipotent (all powerful) or omniscient (all knowing). But some of God's qualities can be seen in any human life particularly in the life of Jesus. Jesus is the decisive revelation of the character and compassion of God.

It follows that wherever and whenever we see these qualities displayed in those around us we see just a glimpse of God. Jesus was the decisive revelation of God but that revelation was not completed in him. At this different time and in this different place God continues to reveal himself. He reveals himself in the people we meet and in the events of our experience. We need to keep our eyes open.

The face of Jesus

In the introduction to his book, *The Human Face of God,* David Cruz reminds us that, while the Old Testament is full of words about the face of God, not much is said in the New Testament. It is clear that the face of Jesus must have been familiar to those who knew him even if we have no detailed descriptions. The face of Jesus can also be familiar to us who have the privilege of meeting him in other ways. David Cruz encourages us to:

> …rediscover and recognise the face of Jesus, as he continues to

> reveal himself in the faces of the young, the old, the poor, the affluent, the wounded, the wise, the neglected, the contented, the abused, the hopeful, the courageous, the despised, the fearful, the sick, the healthy, and the ordinary. It is in these ordinary faces that he is continually trying to reveal himself to us and to the world (Cruz, 2007: viii).

But it works both ways:

> Similarly, we Christians believe and hope that others will come to recognise the living presence of Jesus in us. To put it another way, if I encounter you, the Christ in you will reveal himself to me, while the Christ in me will reveal himself to you. How different the world (and our lives) would be if only we could embrace this ideal (Cruz, 2007:24).

Cruz goes on to illustrate how we can see the particular qualities of Trust, Mercy, Compassion, Forgiveness, Courage and Hope in the faces of those around us All these qualities have a human face.

In the chapter, *Mercy Has a Face*, Cruz reminds us of the Polish priest Maximilian Kolbe who was imprisoned in Auschwitz and who offered to exchange his life for a man about to be executed as a reprisal for the escape of a prisoner during the night:

> When Frank Gajowniczek cried out in despair that he would never again see his wife and children, Maximilian came forward and said, "I am a Catholic priest. I wish to die for that man. I am old; he has a wife and children." Days later, Maximilian, and the other condemned men, died when they were starved to death as a deterrent to prevent further escapes. When John Paul II elevated Maximilian Kolbe to sainthood many years later, in attendance at the ceremony was Frank Gajowniczek, the man whose life Maximilian had

saved (Cruz, 2007: 29).

In the chapter, *Forgiveness Has a Face,* Cruz recalls the tragic events of 2006 when a gunman walked into a rural Pennsylvania school and took ten children hostage. The children belonged to the Amish community and at the end of the siege five girls were dead and the gunman had taken his own life. In the days that followed a local newspaper recalled the details of the funeral of the killer:

> What was striking, indeed remarkable, was that of the seventy-five mourners in attendance approximately half were from the Amish community. In spite of the terrible and tragic events that had befallen them… their presence underscored their remarkable faith in God and humanity. Indeed it was noted by more than one mourner that the example of unconditional love and forgiveness offered by the Amish to the wife of the man who had done so much harm simply made them break down in tears (Cruz, 2007: 66).

In other sections of this book are stories from other chapters of Cruz's book, each of which illustrate other aspects of the face of Jesus or the human face of God.

The Primacy of Humanity

> To be a Christian does not mean to be religious in any particular way, to cultivate some particular form of asceticism (as a sinner, a penitent or a saint), but to be a man. It is not some religious act which makes a Christian what he is, but participation in the suffering of God in the life of the world… (Bonhoeffer 1965: 123).

The story of Marcello

In her book, *The Human Brain*, the eminent neuroscientist, Susan Greenfield, tells the story of a little Italian boy whom I will call Marcello (Greenfield, 1997:114).

Marcello was six years old. He lived with his parents in a small village in Italy. In many ways he was a normal little boy, full of energy and mischief. But in one important way he was different to the other boys in the village. Marcello was blind in one eye. He had been blind since birth and the cause of his blindness was a medical mystery. As far as the doctors could tell his eye was perfectly normal. He had been in and out of hospital as specialists tried to find out the cause of his blindness. He had been examined by many people all of whom felt sure that he ought to be able to see. But as Marcello kept telling them, with his normal eye closed he could see nothing.

Eventually, the mystery was solved. It emerged that as a baby Marcello's eye was bandaged for two weeks. It was bandaged as part of the treatment for a minor infection. Such treatment would have had no lasting effect on an older person. But with a very young boy so soon after birth the eye was at a critical stage of development, as the links between eye and brain began to be formed. Because the bandaged eye was not able to do its job, the brain assumed that the boy would not be using that eye for the rest of his life and failed to make the necessary connections. It was now too late and Marcello would be blind in one eye for ever.

The brain is a highly complicated part of the body. It works as electrical and chemical messages are transferred by neurones making connections between different parts of the brain. There are millions of neurones and millions of connections. Up to the age of about sixteen the brain is a 'battle ground' for establishing connections. Neurones 'compete' for connections. If a new neurone does not make contact with a target neurone then it dies. In Marcello's case, as the bandaged eye was not used, neurone connections were not made. The eye became isolated and useless. Brain research has shown that even small changes in our lifestyle can cause physical changes in the growing brain. Studies have shown an increase in the number of neurone connections in those parts of the brain which have been particularly stimulated or well used. For example, if you are a talented sportsman, then in those parts of the brain associated with the co-ordination of your arms and legs, the neurone connections will be particularly well developed.

So, as we grow up our brain is developing in this important way and it is at risk. There are three ways in which we can interfere with the healthy development of our brain. Firstly, there are accidents. The brain is one of most vulnerable parts of the body and in a car accident is very easily damaged. Secondly, there is abuse. The abuse of drugs can cause permanent damage to the brain. Thirdly, it is clearly possible to affect the development of our brain through lack of use. Marcello's faculty of sight was damaged by lack of use during early childhood. If it is possible to damage major faculties like sight or hearing in this way, then it is also possible to damage our ability to perform other physical and mental functions. It is therefore possible to damage just those skills and talents that make us such unique individuals. If we fail to develop these skills then we may lose them forever.

Most of us recognise emerging strengths and talents in

ourselves and in each other as we grow up. Many of us have physical talents and are good at sport. Others have intellectual talents and are academically strong. Some mix well with other people and have good personal skills. And so it goes on. Each of us also has enormous potential to achieve great things in a wide range of different situations and circumstances. But if the development of that potential is neglected we fail to be the people God made us to be. If we fail to engage with the fullness of our humanity we fail in the service of love to each other to which we are called.

The primacy of humanity

It is an essential premise of this book that any discussion of the Christian enterprise must start with a human rather than a divine perspective. There are two reasons for this. First, it is as human beings that we are embodied as persons, it is as human beings that we engage with the world around us and it is as human beings that we form relationships with the rest of the created order. Second, it as a human being that that which we understand as God was embodied in the form of Jesus of Nazareth, thereby placing humanity at the pinnacle of creation, giving humanity the responsibility for the stewardship of the created order and giving humanity the obligation to nurture and develop it. Despite this, humanity has not been seen positively within the tradition of the Christian Church and the humanity of Jesus has been given much less emphasis than his divinity. This has much to do with the theology of the Fall.

For John Shelby Spong, former Bishop of Newark, this has to change. In a world which almost universally accepts that all creatures have evolved from primitive organisms and that there never was any 'special creation' that suddenly placed fully formed animals and humans on the planet by divine degree, the traditional theology of the 'fall downwards' makes no sense. Instead, it is to a 'fall upwards', as some have described it, that we must turn. In his book, *A New Christianity for a New World,* Spong puts it this way:

> The Darwinian view says that there never was a perfect and completed creation. The universe is not yet finished. It is still evolving and expanding. New galaxies continue to be formed. The post-Darwinian world also recognises that there never was a perfect man or a perfect woman who fell into sin in an act of disobedience. That account is not true either historically or metaphorically. Human beings are *emerging* creatures; they are a work in progress. Neither perfect or fallen, they are simply *incomplete* (Spong, 2002: 123-4).

He goes on to show how damaging this traditional theology has been and how negative a view of humanity it has given us. His point is that although humans are obviously capable of sin, they are not stained by 'original sin':

> It is time, I am convinced, to move Christianity beyond that historically inaccurate and psychologically damaging definition of humanity that has resulted in a constant denigration of human life as helpless, depraved, sinful, and in need of divine rescue. The suggestion made by so much of the Christian theology of the past that every baby is born with the stain of original sin distorting his or her goodness is abhorrent to me. I now regard the traditional Christian interpretation of the account of the fall of humanity, told in the narrative of the Garden of Eden, as the ultimate example of distorted negative thinking (Spong, 2002:149-150).

He argues instead for a positive view of the human condition, and one that really does allow humanity to move forward:

> I prefer to look at the wonder of humanity and to celebrate the

> incredible gift of self-conscious life that has emerged from our earliest living ancestor... To spend my energy concentrating on the presumed lostness, the moral depravity, or the hopelessness of human beings, so easily called sinners by traditional Christianity, is to fail to appreciate the most incredible product of the whole created order – namely the human mind. When I look at what humans have achieved, from great works of art to magnificent symphonies, from architectural wonders to surgical and medical skills that are breathtaking, I stand in awe of human life (Spong, 2002:150).

It is partly for these reasons that this book is primarily concerned with humanity and with the insights that the human condition gives to us in our journey towards God. Our journey begins in an understanding of what it means to refer to the dignity of the human person.

The dignity of man

The incarnation shows that God has faith in man and is prepared to invest in him. And what he invests is love and it is this which gives man his being and value. That love manifests itself in a multitude of different ways and gives man those qualities of freedom, integrity, generosity, and indeed all those qualities that are outlined in this book. Each of these qualities builds him up and enables him to share these qualities with others. For God does not invest in man for himself but to enable him to extend that investment to others. And so man is not only not man without God, but is not man without men.

If man's dignity arises from God, does that mean that all men have equal dignity in the eyes of God? And do all men have equal dignity in the eyes of other men? In his book, *Neither Beast Nor God: The dignity of the human person*, Gilbert Meilaender seeks to clarify meanings by drawing a distinction between human dignity and personal dignity:

> The concept of human dignity is simply a placeholder for what is thought to be characteristically human – and to be honoured and upheld because it is human. The concept of personal dignity is needed to make clear that, however different we may be in the degree to which we possess some of the characteristically human capacities, we are equal persons whose comparative 'worth' cannot and ought not to be assessed (Meilaender 2009: 1).

This distinction is important because we wish at the same time to celebrate qualities that are essentially human and to celebrate the humanity of each individual person. Clearly people differ in the extent to which they demonstrate these human qualities and it would be naïve to suggest otherwise. Physical, mental and spiritual capacities vary from one person to another in all sorts of ways and for all sorts of reasons. But it would be invidious to use these differences to produce an 'anthropological league table'. We are all too aware of what happens when some people are given more 'worth' than others. In Nazi Germany, those who were considered to be of less worth, like mental patients, were ruthlessly exterminated.

Even in so called 'enlightened societies' we are all guilty of placing people in a hierarchy because we have blurred the distinction between these two important perspectives. In employment we are inclined to give greater worth to those with academic ability than those with technical skills. It is perfectly reasonable to give greater worth to the abilities of one person over another for that person may give greater added value to the company because of their advanced skills. But we must not give greater worth to that person as a person for that would be to deny the distinction that has been so carefully made and would deny their equality with other persons in the sight of God.

The notion of equality is a fundamental outcome of the distinction between human and personal dignity:

> Between the concepts of human dignity and personal dignity there is a dialectical relationship. Each needs the other to supplement its central concern. We need the language of human dignity to talk about matters that involve the integrity and flourishing of the human species, and we need the language of personal dignity to express respect for persons regarded as equal and non-interchangeable individuals (Meilaender 2009: 87).

This equality is enshrined in the Universal Declaration of Human Rights adopted by the United Nations in 1948. In the process of preparing the Declaration, the United Nations Educational, Scientific and Cultural Organisation (UNESCO) convened a committee of philosophers to examine the theoretical basis for universal claims about human dignity and rights. Although they were able to agree on these claims, they were unable to agree on 'why' these claims are true. That is not altogether surprising because the philosophers came from different ethnic, cultural and religious backgrounds. Those from a Christian background would point to the nature of God and the way these claims arise directly from the world he has created.

There have been many who have sought to bring dignity to the lives of those who suffer oppression or are otherwise on the margins of society. John Shelby Spong wrote of Nelson Mandela, 'This man expanded the potential of what it means to be human in ways that most people can still hardly imagine' (Spong, 2014).

Human Rights

Human rights arise from the understanding that there is something that we all share because we are all human. We could label it 'personal rights' to preserve Meilaender's distinction but 'human rights' is the phrase in common usage. Human rights are universal claims regardless of whether they are recognised in law or not but for those rights to be respected a framework of national and international law is essential.

The modern human rights movement originated in the Second World War and the subsequent trials of those who had committed crimes against whole communities established new perspectives in national and international law. The Nuremberg Trials were a series of military tribunals set up in 1945-6 to try Nazi war criminals and were particularly significant. Up to that point, Churchill would have preferred to take the perpetrators out and have had them shot as had been British policy in the last years of the war. In *The No-Nonsense Guide to Human Rights,* Olivia Ball and Paul Gready write:

> The Nuremberg Tribunal was a watershed in the fight against impunity for flagrant human rights violations for a number of reasons: It held individuals responsible for the actions of states and other collective entities, it underlined concrete duties we all have under international law, and it overruled 'just following orders' as a defence (Ball and Gready 2006).

The closest there is to a founding document for human rights is the 1948 *Universal Declaration of Human Rights* (UDHR) associated with the founding of the United Nations. The first three articles of the Declaration then give a flavour of the whole:

> All human beings are born free and equal in dignity and rights. They are endowed with reason and conscience and should act towards one another in a spirit of brotherhood. Everyone is entitled to all the rights and freedoms set forth in this Declaration, without distinction of any kind, such as race, colour, sex, language, religion, political or other opinion, national or social origin, property, birth or other status... Everyone has the right to life, liberty and security of person... (United Nations 1948).

Antecedents to human rights can of course be found in all cultures and religions. The *Ten Commandments* are a basis for Jewish, Christian and Muslim ethics. They express the right to life and property in terms of duties as, for example, in 'Thou shalt not kill'. The rule of law, which is so fundamental to the protection of human rights, can be traced back to the *Hammurabi's Code* from the eighteenth century BCE in which King Hammurabi of Babylonia and Mesopotamia attempted to systemise and publicise the laws of his realm. It marked a significant departure from arbitrary rule.

The development of human rights followed a chequered path in the centuries that followed early declarations. Christian doctrine would for centuries assert that kings were divinely appointed with absolute power which was accountable to no one. For long periods there were flagrant breaches of the human rights of individuals in the face of powerful movements in both Church and State. Imprisonment, torture and execution were routine throughout the Middle Ages. Yet the human rights imperative was never altogether lost.

That major intellectual movement of eighteenth-century Europe which we call the Enlightenment heralded new approaches to human rights:

> Jean-Jacques Rousseau typified the Enlightenment. He hypothesised a 'state of nature' in which our species might have existed prior to the creation of society and government. Complete freedom and equality between all humans was the natural state of things. Democratic government and political rights spring from equality, when we reject the idea that any person or group is born to rule (Ball and Gready 2006).

But many a human rights movement fell well short of what Ball and Gready describe as 'the true meaning of its creed'.

> The French Republic, for example, refused to abolish slavery in its colonies or give women the vote… Mary Wollstonecraft also tried to inject sexual equality into the first human rights revolution… Sojourner Truth worked to get the rights of black women on the liberal agenda in the US (Ball and Gready 2006).

In the nineteenth century, movements to extend human rights in practice included the successful campaign to abolish slavery. Although for a long time many in the church argued against abolition, members of the Clapham Sect did much to further the movement. They were a group of influential like-minded Church of England social reformers based in Clapham, London at the beginning of the century and William Wilberforce was one of their leading lights. At the same time, those with similar motives fought for labour rights, child welfare, the right to education and universal, or at least adult male, suffrage.

Human rights were never more widely accepted or grossly violated than in the twentieth century with the genocide of Armenians, Jews and Tutsis and others, and with the two most destructive wars in history killing millions and denying basic human rights to millions more. On the other hand, colonies achieved independence, women's rights gained unprecedented recognition and the welfare state was born. The latter part of the century was notable for an incomparable worldwide effort to further human rights and to make human rights the 'litmus test' of a civilised society.

Many of the great men and women of the twentieth century have written about human rights, most notably some of our most prominent church leaders. The joint canonisations of Pope John XX111 and Pope John 11 in April 2014 reminds us that, although they approached Catholic Social Teaching from very different directions and came to very different conclusions, both popes were concerned for human flourishing and both wrote and spoke extensively in defence of human rights.

In his final encyclical, *Pacem in Terris* (Peace on Earth), promulgated in 1963 just before he died, John XX111 writes:

> Any well-regulated and productive association of men in society demands the acceptance of one fundamental principle: that each individual man is truly a person. His is a nature, that is, endowed with intelligence and free will. As such he has rights and duties, which together flow as a direct consequence from his nature. These rights and duties are universal and inviolable, and therefore altogether inalienable (John XX111, 1963).

For both popes, the notion of human rights arises from their understanding of Natural Law. This refers to the view that morality arises from the very nature of human beings. For example, they would both agree that the United Nations Declaration on Human Rights proposes a set of rights which belong to human beings because of what human beings are, and which ought to be respected for that reason. Natural Law lies at the heart of Roman Catholic teaching on Christian Ethics.

In his address to the fiftieth anniversary gathering of the General Assembly of the United Nations in New York in October 1995, John Paul 11 said this:

> During my previous visit to the United Nations on 2 October 1979, I noted that the quest for freedom in our time has its basis in those *universal rights* which human beings enjoy by the very fact of their humanity. It was precisely outrages against human dignity which led the United Nations Organization to formulate, barely three years after its establishment, that Universal Declaration of Human Rights which remains one of the highest expressions of the human conscience of our time (John Paul 11, 1995).

Although neither pope would be in sympathy with the main thrust of this book, they would both agree that any enterprise of this kind must start with the nature of the human person.

Is the human rights era ending?

Once human rights were taken more seriously and violations were under more control, conflicts emerged between those human rights and other universal principles which could not easily be ignored. In an age of terrorism it became difficult to achieve the right balance between the rights of the individual and the rights of society as a whole, particularly in relation to the security of the state. It is clearly difficult to protect a population from terrorist attacks without severe curtailment of freedom of movement and association. But in some countries the 'war against terrorism' has been used as an excuse for the suppression of human rights.

These developments have prompted Michael Ignatieff to ask the question, '*Is the human rights era ending?*' in an article in the New York Times of February 2002.

> Since the end of the cold war, human rights has become the dominant moral vocabulary in foreign affairs. The question after Sept. 11 is whether the era of human rights has come and gone. If that sounds alarmist, consider some of the evidence. Western pressure on China to honor human rights, never especially effective, has stopped altogether. Australia's government uses the threat of terrorism to justify incarcerating Afghan refugees in a desert compound. Tajikistan and Uzbekistan have leveraged their provision of bases and intelligence into a carte blanche for domestic repression. Egypt, which for many years has used detention without trial, military courts and torture to keep control of militants, now demands an even freer hand. Sudan, which was under attack from a coalition of liberals and black churches determined to

> end slavery and stop Khartoum's war against the south, is now accepted as an ally against Osama bin Laden. And President Robert Mugabe of Zimbabwe has decided that his longtime political opponents are really ''terrorists'' (Ignatieff 2002).

Human Rights Watch is an international non-governmental organisation that conducts research and advocacy on human rights:

> Human Rights Watch has condemned these developments as opportunism, but something more durable than that may be at work. Rome has been attacked, and Rome is fighting to re-establish its security and its hegemony. This may permanently demote human rights in the hierarchy of America's foreign policy priorities. Of course, just because the United States has other priorities doesn't have to mean that, in global terms, the era of this movement is over. Human rights has gone global by going local, anchoring itself in struggles for justice that can survive without American inspiration or leadership. The movement does not have its headquarters in Washington. But if Washington turns away, the movement loses the one government whose power can be decisive in stopping human rights abuses. But the movement will have to engage soon in the battle of ideas: it has to challenge directly the claim that national security trumps human rights. The argument to make is that human rights is the best guarantor of national security (Ignatieff 2002).

The European Court of Human Rights was established in 1959 and hears complaints that a contracting state has violated the human rights enshrined in the Convention and its protocols. Complaints can be brought by individuals or other contracting states, and the Court can also issue advisory opinions. In recent years it has come under criticism for going beyond basic human rights in its judgements. As a last resort in the appeal process it has sometimes given such weight to the human rights of offenders that states have been faced with an inability to deport those whom they believe are a threat to national security.

Amnesty International is the most prominent pressure group for human rights. The movement started in 1961 when the British lawyer Peter Benenson wrote a newspaper appeal, *The Forgotten Prisoners*, calling for an international campaign to protest against the imprisonment of men and women for their political or religious beliefs. Within six months this initiative had developed into a permanent international movement:

> Historically our campaigning has focused on prisoners, but we have responded to the changing patterns of human rights violations in the world. Today people are more likely to become victims of abuse because of who they are, rather than for what they think, say or do – the biggest threat to human rights are the mass violations committed during armed conflicts (Amnesty International 2012).

Amnesty International works to achieve its aims by promoting general awareness of human rights and by opposing specific abuses of human rights as and when they arise. The organisation is well known for organising petitions in support of victims of oppression and for encouraging people to write to those with influence about the plight of these victims and writing to the individuals concerned to express solidarity with them.

The demand for human rights is also about the need for people to be able to have and to express their own individual identity.

Searching for identity

'Who do you think you are?' is the title of a series of BBC

television programmes that explores the family history of well-known personalities. Recently it was the turn of J K Rowling the creator of Harry Potter. Family History has become a very popular pastime and is well supported by online access to registers of births, marriages and deaths, and to parochial records and to census returns. Part of the attraction is that there just might be a good story or perhaps even a royal connection somewhere in our past. But the television programme goes beyond a study of the past. The implication of the title 'Who do you think you are' is that by studying our past we learn something about our present. By looking at former members of our family we learn something about ourselves. We learn something about our identity.

Identity is an underlying theme throughout the New Testament. Both Jesus and Paul are asking us to look at ourselves and consider the question, Who do we think we are? What kind of people are we? What are our strengths and weaknesses? What are the opportunities and threats around us? What identity do we aspire to and how can that be achieved? To what extent do we measure up to Jesus? These are complex questions but they start with that very telling phrase 'Who do you think you are?'

The Jesuits are a religious order within the Roman Catholic Church. In his book, *The Jesuits,* Jonathan Wright, who trained as a Jesuit priest before leaving for a career as an investment banker, explains that the thing which has allowed the Jesuits to be so successful over more than 450 years, is their focus not on what they do, but on who they are. His claim is that their core strength as an organization originates not in their mission, but in their developing of self-awareness. Every Jesuit goes through a long period of formation including spiritual exercises which help them understand their strengths, weaknesses, values and worldview – in short, their identity (J. Wright, 2004).

Karen Armstrong is a well-respected religious historian. In her most recent book, *Twelve Steps to a Compassionate Life,* she seeks to put flesh on the bones of a recent global initiative called a *Charter for Compassion* which seeks to encourage us to put compassion at the heart of our lives. In this book, she uses the pattern of Alcoholics Anonymous and other 'twelve-step movements' and begins by inviting us to examine ourselves. Who are we? Such approaches help us not only uncover our present identity but point us towards a new identity. Who do we want to be? Do we want to be free from alcohol addiction? Do we want to be a more compassionate society? What identifies us? (Armstrong, 2011).

The riots of August 2011 brought into sharp focus the absence of identity in the lives of so many youngsters in our inner city areas. So many have no identity conveyed by their families because they are so dysfunctional. So many have no identity conveyed by their school because they are permanently absent. So many have no identity conveyed by their work because they are unemployed. In a desperate attempt to gain identity, some join gangs and engage in the kind of violence, looting and arson we have seen.

Camila Batmanghelidjh is well known for her work with young people and her charity Kids Company must be one of the most inspirational and successful enterprises working in our inner cities. Kids Company currently mentors 14,000 young people in London alone and only two are known to have taken part in the riots. Joseph, one of those whom she had helped, is quoted as saying that he might well have been amongst the rioters had it not been for Kids Company which gave him 'the hope that I could be a respected member of society'. That was something that he did not want to lose – his identity.

The need to help youngsters in particular to gain self-esteem and a sense of identity has been sadly neglected and the periodic unrest should serve as a wakeup call for all of us. That is not to say that we must ignore the violence, looting and arson that invaded our streets in 2011 or fail to prosecute those involved with custodial sentences if necessary. It means that when the immediate tasks are completed then there is a very big long-term job to be done. We have an identity. So many others do not.

Christian Humanism

In a previous chapter we have explored the claim that Jesus was both human and divine. Christian Humanism is the movement within Christianity which seeks to explore the ground between the human and the divine. It is a long tradition and has been expressed in a multitude of different ways. In an essay entitled *Humanism After Tillich*, Max Stackhouse writes:

> The most creative dimensions of Western spirituality are rooted in a deep interaction between the biblically informed understanding of God, creation, and time and a humanist view of the true, the good, and the beautiful. Although tensions were sometimes acute, the affinities are many, and the interaction generated the deepest inner architecture of our civilisation... Humanity cannot be understood without reference to God; and neither God nor God's revelation can be understood except through the lens of thought and experience. That conviction shaped not only the great Catholic and Protestant traditions, but everything that Paul Tillich did as perhaps the greatest of the twentieth-century 'liberal' theologians (Stackhouse, 1997).

In the history of Western civilisation, Christian humanism has made only infrequent appearances and has rarely occupied centre stage. It is also a tradition that is not well understood, yet it is a tradition that has a long history. It is about the relationship between humanity and divinity and describes the tension that exists between two apparently very different approaches. This 'tension' comes into focus in the doctrine of the incarnation and the claim that Jesus was both human and divine but it is a creative tension. This apparent paradox of the two natures of Christ is the framework within which we begin to understand the many dualities we experience: flesh and spirit, nature and grace, faith and reason, justice and mercy.

For some people this tension in the person of Christ is unbearable and they tend towards one extreme or the other. When emphasis is placed on the divine at the expense of the human – the conservative fault – Jesus becomes an ethereal authority figure who is remote from earthly life and experience. When he is thought of as merely human – the liberal error – he becomes nothing more than a superior social worker or popular guru. Christian humanists are interested in the middle ground because that is where they believe truth is to be found.

There are shifting sands in this middle ground but Christian humanists are fully prepared to deal with the difficult questions that arise because they believe that in struggling with these issues they are more likely to make progress in their journey. This means that Christian humanists are not prepared to simply accept the statement that Jesus was both fully human and fully divine without exploring what that statement might actually mean.

The Crisis of Religious Integrity

> One person with integrity, even living the most private life, affects the entire behaviour of the universe. That is God's promise, and it is among modern psychology's great lessons. But the converse is also true. So with each of us empowered with this awesome ability, will we dare be less than as fully Christians as we can?
> Harry James Cargas, *Encountering Myself*

The Crucible

Written in 1953, Arthur Miller's play, *The Crucible,* is set in Salem, Massachusetts in 1692 and dramatises the events surrounding the Salem Witch Trials of that period. Moral integrity, or lack of it, is at the heart of this play as it was of the historical events which it portrays. The play is concerned with the accusations of witchcraft made against members of the Salem community at a time when paranoia and hysteria gripped many of the Puritan towns of New England. The lack of moral integrity displayed by characters in the play causes a string of destructive events as accusations multiply culminating in the deaths of many innocent people. The recovery of moral integrity amongst some of the characters eventually stops the madness that has overtaken the community from devouring more victims. Towards the end of the play John Proctor, the protagonist, wrestles with his conscience over whether to confess to witchcraft and thereby save himself from the gallows:

> Because it is my name! Because I cannot have another in my life! Because I lie and sign myself to lies! Because I am not worth the dust on the feet of them that hang! How may I live without my name? I have given you my soul; leave me my name! (Miller, 2008)

The last stumbling block is his signature on the confession, which he cannot bring himself to give. In part, this unwillingness reflects his desire not to dishonour his fellow prisoners: he would not be able to live with himself knowing that other innocents died while he flinched at death's door and fled. More important, it illustrates his obsession with his good name. Early in the play, Proctor's desire to preserve his good name keeps him from testifying against Abigail, the leader of the antagonists whom he has earlier seduced. Now, however, he has come to a true understanding of what a good reputation means and what course of action is required – namely, that he tell the truth, not lie to save himself. "I have given you my soul; leave me my name!" he rages; this defence of his name enables him to muster the courage to die with his integrity intact.

Integrity as balance

It is all very well to declare that love is the guiding principle of our lives, but, that love can only be effective if our personalities nurture it and enable it to be expressed. Nurturing of any sentiment takes place through every aspect of our personalities, most notably through the cognitive, affective and volitional aspects of our character. If that nurturing is to be effective then those aspects must be balanced and there must be integrity of the whole. Or to put it another way, 'head' and 'heart' need to work together.

'Head', cognition, or the faculty of thinking, knowing and perceiving, is the dominant aspect of personality in the western intellectual tradition. This is reflected in the way many people in the Western Church approach their religious life and is quite distinct from the approach of the Eastern Church. Having said that, there are many who would suggest that churchgoers in the West too often suspend the rational. It is, for example, difficult for people in the UK to understand why so many intelligent people in the US claim the literal truth of the creation myth.

'Heart', affection, or the faculty of feeling, emotion, or mood, may at times dominate our personality but in the western tradition we look on it disapprovingly and too readily label it as excess. This is reflected in the attitude of many Christians to what they would describe as displays of emotion in Charismatic and Pentecostal churches. Members of those churches would disagree and claim that such displays are the result of the direct intervention of the Holy Spirit, an intervention which bypasses normal psychic behaviour.

Volition, or the exercise of the will, is the faculty which decides upon and commits to a particular course of action. It is important that our actions arise from our own conscious decisions and do not arise by default or as a result of pressure from elsewhere. It is arguable that too many churchgoers are too ready to fall in with decisions made by others in the way they exercise their faith. Some respond in this way because of fear of being different, others because of a perceived need to follow a particular line, yet others simply follow the herd.

So, if there is to be successful nurturing of the imperative to love, then there needs to be balance between the various aspects of our personalities. But integrity is not just balance, it is something much more.

Integrity as something more

Etymologically, 'integrity' is related to 'integer', a whole number, and to integration, the unification of parts into a whole. Understood in this way, the integrity of persons is primarily a matter of keeping the self intact. However, such a definition has only limited value because it implies that successful integration is both necessary and sufficient for integrity. In most cases, it will be neither necessary, nor desirable for full integration to take place. Furthermore, even if it were possible for full integration to take place, it would still leave integrity with only a limited meaning. It is also important to note that this aspect of the definition makes no evaluative judgement about the states that are integrated.

It is possible to go further and understand integrity as associated with the maintenance of identity. Integrity is then not just about ordering our personality but about holding fast to those things which matter most to us and which determine our character. We are committed to many different kinds of things – people, institutions, traditions and so on – and some are held more strongly than others. The prioritising of those commitments and the maintenance of them constitutes another level of understanding of integrity. Although, it may say something about who we are, such an enhanced definition still says nothing about the moral quality of those commitments. Understood in this way, people with integrity can do horrendous things and maintain their integrity so long as they are acting in accordance with their core commitments. Such a definition is therefore still inadequate.

So far, integrity has been defined in personal terms, but it is also possible to see integrity in social terms. Persons of integrity do not just act consistently, they stand for something: they stand up for their best judgement within a community of people trying to discover what in life is worth doing. That means, of course, proper respect for the judgements of others, but again this says nothing about the moral quality of those judgements.

In common usage, however, integrity has moral connotations. In his book, *Integrity: A Philosophical Inquiry,* Mark Halfon writes that persons of integrity:

> …embrace a moral point of view that urges them to be conceptually clear, logically consistent, appraised of relevant empirical evidence, and careful about acknowledging as well as weighing relevant moral considerations. Persons of integrity impose these restrictions on themselves since they are concerned, not simply with taking any moral position, but with pursuing a commitment to do what is best (Halfon,

1989:37).

It is possible to take the understanding of integrity yet one stage further. In their book, *Integrity and the Fragile Self,* the authors of the Stanford Encyclopaedia article, argue that integrity is a virtue, but one that is not reducible to the workings of a single moral capacity or the wholesale pursuit of an identifiable moral end. They take 'integrity' to be a 'complex and thick virtue term'. They also take 'integrity' to mean something that is dynamic rather than static:

> As we conceive it, integrity… involves a capacity to respond to change in one's values or circumstances, a kind of continual remaking of the self, as well as the capacity to balance competing commitments and values and to take responsibility for one's work and thought. Understanding integrity involves taking the self to be always in process, rather than static and unchanging or containing an inner 'core' around which reasonably superficial changes are made (Cox, Levine, & La Caze, 2003:41).

In this analysis, the word 'integrity' has been assumed to apply to the general character of a person. However, it should be possible to speak of the integrity of a person from a particular perspective. It is certainly possible to speak of the integrity of objects in that way. A building can have architectural integrity but unless it also has structural integrity it will fall down. A person may be said to have professional integrity but unless they also have moral integrity they may well be unreliable.

Moral integrity

If, however, all integrity has a moral component then a particular distinction must be made between moral integrity and other forms of integrity. In the case of moral integrity, the commitment is to moral ends, principles or ideals. In the case of other kinds of integrity, the commitment lies elsewhere. The general moral component in all forms of integrity therefore does not lie in the object of commitment but in the nature of that commitment, that is, in the character of the person:

> ...a willingness to make and uphold commitments, a steadfast devotion to one's objectives, and the intention to do what is best are all character traits that ought to be cultivated. If the possession of these traits reflects normally desirable characteristics, then all ascriptions of integrity that apply to persons will have a moral component since each of the different kinds of integrity normally requires a commitment, consistency and the intention to do what is best... (Halfon, 1989:57).

For objects there can be a clear distinction between one perspective and another. For persons this is most unlikely. It is often argued that as long as government ministers have integrity in their public life, what they do in their private life is their own affair and has no bearing on their public duty. This argument that professional integrity and personal integrity have no bearing on each other is unconvincing. If people are unreliable in one part of their life there is at least a chance that they will be unreliable in other parts. In other words it is not possible to completely isolate one perspective of integrity from another. It is not possible for a parish priest to have religious integrity if he is at the same time abusing a child and has therefore forfeited his moral integrity.

Religious integrity

In his book, *Religious Integrity for Everyone,* Fred Campbell writes:

> People have integrity when their words communicate a congruence with their experience and the experience of other

> people, that is, they say what they mean and do what they say, and their words describe reality as others remember and experience it (Campbell 2000:167).

This is another way of saying that, for those with integrity, their words match their commitment, whatever that commitment might be. If that commitment is religious, then they suffer a crisis of religious integrity when there is a mismatch between the language they use about religion and the world as they know it. If we are part of a congregation and find ourselves unable to say or believe the words of the creed or the verses of a hymn because it does not reflect reality as we know it, then we are experiencing that crisis:

> Religion has integrity when it enables human beings to enact the drama of living, aging and dying with understanding and acceptance, meaning and purpose, trust and love, faith and hope. A religion has integrity when its articulated understandings about our world and our living 'make sense'. A religion suffers a crisis of integrity only when its spoken truths and practices no longer meet the needs of the people it seeks to serve (Campbell, 2000:2-3).

Some people have no difficulty with congruence between the language of their faith and the reality of their experience. Others find considerable difficulty with that language and feel that at best it is not helpful and that at worst it is misleading. This difficulty may arise because the words are archaic and lack contemporary meaning. It may arise because the words lack clarity or are ambiguous. It may be that the words are so narrowly defined that they reflect the understanding of only one part of the community. It may be that the words are given a literal interpretation when we believe that they should be understood metaphorically. It may be that we simply do not accept the truth of what the words seem to convey. Whatever the circumstances, there is tension.

This crisis of integrity is now more acute than in the past because of the profound societal changes that have taken place. There is now a much greater diversity of religious commitment in society and a greater awareness of that diversity. The Moslem population in Britain has increased considerably in recent years as have the number of those who practice Hinduism, Buddhism and other world religions. The number of those who practice no religion has also increased and we live in an increasingly secular society. Mass communication has increased our awareness of other traditions and serious tensions have arisen between communities. This increased diversity contributes to the problem that religious communities and the individuals within them have in maintaining their integrity.

Campbell describes his experience with those who have been unable to find integrity within traditional Christian communities.'They know they need a source of meaning in their lives and a community to validate their personal identity, values, and ways of understanding life and being human' (Campbell, 2000: ix); but… traditional religious communities should be able to supply these needs but increasingly they are quite unable to do so. Campbell is forced to the conclusion that for many people integrity can only be found within different faith perspectives. These perspectives are not new branches of the Christian Church but perspectives that cut across the boundaries of different faith traditions. He identifies four – humanism, naturalism, mysticism, and theism.

The Four 'Faiths'

Campbell himself has worked for many years as minister of Unitarian Universalist Church congregations. Such congregations are noted for their willingness to embrace diversity:

> I have preached openness to individual freedom of religious belief and welcomed people who need a religious community that allows and encourages them to be themselves within our secular culture. At some point in their lives, most had attended one or several Christian churches and found that their personal integrity would not allow them to continue. The cost of honouring one's religious integrity in terms of family relationships has been high for many of these individuals (Campbell, 2000:147).

Humanism, naturalism, mysticism, and theism describe the four strands of faith that Campbell has identified in those within these congregations. He describes them as four different ways in which people deal with their human condition:

> Humanists find life's meaning within the human community – past present and future; Naturalists understand that humans are part of the natural world and draw their meaning of living from this context; Mystics have had an experience of 'union with some transcendent whole' an experience so powerful that it shapes their values; Theists know that God exists, and their values derive from this knowledge and relationship (Campbell, 2000: 11).

In order to test his thesis, Campbell created an adult education course called *The Four Faiths Workshop*, He tested his hypothesis with over 500 people and found that it helped people to formulate their faith in a way that no longer compromised their integrity. He believes that this model has the ability to respond to the crisis of religious integrity. The extent to which the institutional churches could accommodate this alternative model is an interesting question.

Religious convictions

In order to put flesh on the bones of this claim that we sometimes suffer from a lack of religious integrity, it is necessary to examine the elements that define our disposition. Traditionally, the Church of England has subscribed to the view that scripture, tradition, reason and experience are broadly the sources for our religious disposition and language. Scripture and tradition are essentially external means of revelation; reason and experience are internal. Different groups within the church place the emphasis in different places. At one end of the spectrum are those who call themselves 'conservative evangelicals'. They would claim that the Bible is the supreme source of revelation and that every other 'revelation' must be tested against it. At the other end of the spectrum are the 'Anglo-Catholics'. They would claim that the history and tradition of the church have equal claim to authority in these matters. Those in the middle ground who might call themselves 'liberal' would place the human faculty of reason high in this 'quadrilateral' of claims.

The argument for integrity is not based on a claim that any one element should be given priority over the other elements of the quadrilateral. It is based on the claim that priority should be given to the integrity of the personality as a whole. This means that although the four 'sides' of the quadrilateral may contribute to the personality of different people in different ways, they can each achieve integrity if the disposition of their religious sentiments are in balance. The nature of this balance will vary and will depend on individual personalities. What matters is not that this disposition is 'right' in the sense that it conforms to one particular school of thought, but that it is 'right' in the sense that it satisfies the integrity of that particular person. For some, that integrity may be achieved by a heavy dependence on 'external' sources of revelation. For others it may be achieved more by dependence on 'internal' sources. Either way, that integrity should command respect even if it does not appear sound or orthodox.

In fact, the search for soundness in religious matters will always be unproductive because it implies that there is some objective measure of soundness that can be applied. The attempt by groups within the Church of England to insist on orthodoxy has always failed because the church as a whole values diversity above conformity. However, the Roman Catholic Church expects its members to follow the teaching of the Church and many do indeed conform. Similarly, some Protestant groups expect their members to follow particular understandings of the Bible and in some parts of the world such groups are gaining in strength. Over the years, the state has also played its part in coercion in one direction or another. The power and control which political, social and religious groups have exerted over each other has a long and ignoble history.

The search for soundness is also undesirable because it attempts to interfere with any personal integrity that has been achieved. I would argue that there is no satisfactory objective measure of soundness and, although some measure of voluntary agreement will exist within particular groups, any attempt to insist on conformity at the expense of integrity is dangerous. It is dangerous because it undermines the religious identity of the human person particularly if that identity is fragile or immature. And any damage to one aspect of human personality causes damage to the integrity of the personality as a whole.

'Testimony to integrity'

In describing their faith, members of the Religious Society of Friends (Quakers) start, not from an institution, or a book or a series of rules, but from human experience. Quakers have a healthy disrespect for any form of external religious authority.

In his book about, *A Light that is Shining*, Harvey Gillman writes about what human experience means for Quakers:

> The attempt is made to live out religion on a day-to-day basis

> and to respect the uniqueness and specialness of each person's experience. It is in this uniqueness that one can often see most clearly that power for love and creativity which is usually called God (Gillman, 2003:14).

In practice this means that Quakers are very distinctive in the way in which they seek to meet with God in worship:

> Quakers feel more able to become aware of this power in the silence of their meetings for worship. In the quiet, they maintain, the still, small voice can speak to them and direct their lives. The experience of quiet waiting upon God gives them strength to go back into the bustle of the world, the better to serve their fellows (Gillman, 2003:17).

Quakers neither separate life into categories of 'sacred' and 'secular', nor divide the world into compartments labelled 'religious', 'political', 'social' and so on. They have a 'holistic' view of experience and when speaking of that experience Quakers frequently use images. The 'inner light' is an important image for them and is a metaphor for Christ's light shining in the human heart. It illustrates the presence of Christ in every human being.

A 'testament to integrity' is the way many Quakers testify or bear witness to their belief that one should live a life that is true to God, true to oneself, and true to others. To Quakers, the concept of integrity includes personal wholeness and consistency as well as honesty and fair dealings. From personal and inward integrity flow the outward signs of integrity, which include honesty and fairness. It is not only about telling the truth – it is applying truth to each situation:

> The word 'testimony' is used by Quakers to describe a witness to the living truth within the human heart as it is acted out in

> everyday life. It is not a form of words, but a way of life based on the realisation that there is that of God in everybody, that all human beings are equal, and that all life is interconnected. The testimonies reflect the corporate beliefs of the Society, however much individual Quakers may interpret them differently according to their own light (Gillman, 2003:54).

Sometimes Quakers have found themselves at odds with society in witnessing to this testimony. They have a strong commitment to peace and have been prominent in pacifist movements and in protests against war. They uphold the sacredness of human life and have been against capital punishment. Quakers have put on one side all that gets in the way of their experience of God and that experience has then become for them the driving force for their life in the world. It is an attractive vision.

'Servant Leadership'

The themes explored in this book appear frequently and informally in the routine of daily lives. They also sometimes appear more formally when they form the basis of particular approaches and techniques within the world of commerce and industry. We have already met Critical Thinking in a discussion about methods of discourse. Here we meet Servant Leadership in our discussion of personal integrity.

The story is told of a company CEO spilling a cup of coffee prior to a board meeting. Instead of summoning someone to clean it up, he asked a colleague to get him a cleaning cloth, something easily found in a company that provided cleaning services. Whereupon he proceeded to get down on his hands and knees to clean up the spill himself. The remarkable thing was that board members and employees alike hardly noticed as he did it. It was as if it was expected in a company which promoted 'servant leadership'.

While servant leadership is a timeless concept, the phrase

'servant leadership' was coined by Robert K. Greenleaf in *The Servant as Leader* published in 1977:

> The servant-leader is servant first... It begins with the natural feeling that one wants to serve, to serve first. Then conscious choice brings one to aspire to lead. That person is sharply different from one who is leader first, perhaps because of the need to assuage an unusual power drive or to acquire material possessions... The leader-first and the servant-first are two extreme types. Between them there are shadings and blends that are part of the infinite variety of human nature. The difference manifests itself in the care taken by the servant-first to make sure that other people's highest priority needs are being served (Greenleaf, 1977).

The 'science' of servant leadership can be expressed in the different ways in which organisations which promote this model are structured. This might be to relate servant leadership to the concept of an inverted pyramid organisation in which top management 'report upwards' to lower levels of management, and so on. The 'art' of servant leadership is more nuanced and is explored in the book, *Leadership is an Art*, by Max Depree:

> The book is about liberating people to do what is required of them in the most effective and humane way possible. It is not a book about facts or history. Since it deals more with ideas and beliefs and relationships, it has to do with the 'why' of institutional and corporate life rather than the 'how' (DePree, 1989:1).

DePree introduces his theme by telling the story of a millwright in his father's company. The millwright was a key person in the organisation but one day he died. His father was a young manager at the time and went to visit the family. During awkward conversations the widow asked if she could read some poetry. For several minutes she read beautiful poetry from a bound volume. When asked who had written the poems she replied that it was her late husband. The young manager was taken aback and left wondering. Was he a poet who did millwright's work, or was he a millwright who wrote poetry?

In our effort to understand corporate life, what is it that we should learn from this story? In addition to all the ratios and goals and parameters and bottom lines, it is fundamental that leaders endorse a concept of persons, This begins with an understanding of the diversity of people's gifts and talents and skills (DePree, 1989:9).

DePree goes on to outline the principles and practice that apply to an organisation that promotes servant leadership. The emphasis throughout is on the best interests of all those with a stake in the company and the need for covenants as well as contracts between them. In an address to students at Harvard College in 1978, Alexander Solzhenitsyn comments on the limitations of contracts:

> A society based on the letter of the law and never reaching any higher, fails to take advantage of the full range of human possibilities. The letter of the law is too cold and formal to have a beneficial influence on society. Whenever the issue of work is woven of legalistic relationships, this creates an atmosphere of spiritual mediocrity that paralyzes men's noblest impulses (Solzhenitsyn, 1978:17-19).

Covenantal relationships, on the other hand, avoid the 'paralysis' that Solzhenitsyn believes legalistic thinking inevitably induces:

> Covenantal relationships, on the other hand, induce freedom, not paralysis. A covenantal relationship rests on a shared

> commitment to ideas, to issues, to values, to goals, and to management processes. Words such as love, warmth, personal chemistry are certainly pertinent. Covenantal relationships enable work to have meaning and to be fulfilling. Covenantal relationships reflect unit and grace and poise. They are an expression of the sacred nature of relationships (DePree, 1989:60).

This brings us back to the question of how such relationships express 'love in action'. In his book, *Servant Leadership*, Robert Greenleaf expresses succinctly what love in the working environment means for him:

> Love has only one absolute condition: unlimited liability! As soon as one's liability for another is qualified to any degree, love is diminished by that much (Greenleaf, 1977:38).

Pope Francis also clearly sees himself as the servant leader of the Roman Catholic Church. And he has recently demonstrated this in a spectacular way. Popes have for centuries washed the feet of the faithful on Maundy Thursday but never before has the pontiff washed the feet of a woman as he did in Holy Week 2013. That one of the female inmates of the prison in Rome where he performed the ceremony was a Serbian Muslim is even more remarkable.

Washing the disciples' feet

If you lived in Texas in the nineteenth century and wanted to travel by stagecoach then you could buy three types of ticket. They were first class, second class, and third class, with the price, of course, descending with each category. However, the distinction between these tickets did not have to do with where you sat or how much you would eat or drink, but rather as to what was required of you in case of an emergency.

At that time most of the roads were unpaved, and many of the hills were very steep, so that even two strong horses could hardly pull a full stagecoach. Therefore when they faced the emergency of a mud-bog or a steep incline then somebody had to help out. If you had a first class ticket you could stay on board, nothing was asked of you; you were in a position of privilege. If you had a second class ticket, you had to get off and walk around the mud, or walk up the hill to lighten the load. If you had a third class ticket you were obliged to get out and help the stagecoach driver either to push the vehicle through the mud, or push it up the hill.

This was certainly a novel way to operate a stagecoach but the principle behind it is very familiar. 'First class' has always been associated with privilege, exemption from hardship, having other people do things for you, while 'third class' has always been associated with having to do the menial task, and having as it were, to deal with the dirt.

But in Jesus of Nazareth we have a very different story and a very different set of priorities. By what he did and what he said, Jesus took this traditional hierarchy of values and turned it upside-down. He took the notion of first class, second class and third class, and literally stood it on its head.

On the last night of his life his ordeal was about to begin, and he very much wanted to share one last meal with the twelve men who had been so close to him. So Jesus carefully arranged for a Passover meal to be served in the Upper Room, and the thirteen of them trooped in just as the sun was going down. Then just when everything seemed ready, a problem developed. None of the disciples seemed willing to do the menial task of washing the feet of the others.

In first-century Palestine, roads were unpaved, and most people wore open sandals, which meant before you could eat a meal in comfort, somehow the dirt on the feet had to be dealt with. In rich families, slaves did this task. In Jesus' circle, they usually shared the responsibility. But on that particular day, the disciples were feeling very competitive. They had argued all that afternoon about who was going to be the greatest – that is who was going to be first class, second class and third class. Therefore no one was in a mood to stoop down and do the task of washing another's feet.

And so we're told in the gospel of John that when they were at a seeming gridlock, nobody willing to do what needed to be done, Jesus got up from the table, laid aside his garment, wrapped himself in a towel, and stooped over and did the work of a slave: he washed all of the feet of the disciples. And when he had finished and put on his garment again, he said, "Do you realise what I have done? Do you recognise that what the world calls greatness means lording it over other people, striving for privilege and exemption, but what I have demonstrated for you this night is that true greatness in my kingdom involves the willingness to be a servant, the willingness to do what needs to be done." In other words, first class in Jesus' hierarchy of values, is not a position of privilege, it is, rather, the willingness to serve others and to do whatever has to be done in order for the common good to be accomplished.

It is often said that there is a 'crisis of authority' in our political, social and economic life, and also in our religious life, and that may be so. What seems clear is that if authority is to have any meaning in our future religious life then it must be refocused and recast in the mould of Jesus. The authority of Jesus did not lie in his power and influence. The authority of Jesus was revealed in a life of love which reflected his authority and stamped it with very clear characteristics. This authority of love was manifested first and foremost in service. We are reminded of the passage in Luke:

> A dispute also arose among them as to which one of them was to be regarded as the greatest. But he said to them, "The kings

of the Gentiles lord it over them; and those in authority over them are called benefactors. But not so with you; rather the greatest among you must become like the youngest, and the leader like one who serves. For who is greater, the one who is at the table or the one who serves? Is it not the one at the table? But I am among you as one who serves (Luke 22:24-27).

The Recovery of Virtue

> All that is necessary for the triumph of evil is that good men do nothing.
> Edmund Burke.

The need for good people

The crises which have engulfed the worlds of finance and politics in the United Kingdom in recent years have a number of things in common, not least the gulf that exists between what appears to be happening on the surface and what is actually going on underneath. On the face of it both banking and politics had been conducted with responsibility and integrity. But when the surface was scratched whole new worlds were uncovered. These were worlds governed not by values but by regulations. And with the failure of the regulations the systems collapsed. And they collapsed because they had no foundations. Moreover, they cannot be fixed by introducing new regulations without attention to those foundations. The culture that rejected common values is responsible for this mess. And only a new culture that affirms such values will clean it up.

This distinction between values and regulations can be understood in the way we approach moral questions. There are generally two ways in which we handle decisions on moral questions and it goes something like this. We either ask ourselves what action will produce the best consequences whatever the guiding principles might be. Or we ask what guiding principles should govern what action we take regardless of the consequences. We can be for abortion in practice whatever the principles might be. Or we can be against abortion in principle whatever the consequences in practice. But sometimes these two ways become polarised and we need to explore a third way. We do this by asking a different set of questions. What kind of people should we be? What traits of character should we aspire to? What virtues should we seek?

It has always seemed to me to be nonsense to suggest that the private life of a person has no bearing on their public performance. And recent events have served to illustrate how close these two worlds actually are. If a man or woman behaves in a particular way in private life then why should they be any different in public life? It is all very well to say that a politician is doing a good job but if they are lining their pockets with taxpayer's money then we can have little confidence in what they achieve. It is all very well to say that a banker is doing a good job but if he is reckless in his investment of other people's money then he cannot be trusted. The quality of a person's character is integral to who they are as a person and to the way they perform their job.

The present crisis will not be resolved overnight whatever we do. But its resolution will be that much more secure if it has firm foundations. And the best foundations are not sound regulations and good management, important as these are. The best foundations are good people with common values.

Traditional approaches to ethical questions

Ethics, or moral philosophy as it is sometimes called, seeks to determine how we make moral decisions about what is good or evil and about what is right or wrong. For Christians, and for others, there have been broadly three approaches to ethical problems – deontological, teleological and personalist.

Deontological arguments – derived from the Greek for 'necessary' or 'imperative' – are absolutist. One cannot argue beyond them. So if one claims that murder is wrong and is asked to give a reason, a deontological response would be: 'Because it is against God's will', or 'Because it is against the law of nature' or 'Because it is simply wrong'. Murder is seen to be wrong regardless of its consequences.

Teleological arguments – from the Greek *telos,* or end –

sometimes termed consequentialist arguments, although the two can be distinct – treat morality, not as an end in itself, but as a means to something else. To return to reasons for believing that murder is wrong, consequential responses typically might be: 'Because murder, if allowed, would destroy society', or 'Because murder does not contribute to general happiness'. Murder is thought to be wrong, not because it is wrong in itself, but because it leads to something else which is thought to be wrong or undesirable.

Personalist arguments view morality, not as obedience to absolute principles or as means to something else, but as an expression of individual feeling, conscience or love. Moral dilemmas cannot be resolved in advance of particular situations. It makes no sense to argue, as an abstract principle, about whether or not killing is wrong. Only in particular circumstances, when the individual is confronted with the possibility of killing, can that individual determine whether it is right or wrong or can be called murder. Dietrich Bonheoffer decided that in facing up to Hitler, the greater evil would have been not to act so he supported the attempted assassination.

'Situation ethics' seeks to combine a general personalist ethical approach with a specifically Christian approach to 'love'. Situation ethics seeks to determine how love will be best served in each situation. Love is the sole norm for decision making. Other principals can be put on one side. But Situation Ethics has been criticised for the lack of guidelines. How do we determine what is the most loving response? In recent years there has been renewed interest in the very different personalist approach of Virtue Ethics.

Something also needs to be said about Natural Law. This tradition refers to the view that our ethical principles arise from the nature of human beings and that what is good or evil and right and wrong can be discerned using the human faculty of reason. For example, documents like the United Nations

Declaration on Human Rights propose a set of rights which belong to human beings because of what human beings are, and which ought to be respected for that reason alone. Natural Law has been very influential in Roman Catholic theology for many centuries and continues to inform contemporary debate.

The approach of Virtue Ethics

Virtue Ethics is not concerned with particular actions. It believes that the real discussion of ethics is not the question 'What should I do?' but 'Who should I become?' If you like, it shifts the emphasis from right actions to good people.

Virtue Ethics has a noble history. As Neil Messer explains in his book, *Christian Ethics,* the concept of virtue goes back to Greek thought, in which the word originally meant any kind of excellence. Plato was the first to identify the four 'cardinal' virtues – prudence, justice, courage and temperance. The term 'cardinal' comes from the Latin *cardo* or hinge; the cardinal virtues are so called because they are hinges upon which the door of the moral life swings. We shall explore the meanings of each of these virtues in due course. Aristotle went further and devoloped the 'doctrine of the mean'. This is the notion that any virtue is a sort of middle way between two extremes, which are vices. For example, courage is the mean between cowardice on the one hand and rashness on the other. The Greeks also bequethed to us the notion that human beings have some sort of goal. For Aristotle, this goal can best be described as 'human flourishing'. The virtues are those qualities that enable us to move towards our goal. In due course Christian thinkers took up this idea but reworked it in distinctly theological ways (Messer, 2006).

Although the Bible does not use the langauge of virtue very much, the New Testament does contain lists of characteristics which be could well be described as virtues. One is found in Galations 5.22-3 and covers love, joy, peace, patience, kindness, generosity, faithfulness, gentleness and self-control. Paul, of course, describes these as 'fruits of the Spirit' which immediately suggests a difference from Greek thought. Another list, perhaps the most famous, is in 1 Corinthians 13.13 and covers faith, hope and love. Augustine, whose thought was deeply influenced by Plato and his followers, argued that virtue can only be truly virtuous if it reflects the knowledge and love of God. Pagan virtues, though praiseworthy in many respects, cannot be truly virtuous as they are not rooted in the love of God.

Christian virtue ethics was most fully developed in the Middle Ages by Thomas Aquinas. Aquinas followed earlier Christian thinkers in adopting a two-tier scheme of virtues – the cardinal virtues of prudence, justice, fortitude and temperance, in that order – and the theological virtues of faith hope and love. He drew on Aristotle's idea that humans have ends or goals and that the virtues direct us towards these goals. For Aquinas these goals were, to exist and maintain our existence, to mate and rear offspring, and to live in ordered societies and know the truth about God. For Aquinas, humans have a natural capacity to develop the cardinal virtues but we need God's grace to develop the theological virtues.

In his book, *The Promise of Christian Humanism*, Dominic Doyle expands on what has become a traditional distinction:

> A virtue, then is a settled disposition that is the source of those good acts which lead to happiness. The infused theological virtues and the acquired natural virtues, despite their different goals, operate through the same inate human capacities of intellect and will... But the differences between the theological and natural virtues vastly exceeds their similarity. The moral and intellectual virtues intend the imperfect happiness proportional to human nature and attainable in this life, while the theological virtues intend the perfect happiness of the vision of God in the next (Doyle, 2011:77).

Despite this distinction in orthodox theology, the theological virtues will be approached in this book through human capacities.

The tradition of the virtues continued to supply the langauge and intellectual framework for understanding morality into the early modern period but as the Enlightenment gathered pace in the eighteenth century these older ways of thinking were increasingly obscured by new appraoches. In his book, *After Vitue,* Alasdair MacIntyre argues that the inevitable failure of the Enlightenment project has left our intellectual and moral life in the mess that it is today. The answer is to recover the tradition of virtue (MacIntyre, 1999).

Unfortunately, in recent times, two movements have tended to marginalise Virtue Ethics. The Secular State has wanted to focus on consequences – teleological ethics. The Christian Church has wanted to focus on obedience to divine law – deontological ethics. In his book, *The Four Cardinal Virtues,* Josef Pieper writes:

> ...the classic origins of the doctrine of virtue later made Christian critics suspicious of it. They warily regarded it as too philosophical and not scriptural enough. Thus they preferred to talk about commandments and duties rather than virtues. To define the obligations of man is certainly a legitimate, even estimable, and no doubt necessary undertaking. With a doctrine of commandments or duties, however, there is always the danger of arbitrarily drawing up a list of requirements and losing sight of the human person who 'ought' to do this or that (Pieper, 2007: xi).

The emphasis in the secular world on utility and consequences in moral debate has increased in recent years almost to the extent that many see this approach as the default understanding of what it means to be a moral person. Yet we need to keep reminding ourselves that moral choices are not made in a vacuum and that it is ultimately the character of persons and the virtues that they possess that will determine the outcome. Virtue Ethics therefore deserves its new 'place in the sun'.

James Keenan, in his chapter on Virtue Ethics in *Christian Ethics: An Introduction* by Bernard Hoose, writes:

> We believe that the real discussion of ethics is not the question 'What should I do?' But 'Who should I become?' In fact virtue ethicists expand that question into three key related ones: 'Who am I?' 'Who ought I to become?' 'How am I to get there?' (Keenan, 1998: 84).

Keenan is one of a number of Roman Catholic theologians who have given much needed structure to the pursuit of Christian Ethics and his approach will be adopted in the this summary.

Who am I?

This is the foundational question but for the virtue ethicist it becomes 'How virtuous am I?' because, for Aquinas, every moral question can be reduced to a consideration of the virtues.

Two important works have assisted us in naming the basic virtues. In the *Nicomachean Ethics,* Aristotle gives us eleven different virtues including friendship, magnanimity and practical wisdom. In the *Summa Theologiae,* Thomas Aquinas summarises the four cardinal virtues: prudence, justice, temperance and fortitude. He then adds the three theological virtues: faith, hope and love. For Aquinas, the cardinal virtues can be acquired by men and women; the theological virtues are gifts from God.

The fundamental question is then 'Am I just, temperate, brave and prudent etc?' To answer that question, Aristotle suggests that it is not enough to believe that we have these qualities. We need to demonstrate them in our response to the events of the world around us. Furthermore, we can only be sure that we have these qualities if we respond accordingly when we are put to the test by unplanned and unexpected events. Even if we choose other virtues, the test must be the same.

Who ought I to become?

If the first question directs our attention to the virtues that we currently possess, the second questions direct us to virtues that we have yet to acquire.

If we know the strengths and weaknesses of our current position then we can build a vision of a future goal. We can seek to achieve a better balance between the demands of those virtues that we believe should form the basis of a virtuous life. We can aspire to our own distinctive 'take' on what it means to live a virtuous life.

If we take this approach then we have implicitly accepted that we need to grow and develop those embryonic virtues that we have identified. We have understood that this process will continue throughout our lives. We have realised that our lives must be dynamic not static. As Keenan points out, this approach is typical of the way parents see the growth of their child. If they identify weakness in growth they seek ways of giving their child greater strength. If they see that their child is insecure then they will find ways of helping him or her to grow in confidence. They are asking the questions, 'Who is my child?' and 'How can he or she grow well?'

Virtue ethicists believe that by examining ourselves in this way and by finding ways of achieving the kind of virtuous life we believe is right for us and our communities then we place ourselves in a much better position to face the big ethical questions of our time. We are in a better position to offer moral guidance to others when we have addressed our own moral disposition. We are more likely to focus on primary rather than secondary issues. We are less likely to let baser instincts prevail. In addressing issues of war and peace it is all too easy for racial and religious prejudice to take over. In addressing issues of life and death it is all too easy for quantity and quality of life to be confused.

How do I get to the end?

Prudence is the key, but it has had a 'bad press'. It is often thought of as 'caution' but that is too narrow a definition:

> Prudence is rather the virtue of a person whose feet are on the ground and who thinks practically and realistically. Prudence belongs to the person who not only sets realistic ends, but sets out to attain them (Keenan 1998: 87).

Prudence is not something that we are born with. It is something that we acquire with experience. It arises from the questions we ask and the answers we receive not only from those who are close to us but also from those who take a different view or pursue a different lifestyle. As Keenan points out, you are not going to develop prudence in your drinking habits if you only listen to those who are equally heavy drinkers. Prudence is about finding the mean. In this example it is about drinking in moderation.

For Aristotle, the mean is the desirable middle between two extremes, one of excess and the other of deficiency. For example courage, if taken to excess would manifest as recklessness and if deficient as cowardice. Keenan puts it this way:

> Getting the mean is not always easy. I remember a friend who was afraid of heights. In order to grow, he needed to face his fear, but he had to do it prudentially. That is, he needed to set a realistic goal that he could attain. But that goal had to be the mean between extremes for him. For instance, if he went too high, say if he went to the observation deck of the World Trade Centre, he would feel no confidence at all, only anxiety. But if he only went to the second-storey balcony of an apartment

> building, he would not feel sufficient tension. Prudence helps then find the mean where there is adequate tension for growth, neither too little nor too much (Keenan, 1998:88).

In his book, *Christian Love*, Bernard Brady quotes from Augustine's famous reflection on the virtues:

> For the fourfold division of virtue I regard as taken from four forms of love... The object of this love is not anything, but only God, the chief good, the highest wisdom, the perfect harmony. So we may express the definition thus: that temperance is love keeping itself entire and incorrupt for God; fortitude is love bearing everything readily for the sake of God; justice is love serving God only, and therefore ruling well all else, as subject to man; prudence is loving making a right distinction between what helps it towards God and what might hinder it (Brady, 2003:122).

Virtues for today

The virtues of Aristotle and Aquinas have stood the test of time but there are other ways in which these fundamental values can be expressed. Keenan suggests his own three cardinal virtues based on the understanding of humans as 'relational' beings:

> 'I conclude by proposing that we conceive of ourselves as relational in three ways: generally, specifically and uniquely, and each of these relational ways of being demands a cardinal virtue: as a relational being in general, we are called to justice and to treat all people fairly; as a relational being specifically, we are called to fidelity and to sustain the specific relationships that we enjoy; as relational beings uniquely, we are called to self-care that no one else can provide' He goes on, 'The fourth cardinal virtue is prudence, which determines what constitutes the just, faithful and self-caring way of life

> for an individual. It also negotiates how the cardinal virtues should interact and which one should override the others in a particular situation, and when and to what degree (Keenan 1998: 92-3).

Keenan's approach is just one way of handling virtue ethics and it is by no means the only way. But it asks the right questions. Whatever we think of the particular virtues identified in these discussions, the general thrust of Virtue Ethics is clear. It shifts the debate from 'right actions' to 'good people' which is where we began.

The Outsiders

Imagine floods surging over the plains of the country. Picture the wild animals congregating for safety on higher ground. Look carefully and you will see animals who are natural enemies, and who at any other time would be fighting each other, standing peacefully together. In their common predicament, they stand on common ground.

In chapter seventeen of the gospel according to Luke Jesus is on the border between Galilee and Samaria and is met by a group of ten lepers. We know that the Jews had no dealings with the Samaritans, yet in this group there was at least one Samaritan. The ultimate symbol of prejudice in first-century Judaism was the Samaritan. The Jews believed that they were the pure-blooded, true believers. In their eyes the Samaritans were half-breed heretics, worthy only of being despised. I won't go into all the historical detail but one of the reasons for this animosity was a dispute about the location of God's temple. But in this case, in their common misfortune, the racial, cultural and religious barriers temporarily disappeared. In the common tragedy of their leprosy they had forgotten they were Jews and Samaritans and remembered only that they were men in need.

For Luke, the Samaritan is the focal point of the story. The

Samaritan Leper who returned to thank Jesus is deeply symbolic for Luke. The action of the Samaritan was a sign. A sign of the breaking down of traditional barriers that kept the Judean people separate from their northern neighbours. As a Samaritan, the figure of the man recalls the familiar parable in which a Samaritan shows compassion to the traveller who falls among thieves. As a Leper, the figure of the man recalls the story from the second book of Kings about the healing of Naaman the Syrian. In an earlier passage in Luke, in a sermon at Nazareth, Jesus uses the example of Naaman to show how the promise of salvation would go to those outside the people of God who rejected it. This theme is continued elsewhere in Luke and the Samaritan prefigures the spread of the Gospel beyond the boundaries of Israel after the death and departure of Jesus.

Throughout his ministry Jesus goes out of his way to break down barriers and to welcome 'outsiders' into his midst. And it is not just that he wants to be inclusive and to bring all into the fold. He opens the doors because he believes that the outsider is something special. A former colleague of mine is a champion of 'Outsider Art'. The term 'Outsider Art' was coined to describe art created outside the boundaries of official culture. Typically, those labelled as Outsider Artists have little or no contact with the institutions of the mainstream art world, and in many cases, their work is 'discovered' only after their deaths. Yet they have much to say. Doris Lessing, the Nobel Laureate, writes passionately in her novels about the outsiders in society particularly those in Africa where she grew up. In Colin Wilson's 1956 book, *The Outsider*, he examines the role of the social outsider in seminal works of various key literary and cultural figures including Albert Camus, Jean-Paul Sartre, Fyodor Dostoyevsky, William James and T. E. Lawrence. You could say that 'the outsider' is a modern preoccupation. Certainly, our consciousness has been raised about those who are marginalised in society.

'The outsider' is a challenge to all of us for we are all guilty of creating outsiders. In our family life, there always seem to be those who upset the equilibrium. In our workplace, there are always those who want to do the job their way. In social life there are always those who just don't fit in. In our churches, there are always those who seem to follow a different creed or adopt a different lifestyle. And yet these are the very people who are often the most energetic. These are the people who are often the most creative. These are often the real visionaries. The prophets are always outsiders. They are not closed in by past traditions. They are open to future possibilities. They enrich our common life and, more importantly we are incomplete without them.

In our life together on this planet we are faced with many dangers and with many threats to our common life. This applies particularly within our religious traditions and churches. Jesus was quite clear about this. We continue to exclude the outsider at our peril. To return to the animals. In their common predicament, the animals of Africa stood on common ground. In our common predicaments, we also need to stand on common ground.

Wisdom

> Accumulated knowledge does not make a wise man. Knowledgeable people are found everywhere, but we are cruelly short of wise people.
> Michel Quoist, *With Open Heart*

The 'cardinal' virtues

We begin our study of the virtues with what Aquinas called the 'cardinal' virtues – wisdom, justice, courage and temperance. The term 'cardinal' comes from the Latin *cardo* or hinge; the cardinal virtues are so called because they are hinges upon which the door of the moral life swings.

Prudence or Wisdom?

Phronesis, is an Ancient Greek word for wisdom or intelligence and is a common topic of discussion in philosophy. In Aristotelian Ethics, for example in the *Nicomachean Ethics,* it is distinguished from other words for wisdom and intellectual virtues – such as *episteme* and *techne* – as the virtue of practical thought. For this reason, when it is not simply translated by words meaning wisdom or intelligence, it is often translated as 'practical wisdom', and sometimes (more traditionally) as 'prudence', from Latin *prudentia.* In this chapter, we will use the word 'wisdom' for the first and most prominent of the cardinal virtues.

Natural wisdom

People for Others – working together to find God in all things, is a 'blog' about 'how, when we strive together to follow Christ, we become men and women for others'. The blog contains a number of 'wisdom stories' of which this is one:

A man found a cocoon of a butterfly. One day a small opening

> appeared, he sat and watched the butterfly for several hours as it struggled to force its body through that little hole. Then it seemed to stop making any progress. It appeared as if it had got as far as it could and it could go no farther. The man decided to help the butterfly, so he took a pair of scissors and snipped off the remaining bit of the cocoon. The butterfly then emerged easily. But it had a swollen body and small, shriveled wings. The man continued to watch the butterfly because he expected that, at any moment, the wings would enlarge and expand to be able to support the body, which would contract in time. Neither happened! In fact, the butterfly spent the rest of its life crawling around with a swollen body and shriveled wings. It never was able to fly. What the man in his kindness and haste did not understand was that the restricting cocoon and the struggle required for the butterfly to get through the tiny opening were God's way of forcing fluid from the body of the butterfly into its wings so that it would be ready for flight once it achieved its freedom from the cocoon (Campbell, 2013).

So, the gap between 'human' and 'divine' wisdom seems wide. But that does not mean that we should not seek to grow in wisdom, not to achieve divinity but to achieve the fullness of our humanity.

Information, knowledge, wisdom...

Being Human, is a report of the Doctrine Commission of the Church of England published in 2003. It may seem strange to draw on such a formal document at the start of this discussion but at the outset this report identifies wisdom as the essential ingredient in human flourishing. Its starting point is the phrase from the Gospel of Luke, 'Jesus increased in wisdom' (Luke 2:52). This short phrase immediately places Jesus at the centre of discussion and makes him our primary reference point for what it means to be human in relation to God and to each other. The document expands on what it means by wisdom:

> Wisdom is about how we live well before God alongside other people in our world. How can we arrive at an understanding that helps to shape good living? What are the best resources for insight into basic features of human existence today? ...Wisdom is not a destination but is classically described as a way, a path, or a journey. There is always more wisdom to be found, and the desire to learn it is a core dynamic in good living... In most societies wisdom has been strongly traditional. It has been deeply rooted in the past, concerned to conserve the best and ensure continuity. Yet most of them have also known times of radical change during which traditional wisdom has been questioned, revised and abandoned or transformed (Doctrine Commission, 2003:3).

Throughout history people have reaffirmed this gift of wisdom and the traditions of the Church have restated it in different ways. We are drawn to the wisdom literature of the Bible and in particular to the Book of Proverbs, but in recent years we seem to have lost something of this tradition. Wisdom literature is not well covered in most lectionaries and we hear little of wisdom from the pulpit. It is not well covered in the teaching schemes of churches or schools. Wisdom in common usage is too often associated with old age and not with the vitality of youth. It deserves a more prominent 'place in the sun'.

Perhaps this has something to do with our approach to learning. Those of us who are privileged to work professionally with children, those of us who take on the responsibility of parentage, and those who have any contact whatever with the young, know that the personal development of a child involves every aspect of their personality. It involves the physical, the emotional, the intellectual, the moral and the spiritual. But how often do we teach children how to discriminate, how to make decisions, how to choose? The society in which we live also seems to have other priorities. It places great emphasis on the fine tuning of the intellect, on the acquisition of skills and on the ambitious striving after power and wealth. It places great emphasis on the ability to use this intellect and these skills to communicate, to persuade and to commit. It seeks to promote the notion of success.

So, for both the innocent and vulnerable child and the sophisticated and successful adult, there is little talk of wisdom and the ability to use intelligence, knowledge and experience to critically evaluate the choices that confront us all and to work for the long term common good of all.

In his pageant play, *The Rock,* T S Eliot writes:

> Where is the wisdom we have lost in knowledge?
> Where is the knowledge we have lost in information?
> (Eliot, 1971:107)

I once had a colleague who often spoke of the respect he had for those with intelligence, for those who had what he called 'a good brain'. Eventually in frustration, I challenged him. 'It is not the person with intelligence that I respect', I told him, 'but the person with wisdom, who knows how to use that intelligence well'.

What is wisdom and who are the wise?

In his book, *Wisdom: From Philosophy to Neuroscience,* Stephen S Hall writes:

> One of the hallmarks of wisdom, what distinguishes it from 'mere' intelligence, is the ability to exercise good judgement in the face of imperfect knowledge. In short, do the right thing – ethically, socially, familiarly, personally (Hall 2011: 4).

Hall makes the point that although it is always possible to attempt a definition of the word 'wisdom', such definitions are bound to be inadequate because of the nature of the underlying concept. 'Wisdom' is not straightforward, it is full of ambiguities and contradictions, but that is the nature of the human condition, and is reflected in all those individuals whom we regard as 'wise':

> These inherent contradictions do not fatally vex a potential definition of wisdom; rather they are embedded in it. One of the best ways to think about wisdom, in fact, is to try to identify those rare individuals who manage to reconcile these contradictions and still embody wisdom. These are (or once were) living, breathing, and, because they are human, imperfect definitions of wisdom, but they are also less abstract, more like wisdom in the flesh. We can learn a lot about wisdom from its exemplars, past and present (Hall 2011:11).

Apparently, some years ago, psychologists in Canada conducted a survey in which subjects were asked to nominate people who struck them as especially wise. Predictably, people like Mahatma Gandhi, Martin Luther King, Mother Teresa and Nelson Mandala were included, and, as with Jesus who was also nominated, most of those who were celebrated for their wisdom were at odds with the prevailing values of the societies in which they lived. This is a salutary reminder that the wise man (or woman) thinks independently and is prepared to challenge the *status quo:*

> Pythagoras – who gave us the word philosophy (literally, 'love of wisdom') –so alienated the populace of Croton, where he lived, that its citizens burned his house down, massacred many of his fellow Pythagoreans, and forced the 'inventor' of

> philosophy to flee for his life. In an early foreshadowing of the Socratic tragedy, we can see that in many cultures, the wise man is a marked man (Hall, 2011:12).

Wisdom then, is not an 'easy' virtue. A favourite passage of mine comes from the work of Lawrence Jacks, an American philosopher and educator, who wrote this:

> There is a dream of human progress which makes it to consist in a gradual easing of the lot of man, in the gradual lightening of his task, until the last straw of difficulty has been lifted out of his path, the last peril extinguished, the last lee-shore weathered and all smooth sailing for ever afterwards. May it never come true! Man is not made to live under those conditions; the lines on which he is built are far too high and large to fit into them. He will never accommodate himself to an easy life unless we are to assume that his nature has degenerated in the meantime.
>
> Ill adapted for living an easy life, he is well adapted for living a difficult one. It is precisely when his circumstances are easiest that he gives the poorest account of himself, and the best when he is fighting against odds. Never is he more at home in this universe that when he finds himself "upon an engagement very difficult". "It behoves the son of man to suffer many things that he may enter into his glory." Give him a life in which suffering plays no part, and you defraud him of the core of his being. You say to him: "Be a hero no more. Henceforth, take your ease; eat drink and be merry, be Fortune's darling and a smiling fool." A wise man turns his head from your offer with loathing (Jacks, 1931).

Nikos Kazantzakis was excommunicated from the Greek Orthodox Church because of his novel, *The Last Temptation of Christ*. The Christ that Kazantzakis wrote about had one last hallucinatory temptation while he was hanging on the cross – the temptation to renounce all this suffering business and instead get married to Mary Magdalene, make love, have babies, and in his old age sit on the porch with his grandchildren. Kazantzakis' Christ said "no" to that temptation, and he died.

The wisdom tradition

The wisdom tradition really begins in what has been described as the 'axial age', the period roughly between 800 BCE and 200 BCE when intellectual life in both East and West was dominated by individuals who promoted new modes of thought and described uniquely human paths to wisdom. Socrates in ancient Greece is one example, as is Confucius in feudal China and the Buddha in the Asian subcontinent. Jesus, of course, comes on the scene a little later:

> Socrates managed to say something monumental in the history of human thought: that wisdom is a human virtue, won like all virtues by hard work, in this case the hard work of experience, error, intuition, detachment, and, above all, critical thinking. It is counterintuitive, adversarial, unsentimental, demythologising, anything but conventional. Most important, Socrates' wisdom is *secular,* perhaps the highest form of excellence any mortal can hope to achieve without the help of the gods (or God) (Hall 2011:21).

We shall return to the implications of this last sentence but for the moment it is important to say a little more about Socrates himself. It is difficult to separate the biographical details of his life from the philosophy that exemplified that life most obviously because his trial and execution arose directly from his pursuit of this theme:

> The arguments Socrates made at his trial and in his later

> deathbed ruminations (recounted in Plato's *Phaedo*) mark philosophy's grand, almost melodramatic annexation of the study of wisdom, in all its gnarly contradictions and insoluble paradoxes. Many of the essential elements we associate with wisdom were introduced as 'evidence' at Socrates' trial: the importance of humility, especially in acknowledging the limits of one's knowledge and expertise; the importance of persistent, discomforting critical thinking and discernment (usually in the form of conversational questions) to unearth the truth; the importance of identifying and pursuing goodness; and, often underappreciated, the acceptance that true wisdom at some level is often an act of hostility against society (Hall 2011:24).

It is not altogether surprising that in his encounters with people and in his debates with them that he generated a good deal of hostility:

> Although, Socrates was formally charged with corrupting the young and refusing to believe in the Athenian gods, nothing less than Socrates' lifelong pursuit of wisdom itself was on trial. Yet his greatest crime – or, perhaps his greatest lapse in social judgement – may well have been the deft, dispassionate inquisitions by which he established that so many of his judges and jurors were not nearly as wise as they thought (Hall 2011:20).

Socrates was convicted and executed at the end of his trial in 399 CE. As far as we know, he wrote nothing down but a record is provided by his pupil Plato in the dialogues, *Phaedo*. In his summary of the wisdom tradition in the axial age, Hall writes:

> To some degree, the natural history of wisdom can be seen as a never-ending battle between the forces of theology and those

> of secularization, between a top-down, benevolent, dispensed, and divine form of wisdom and a bottom-up, organic, hard-earned human form of wisdom. Put simply, is wisdom a human quality, achieved by human intelligence and insight? Or is wisdom a heavenly gift, bestowed by the gods (or God), utterly inaccessible to mortals who do not subscribe to one or another of the world's religions? This question... became especially thorny with the rise of Christianity, which restored an era of authority, nonhuman agency, and religious mysticism. In such a setting, Wisdom (with a capital W) comes from on high, and wisdom (with a small w) contracts to the rather more modest spheres of familial and communal enterprise (Hall 2011:34).

The idea of wisdom was transported from antiquity to the Middle Ages by eminent religious thinkers within the Judeo-Christian tradition who placed the primary emphasis on wisdom as a gift from God. Augustine and Aquinas were the two towering figures who dominated the landscape during this period. Hall writes:

> No single person embodied theology's recapture of wisdom more than Augustine, who single-handedly demoted secular wisdom to a lower, more inferior plane in the hierarchy of human achievement. Saint Augustine distinguished between *sapientia,* a timeless, eternal wisdom about human conduct and moral perfection bestowed by God, and *scientia,* which reflected mere knowledge of the material world. Taking their cue from Augustine, religious authorities drew an increasingly sharp (and intolerant) distinction between the material wisdom based on reason and knowledge on the one hand and, on the other, the spiritual wisdom and knowledge associated with faith and ecclesiastical authority (Hall 2011: 35).

The distinction between 'human' and 'divine' wisdom was treated rather differently by Aquinas who believed that although there was a distinction, the pursuit of human wisdom could thrive within the context of divine wisdom. In an unpublished article, *Wisdom as orchestration of mind and virtue*, Paul Baltes, the German psychologist, puts it this way:

> According to Aquinas, human reason was autonomous… but its autonomy was preconditioned by faith and the order of the world as created and revealed by God. Thus reason could operate within faith and yet according to its own laws. In other words, Aquinas proposed that the theologian accepts God and his supreme knowledge as a metaframework and then elaborates conclusions using human reason… Thus, although Aquinas presumed that divine wisdom is a higher form of wisdom, he brought a part of wisdom from heaven to earth (Baltes, 2004).

The Renaissance was a turning point and it is difficult to overstate the significance of this turning point for western thought:

> It took many centuries, but Renaissance thought restored the central secular importance of wisdom… In *The Renaissance Idea of Wisdom,* Eugene Rice wrote, "Augustine tied *sapientia* and Christianity together with knots which held a thousand years. The Renaissance patiently loosed them, and restored wisdom to its old autonomy and its purely human dignities" (Hall, 2011:36).

This shift of focus enabled the concept of human reason to flourish but the concept of divine wisdom made little progress as it became engulfed in the doctrine of the Church.

The tension between these two understandings of wisdom

become strained as institutional religion sought to constrain the development of human wisdom in order to maintain the focus on divine wisdom. Some would go further and suggest that ecclesiastical authorities have been ruthless in their determination to maintain an inflexible doctrine. Paul Baltes, 'arguably the foremost scientific scholar of wisdom':

> wondered aloud later in life whether religion, because of its insistence on a fixed set of values, was an 'intellectual enemy' of wisdom. While acknowledging that organised religion makes wisdom a cultural and spiritual priority, he concluded that 'religions constrain how far wisdom is developed...' (Hall, 2011).

This distinction remains within orthodox Christianity but in an age when an increasing number of people reject a theistic faith this tension does not necessarily hold. Those who are inclined to some forms of Christian Humanism reject the supernatural God. For them, divinity is approached through humanity. God becomes not a separate Being but being itself. The two understandings of wisdom then merge to be the ideal to which humankind can aspire on the one hand and a manifestation of God in the depths of our being on the other.

The wisdom literature

The period roughly between 597 BCE and 538 BCE when the Jews were exiled in Babylon was a very low point in their history. The development of wisdom literature at that time was a response to what John Shelby Spong describes as the 'ache of emptiness in the Jewish soul'. For him, it was 'the recovery of the immanence of God' and a new dimension of Jewish thought. In his book, *The Fourth Gospel: Tales of a Jewish Mystic*, Spong writes:

> Wisdom was perceived as an aspect of God who was

> immanent, within them, a God who could touch their lives deeply. To walk in wisdom for the Jews came to mean to walk in or with God. To learn wisdom was to learn God. To listen to wisdom was to listen to God. The God that the universe itself could not contain, much less a temple made by their own hands, began to be perceived not only as a 'being' present with them, but as a permeating presence in all of life. So in the literature of this period of Jewish history, wisdom came to be made very human and very personal. Wisdom was perceived as a manifestation of God that informed even the tiniest events of daily life. God had come out of the heavens and had become a reality closer than their breath. People walked with God's wisdom. People lived inside God's wisdom. People partook of God as they partook of God's wisdom. Wisdom was thus another aspect of God, like the law given on Mount Sinai (Spong, 2013: 56).

Wisdom was a new and very different dimension of Jewish thought. Law was external and to be studied; wisdom was internal and to be lived.

There are over 200 references to 'wisdom' in the Bible and it is one of the great themes of the biblical corpus. The Old Testament books usually classified as wisdom literature are Job, Psalms, Proverbs, Ecclesiastes and the Song of Solomon. Wisdom (or The Wisdom of Solomon) and Sirach (or Ecclesiasticus) are included in some versions of the Bible but not others. In the Protestant Bible they are placed in the Apocrypha. Wisdom references also occur in other parts of the Old Testament, most notably in the story of Solomon in the Book of Kings.The wisdom of Solomon is legendary. 'God gave Solomon very great wisdom, discernment, and breadth of understanding as vast as the sand on the sea shore' (1 Kings 4: 29).

Solomon's great wisdom is traditionally illustrated by his decision in the case of two women who claimed the same baby.

The story goes that Solomon proposed to settle the argument by cutting the baby in two with a sword, giving half to one woman and half to the other. At this point the real mother of the child offered to surrender the baby, and Solomon, with psychological understanding of a mother's love, rendered the verdict in her favour. This folktale, one of the finest in the wisdom tradition, is rounded off with a statement of the community's response to the king's act:

> All Israel heard of the judgement which the king had rendered; and they stood in awe of the king, because they perceived that the wisdom of God was in him, to execute justice (1 Kings 3: 28).

It is important to note that although the Bible credits Solomon with great wisdom, he was also a man of great folly, ultimately leading to the division of his kingdom during the reign of his son Rehoboam.

The book of Proverbs is a rich source of writing on wisdom. It is generally agreed that this book in its final form comes from a much later period and represents the final stage of a tradition but one that goes back to Solomon. Indeed he may have composed or collected the original nucleus of material. Here is one of many passages:

> Listen, children, to a father's instruction, and be attentive, that you may gain insight; for I give you good precepts: do not forsake my teaching. When I was a son with my father, tender, and my mother's favourite, he taught me, and said to me, "Let your heart hold fast my words; keep my commandments, and live. Get wisdom; get insight: do not forget, nor turn away from the words of my mouth. Do not forsake her, and she will keep you; love her, and she will guard you. The beginning of wisdom is this: Get wisdom, and whatever else

> you get, get insight. Prize her highly, and she will exalt you; she will honour you if you embrace her. She will place on your head a fair garland; she will bestow on you a beautiful crown" (Proverbs 4:1-9).

In this passage, the search for wisdom is portrayed as a parent's loving guidance and the child's affectionate response or, as one commentator paraphrases it, 'The taste for wisdom is a father's noblest legacy; the pursuit of understanding is the highest mark of filial respect.'

Wisdom was also highly regarded by the writers of the New Testament. It was regarded by Paul as one of the highest gifts that God could bestow:

> Now there are varieties of gifts, but the same Spirit; and there are varieties of services, but the same Lord; and there are varieties of activities, but it is the same God who activates all of them in everyone. To each is given the manifestation of the Spirit for the common good. To one is given through the Spirit the utterance of wisdom, and to another the utterance of knowledge according to the same Spirit (1 Corinthians 4-8).

But Paul draws a sharp distinction between human wisdom and divine wisdom, a distinction we have already met, and which pervades discussion of these issues:

> Do not deceive yourselves. If you think that you are wise in this age, you should become fools so that you may become wise. For the wisdom of this world is foolishness with God. For it is written, 'He catches the wise in their craftiness', and again, 'The Lord knows the thoughts of the wise, that they are futile' (1 Cor 3: 18-20).

On the face of it, these verses increase the tension between divine and human wisdom but the context is crucial and these texts mean very little if taken out of that context.

It seems clear that Paul was dealing with a tense situation in Corinth and felt he needed to exert his authority over the various factions within the Christian community. He was also faced by a number of other competing groups and philosophies. He was faced by Sophists who regarded wisdom as essentially to do with eloquence and rhetoric and who favoured form over content. He was faced by Gnostics who claimed that wisdom could only be achieved by those who had achieved spiritual advancement. He needed to assert that wisdom was a gift from God not the achievement of human reason. He wanted to refute heresy but also to prevent strife.

Another reference to the distinction between 'divine' and 'earthly' wisdom occurs in this self-contained passage from *The Letter of James,* a passage consistent with the message of the Gospels and with Paul:

> Who is wise and understanding among you? Show by your good life that your works are done with gentleness born of wisdom. But if you have bitter envy and selfish ambition in your hearts, do not be boastful and false to the truth. Such wisdom does not come down from above, but is earthly, unspiritual, devilish. For where there is envy and selfish ambition, there will also be disorder and wickedness of every kind. But the wisdom from above is first pure, then peaceable, gentle, willing to yield, full of mercy and good fruits, without a trace of partiality or hypocrisy. And a harvest of righteousness is sown in peace for those who make peace (James 3:13-18).

It is important to note that some of these words have a slightly different emphasis in the modern world. In some translations, 'meekness' is used as an epithet for 'wisdom'. This is a word that has lost some of its nobility and become somewhat 'limp' in modern usage.

Wisdom Research

Until recently wisdom has been relatively overlooked as a topic for serious academic study and scientific investigation. But it is difficult to imagine a subject more central to the highest aspirations of being human. The study of wisdom holds great promise for shedding light on and opening up new insights for human flourishing.

Supported with funding from the John Templeton Foundation, research projects led by the University of Chicago, in collaboration with scientists at other institutions, are investigating questions that arise in the serious academic study of wisdom. Further information can be found on the website www.wisdomresearch.org.

In an article on the website entitled, *The Wisdom of Oz: A Metaphor of Moral Courage and Self-Compassion,* Brenda Huskey writes:

> In her famous words at the end of the 1939 film production of *The Wizard of Oz,* Dorothy Gale helps us to realize that wisdom is not granted by a wizard or teacher so much as it is realized by the individual by searching within,
>
> "…if I ever go looking for my heart's desire again, I won't look any further than my own backyard; because if it isn't there, I never really lost it to begin with."
>
> *The Wonderful Wizard of Oz* was first published in 1900 long before the MGM movie was released in 1939. This timeless story must be timeless for a reason. In fact, the author L. Frank Baum believed the story may have been divinely inspired: "It was pure inspiration. It came to me right out of the blue. I think that sometimes the Great Author had a message to get across and He was to use the instrument at hand". Indeed, the

story of Oz sends a timeless message of faith and courage to all who struggle with life's challenges, and to teach us to look within to discover that wisdom was always there to begin with (Huskey, 2013).

The Little Book of Wisdom

The Little Book of Wisdom is a collection of sayings of the Dalai Lama which together provide an insight into his understanding of what it means to be wise. Alongside people like Mahatma Gandhi and Mother Teresa he ranks as one of the great spiritual leaders of our time. Like them he reaches beyond his Buddhist roots to find a universal relevance. Those who follow him do not necessarily adopt Buddhist practices but all derive enrichment from his insights on inner peace, daily living, compassion and justice.

For the Dalai Lama it is the quality of our inner spiritual life which determines the character of our actions in the world beyond ourselves, and for him:

> The foundation of all spiritual practice is love.
>
> The essence of all spiritual life is your emotion, your attitude towards others. Once you have pure and sincere motivation, all the rest follows.
>
> The dominant force of our mind is compassion and human affection. Therefore I call these human qualities spirituality (Dalai, 2000:9, 17,18).

Or to put it another way, spirituality is a human quality.

Justice

Injustice anywhere is a threat to justice everywhere.
Martin Luther King, Jr.

Death of a Dream

The Diane Lang Foundation Children's Home was in a township outside Middelburg in South Africa. It looked after abandoned, abused and neglected children for a number of years; sadly it has now been closed. Dianne Lang tells her story in the book, *Saving Mandela's Children*. Two girls, Kelly and Jane, spent some time in the home:

> I found nine year-old Kelly one ice-cold winter's night in May 2002 in Lusaka, a shanty township made up of dwellings built from corrugated iron, bits of wood, plastic, cardboard or anything that can serve as cover for the severe winters and summers. The township is adjacent to Middelburg, a Karoo town in the Eastern Cape, and is the oldest township in South Africa.
>
> Kelly was sitting with her seven year-old friend, Jane, in what would serve as a street, which is nothing more than a strip of gravel between dwellings. They had covered themselves with a piece of cardboard to keep themselves warm. Kelly was dressed in a tracksuit top that only reached her elbows and had on a pair of track pants that reached her knees. Jane had a school dress on. Neither girl had any underwear nor had they shoes. Kelly had a very large scar running along her face where she had been stabbed by a youth in the township when she had been gang raped.
>
> Both girls had lice and scabies. Both had been raped. Neither girl had had anything to eat in four days. Their last meal had been on the rubbish dump, the place known to the street children as 'The Restaurant': They had also never

> attended school. I reported the child abuse and rape to the police and a docket was opened (Lang, 2008:9-10).

Despite Nelson Mandela's work to secure a peaceful transition to majority rule in South Africa, huge injustices remain in the social fabric of that country and as ever it is the children that suffer most. Many children have lost their parents to AIDS and the authorities have not risen to the challenge. Corruption and mismanagement are rife. Kelly and Jane never received the justice they deserved.

Letter from Birmingham Jail

In April 1963 Martin Luther King and others were arrested in Birmingham, Alabama following a Civil Rights march which had been banned. In *Letter from Birmingham Jail,* King responds to a newspaper article from white clergymen criticising King and his methods. They agree that social injustices exist but argue that the battle against racial segregation should be fought solely in the courts, not in the streets. King answers the question, 'Why direct action?'

> Nonviolent direct action seeks to create such a crisis and foster such a tension that a community which has consistently refused to negotiate is forced to confront the issue. It seeks so to dramatize the issue that it can no longer be ignored... I have earnestly opposed violent tension, but there is a type of constructive nonviolent tension which is necessary for growth. Just as Socrates felt that it was necessary to create a tension in the mind so that individuals could rise from the bondage of myths and half-truths to the unfettered realm of creative analysis and objective appraisal, so we must see the need for nonviolent gadflies to create the kind of tension in society that will help men rise from the dark depths of prejudice and racism to the majestic heights of understanding

and brotherhood (King, 1963b).

King goes on to say that it is not the extremists who are the greatest stumbling block to change but the white moderates who are 'more devoted to order than to justice; who prefer a negative peace which is the absence of tension to a positive peace which is the presence of justice'. King explains why he has returned to Birmingham, Alabama and concludes, 'I am in Birmingham because injustice is here' (King 1963b).

Justice and injustice

There is more than a tendency in our tradition to separate the worship of God from welfare of people. In our liturgy we add the needs of the world as an afterthought. In our intercessions, prayers for those who suffer from injustice and oppression and those who are denied dignity and respect come at the end. It is as if we can somehow engage with God without engaging with others at the same time. Is this really what we believe?

Justice is a word that has a rich heritage in the intellectual tradition but it is notoriously difficult to define and means different things to different people. For some, justice is about retribution and punishment. For others, it is about reparation and restitution. For yet others, it is about fairness and the redistribution of wealth. All of these are important strands in the western philosophical tradition. But in the Christian tradition there are additional elements. One has to do with the way in which society must be structured. Another has to do with the way individuals should behave. At the end of the day, however, a comprehensive and coherent account of justice remains elusive.

But there is another way. In her book, *Justice in an Unjust World*, Karen Lebacqz suggests an alternative approach that focuses on injustice. She writes:

My reflections on justice must begin with the realities of

> injustice. I have long been convinced that injustice is our lived reality, and that it is therefore our primary category. Justice emerges as the cry of revolt against injustice. An approach to justice must therefore begin with injustice (Lebacqz 2007:7).

She then proceeds to outline examples of injustice and to provide an interpretive framework that enables us to move forward. This is clearly only one way of approaching an understanding of what justice might mean, but it has the merit of being grounded in our lived experience which is the surest of all foundations.

Lebacqz identifies six forms of injustice that are endemic.

First, racism or ethnic injustice. She argues that at the heart of racism is 'the denial of personhood. Racism involves prejudice blown up into myth. The myth establishes the inferiority of others to justify their exclusion, discrimination, mistreatment and ultimately their death' (Lebacqz 2007:17). Injustice has much to do with the misuse of power which often leads to violence. Examples are drawn from the struggle for civil rights in the United States.

Second, rape and other forms of sexual and gender injustice. Rape is a form of violence directed at both women and men. Such violence also extends to those who are gay or lesbian or who exhibit 'different' lifestyles. Violence extends to women who also suffer oppression, discrimination and marginalisation in many parts of the world. Examples are drawn from societies in which this kind of injustice is endemic.

Third, repression and political and social injustice. People are denied the due process of law or suffer from corruption of the legal system. Others are trapped within government policies and programmes that institutionalise social injustice. Some are denied access to education, health and welfare. Life under apartheid in South Africa provides a powerful example of this form of injustice.

Fourth, robbery and economic injustice. People work hard for little return and are often not protected by a minimum wage. Others are unemployed and are unlikely to find jobs in a climate that tends to favour the rich over the poor. Poverty leads to poor diet declining health and debilitating disease. Many die of starvation. Examples are drawn from the experiences of the poor in Brazil and the Philippines.

Fifth, removal or cultural injustice. People are forcibly removed from their homelands and a different way of life is imposed. They lose culture, tradition and a sense of identity. History is rewritten. Children lose their heritage. The removal of tribes from their lands in the United States is just one example of 'ethnic cleansing'. Recent events in the Balkans and elsewhere provide other examples.

Sixth, rhetoric or verbal injustice. Language is used as an instrument of oppression. It is used to manipulate the truth. Stereotypes are reinforced. News media can sometimes be complicit. Nazi propaganda against the Jews provides one example but there are many others.

Lebacqz goes on to outline some of the ways in which Christian communities have been complicit in each of these forms of injustice. She points out that the justification for slavery was born in the Christian tradition of Noah and nurtured by groups like the Dutch Reformed Church of South Africa in its support for successive regimes of apartheid.

The South African experience

We can now reflect on these examples of injustice in the context of our convictions of how things ought to be. For the Christian, such reflection will be rooted in scripture, tradition, reason and experience, what is sometimes called the Weslyan Quadrilateral. The primary source will be the Bible. Despite the fact that we will disagree about methods of interpretation and may be suspicious of the bias built into the Bible by the communities which formed it, the study of scripture is necessary for any Christian approach to justice.

For Karen Lebacqz, such a study must be undertaken from the perspective of the poor and oppressed. Traditional methods of historical-critical scholarship have looked towards universal and authoritative understandings. A new hermeneutics is now needed that unashamedly starts from a particular perspective:

> The starting point both for theology and for exegesis and textual interpretation is the lived experience of those who struggle against oceans of injustice. As Dorothy Solle puts it, "Bible texts are best read with a pair of glasses made out of today's newspaper" (Lebacqz 2007:60).

Desmond Tutu, speaking about the role of the Church in South Africa in his book *Hope and Suffering*, argues that its theology must be grounded in the experience of real communities:

> Western theology is no more universal than another brand of theology can ever hope to be… Theology is a human activity possessing the limitations and particularities of those who are theologising. It can speak relevantly only when it speaks to a particular historically and spatio-temporally conditioned Christian community… (Tutu 1984: 75).

It is well known that the black population of South Africa suffered under Apartheid but the nature of that suffering is not always well understood. It is really only by listening to people like Desmond Tutu that it is possible to go beyond a superficial condemnation of the policies of the Nationalist Government that ruled South Africa for so many years and achieve greater insight. Behind claims that the security of the state was threatened by communists and subversives of every kind, the minority white community and its elected representatives adopted a quite untenable position of entrenchment. To reinforce their position they did everything in their power to marginalise the majority black community and ensure its impotence in the decision making process. This started with the inculcation of attitudes and continued with the implementation of policies.

The black population were regarded by many in the white community as inferior in every respect. They were not worthy even to be addressed in the same terms as their white compatriots. It was rare for a black man to be addressed as 'Mr'! Some genuinely believed that the black races had been born with a natural inferiority. They were regarded as less intelligent, less cultured and less civilised and so had to be treated quite differently from the rest. Others were simply prejudiced against them or displayed the fear and ignorance typically associated with such attitudes. And because blacks were in the majority, they posed a threat. They needed more policing, more control and more separation. Many white communities were paranoid about the survival of their privileges and did everything possible to retain their hold on power. They were terrified of anything that threatened to disturb their secure and comfortable way of life.

In practice this meant that for whatever reason, the black community found themselves with inferior housing, inferior services, inferior education and inferior employment opportunities. Moreover, they had inferior means of representation, inferior access to the justice system and an inferior ability to control their own destiny. This increased as the policy of separate development caused many thousands to be uprooted from their homes and relocated in unfamiliar surroundings where infrastructure was inadequate and employment opportunities were limited. Families were put under considerable strain by the need for the breadwinner to travel long distances to find work. Many thousands were away from those families for very long periods.

All this had a huge impact on the self-confidence and human dignity of individuals and communities with the result that although some became compliant others were increasingly not prepared to be continually abused in this way. This increased when all blacks were required to carry passes. This treatment of the black by the white population also had an impact on the self-control and patience of those under oppression particularly the younger members of communities. Inevitably this treatment bred frustration, resentment and violence towards all forms of authority particularly the police and the agencies of government. When the government responded with harsher measures of repression, some responded with more aggression and so the cycle of violence increased. There was a certain inevitability about the future if policies did not change. In an open letter to the Prime Minister in 1976, Desmond Tutu wrote:

> I have a growing nightmarish fear that unless something drastic is done very soon then bloodshed and violence are going to happen in South Africa almost inevitably. A people can take only so much and no more (Tutu 1984: 32).

In the end, it was not a change of heart that caused Apartheid to collapse but external and internal pressure. The international community were increasingly unwilling to tolerate this blatant denial of human rights and were escalating political, economic and other sanctions on the country. The internal tensions were increasingly spiralling out of control and the South African government could see that they had a choice between peaceful or violent change. To maintain the *status quo* was simply not an option. In the event there was a relatively peaceful transition to majority government. And the release of Nelson Mandela and his benign influence on events was a significant contributory factor. This did not mean that problems disappeared overnight and many years later the country is still divided between rich and poor. And the crime rates of South African cities are amongst the highest in the world. However, the basic premise of equality on which the new constitution is based gives everyone hope for the future.

The Biblical Context

But, for Karen Lebacq, 'Human laws and institutions are not the beginning point for understanding justice; rather, we must attend to the narratives that give shape to the history of God's interventions in human life...'

> The justice of God begins in the mighty act of exodus. It begins in the rescue of slaves. From then on the Israelites saw everything in the light of this single event; it became for them the paradigm for describing God's activity in human history. The God of the Bible is therefore first and foremost the God of liberation (Lebacqz 2007:70).

But as William Johnson points out in his study guide, *Exodus*, the biblical account of the exodus is not primarily an historical narrative:

> Israel's religion is not founded on historical events; rather, Israel's religious writers are using a narrative form of presentation in which history provides the general framework; for the filling in of the detail, historical circumstances are only one source among many. This complex narrative is the medium for expressing a prior religious tradition: the historical events in Exodus are not the source but the vehicle, not the basis but the confirmation, not the proof but the proving-ground (Johnstone, 1995:36).

That is, of course, not to say that the historical event itself is unimportant but it is to say that the narrative has a higher purpose. In any case we cannot take the biblical account at face value and scholars continue to debate the historical detail. Nevertheless, for Desmond Tutu:

> This gracious act of divine intervention was to be indelibly impressed on the corporate memory of Israel, so that from that time on they would see everything... from the perspective of this signal event. It was for them the founding event of their existence as a people *par excellence*. It would be for them the paradigm for describing God's activity in human history (Tutu, 1984:54).

For Lebacqz, the narrative of the exodus is 'the base for interpreting the remainder of the Hebrew Scriptures' and it provides a clear guide to the nature of God's response to injustice. She goes on:

> The centrality of the Exodus tradition suggests that rescue, or deliverance, becomes the first form of God's response to injustice and therefore the first form of justice (Lebacqz, 2007:73).

This is also reflected in the New Testament where Jesus describes his ministry 'in terms reminiscent of the liberation tradition':

> The Spirit of the Lord is upon me, because he has anointed me to preach good news to the poor. He has sent me to proclaim freedom for the prisoners and recovery of sight to the blind, to release the oppressed, and to proclaim the year of the Lord's favour (Luke 4:18-19).

Although, justice is expressed in other ways, for Tutu, the God of the Bible is primarily a God of liberation:

> He leads his people out of every kind of bondage, spiritual, political, social and economic, and nothing will thwart Him from achieving the goal of liberation of all His people and the whole of His creation (Tutu 1984:155).

For many, this biblical message of liberation extends to all times and to all places. It has been the inspiration for what has become known as Liberation Theology.

Liberation Theology

Liberation Theology has its origins in the reality of the premature death and acute suffering of the poor people of South America. In 1968, the Roman Catholic bishops of Latin America gathered for a congress at Medellin, Columbia. This meeting sent shock waves throughout the region by acknowledging that the church had often sided with oppressive regimes in the region, and declaring that in future it would be on the side of the poor. This position was soon complemented by a solid theological foundation. In his *Theology of Liberation*, Gustavo Gutierrez introduced the characteristic themes that would define the movement. Gutierrez is a Peruvian priest and theologian who lives and works among the poor of Lima:

> The theology of liberation offers us not so much a new theme for reflection as a new way to do theology... This is a theology which does not stop with reflecting on the world, but rather tries to be part of the process through which the world is transformed. It is a theology which is open – in the protest against trampled human dignity, in the struggle against the plunder of the vast majority of humankind, in liberating love, and in the building of a new, just, and comradely society – to the gift of the Kingdom of God (Gutierrez, 2001:59).

Poverty in Latin America is widespread. The indigenous peasants are the poorest people, and their extreme poverty is mainly due to unfair distribution of wealth and corruption within government. These countries have generally attracted more foreign investment than Africa or Asia but this often makes them reliant on unstable short-term speculative foreign investment.

Allied with expensive high interest rate aid loans, this has made escaping poverty difficult for many governments. Poverty in some Latin American countries has been worsened by migrations, internal conflicts and bad government. In some areas poverty is due to the pressure of population growth on scarce resources. In some regions, drug-related social and political instability helps maintain poverty. Latin American countries have recently been increasing military spending, as poverty has started increasing again. And Latin America is an area where aid debt also seems a major obstacle to progress.

Liberation theology not only argues that the church should be on the side of the poor but declares that the poor occupy a special place in God's plan. This is not the 'top down' theology of classical theology but a 'bottom up' approach. Whereas classical theology regards social action as arising from theological reflection, liberation theology inverts this and places action first, followed by reflection. It claims that true knowledge of God and his ways can never be disinterested or detached and can only arise from a commitment to the poor and oppressed. Gutierrez popularized the phrase 'preferential option for the poor'; it became the slogan of liberation theology.

For liberation theologians, this 'preferential option for the poor' is a fundamental aspect of the biblical gospel. Scripture is read as a narrative of liberation with a particular emphasis placed on the Exodus, the prophet's denunciation of oppression and on Jesus' support for the poor and oppressed. Again, there is a certain inversion of biblical hermeneutics taking place here. The aim is not so much to apply the principles of biblical interpretation to these passages but to apply their liberating insights to the Latin American situation. Inevitably, some academic theologians are unhappy with this approach.

There are also other issues, most notably the liberation theologian's understanding of the nature of salvation. In *Christian Theology: An Introduction,* Alister McGrath writes:

> Liberation theology has tended to equate salvation with liberation, and stressed the social, political and economic aspects of salvation. The movement has laid particular emphasis upon the notion of 'structural sin', noting that it is society, rather than individuals, that is corrupted and requires redemption. To its critics, liberation theology has reduced salvation to a purely worldly affair, and neglected its transcendent and eternal dimensions (McGrath, 1997:117).

The Roman Catholic Church hierarchy initially welcomed liberation theology but in recent years they have been more critical claiming, for example, that the movement places too much emphasis on the humanity and too little emphasis on the divinity of Jesus. The Jesuit theologian Jon Sobrino has been a particular target and in 2007 his award-winning books, *Jesus the Liberator* and *Christ the Liberator,* were censured by the Vatican. These books were described as 'erroneous or dangerous' and 'may cause harm to the faithful'. Needless to say these comments hugely increased circulation. He has been the subject of attacks not just by the Church but also by the Military. In 1989 he was the sole survivor after the Salvadoran Military murdered his six Jesuit colleagues, their housekeeper and her daughter at his home on the campus of the University of Central America.

In his most recent book, *The Eye of the Needle,* published in 2008, Sobrino argues that:

> ...global capitalism is driven by a cruel dynamic of oppression and greed, which inevitably dehumanises people, destroys the human family, and threatens mother earth. Yet, he argues, it is the poor themselves, who, paradoxically, offer the only way to salvation for the world. We must work for a new civilisation that will give everyone access to the material and cultural goods that make for a truly human life, and reduce the enormous and growing gap between those who have and

> those who haven't (Sobrino 2008).

These ideas represent a major shift which grounds theological discourse in the real world of the human condition and redefines the notion of salvation. The sub-title of Sobrino's book is *No Salvation Outside the Poor.* He explains that:

> ...we are not saying that with the poor salvation already exists automatically, but that without them it cannot exist at all. We are saying that there is always 'something' of salvation with the poor. What we want to do is offer hope, despite everything: salvation for a very sick world can come from the world of the poor and the victims (Sobrino 2008:41).

This is very different from the traditional notion of personal salvation for it claims that salvation can only arise in our relationships with each other and in particular with those who suffer.

Looking from the outside we are used to describing the world of the poor as wholly negative. They are described as lacking food, clothing and shelter. They suffer from discrimination and unemployment. They lack civilisation, and culture. The list is endless. Yet those who venture into the world of the poor find something quite unexpected and positive. They find a vitality in the struggle of the poor to survive. They find an ingenuity in their efforts to improve their conditions. They find a communal way of life that respects the individual. They find a culture with its own art, music and poetry.

Sobrino quotes from the experience of one who saw both the positive and negative in the world of the poor during the Asian tsunami of 2004:

> Coping with suffering and responding with compassion has developed in the victims some of the values we need for a

> different world: solidarity, humanity, a spirit of sharing, survival skills, dogged resistance to adversity. Unlike the world of the Empire and globalisation, in the world of the victims the good is not seen as mere 'success'. The good and the just are ideals the world needs in its struggle to attain something vital. The cultural resources of the poor reflect the values and ideals of a future world and help them to face life bravely, individually and together (Sobrino, 2008:47).

It is Sobrino's claim that salvation can only come from within the suffering community when individuals and communities are liberated from oppression whatever form it may take. Furthermore, the seeds of that salvation come from the response of the suffering community where the qualities that make for salvation are forged. The preferential option for the poor is therefore not a 'top down' approach but 'bottom up'. In the colloquialism of our time, we must 'start where they are at'.

As a postscript, it is heartening to note a change of direction in the Roman Catholic Church with the election of Pope Francis. Not only is he more sympathetic to Liberation Theology than his predecessor, but he is also more positive towards the 'preferential option for the poor' than his previous statements on the subject. Paul Vallely, describes this change of heart in his book *Pope Francis: Untying the Knots*, and it really does seem to be a 'conversion' (Vallely, 2013):

> History has been a major factor in the transmutation of Bergoglio (Fr Jorge Mario Bergoglio SJ, now Pope Francis 1), for the world has changed significantly around him. His opposition to Liberation Theology was very much rooted in the mind-set of the Cold War and the fear that atheistic Soviet-style communism would supplant both capitalism and Catholicism in Latin America, with Cuba as its toehold. But

> then the Berlin Wall came down. The Soviet Union and its empire collapsed. A new international *realpolitik* was ushered in… The globalisation of the world's economy prompted Bergoglio to think differently about extreme poverty. To recognise the exploitation of the poor, or their wilful marginalisation, was no longer to risk being seen to side with the forces of an anti-religious Marxism. Rather it began to sound like a form of solidarity which was part of bringing the good news to the poor… A key part of Bergoglio's growth has been the development of an understanding that what the poor need is not charity but justice (Vallely, 2013:129).

'The unjust judge'

The story goes that Mother Teresa went to visit Edward Williams, a legendary Washington criminal lawyer. He was a powerful man and worked for Frank Sinatra and Richard Nixon, among others. Mother Teresa was raising money for an AIDS hospice. Williams was in charge of a small charitable foundation that she hoped would help. Before she arrived for the appointment, Williams said to his partner, Paul Dietrich, "You know, Paul, AIDS is not my favourite disease. I don't really want to make a contribution, but I've got this Catholic saint coming to see me, and I don't know what to do." They agreed that they would be polite, hear her out, but then say "No".

Well, Mother Teresa arrived. She was a little sparrow sitting on the other side of the big mahogany desk. She made her appeal for the hospice, and Williams said, "We're touched by your appeal, but, No." Mother Teresa said simply, "Let us pray." Williams looked at Dietrich; they bowed their heads and after the prayer, Mother Teresa made the same pitch, word for word, for the hospice. Again Williams politely said "No". Mother Teresa said, "Let us pray." Williams, exasperated, looked up at the ceiling, "All right, all right, get me my cheque book!"

The parable at the beginning of Luke 18 is sometimes called

'the parable of the unjust judge' but that is not fair. The judge in the parable is not perverting the course of justice but is simply slow or dilatory in carrying it through. Jewish judges received no payment so attention to their task rested on a high sense of duty. Where a judge had no such sense of duty the process was likely to be delayed. And it was more likely to be delayed in the case of someone on the margins of society with no 'clout' to move things on. Typically this was someone who was weak and vulnerable like the widow.

But note that the judge does eventually give her justice because of her tenacity and persistence despite his character and inclinations. And part of the aim of this parable is to highlight the contrast. How much more will God dispense justice to those who 'cry to him day and night'. Those who suffer injustice should not lose heart or give up crying out for the justice that God is sure to give. Moreover, that justice may come in unexpected ways and through unexpected people.

This story has been shaped in the cruelty of exploitation and the arbitrary abuse of power that was as prevalent in first-century Palestine as it is today. It belongs in the world which Jesus is addressing and in which he lived. Jesus is reading the signs in the wounds of the people and the contours of their devastation shape the structures of his thought. Jesus being Jesus was acutely aware of the needs of the people of his time.

And it is our role to be as acutely aware as we can of the needs of the people of our time. This means being in touch with the struggles, with the poverty, with all that makes people cry out in our world. It also means living with the affirmation of a God who cares, even though the solution may not come speedily. It means building supportive communities where people can sustain the crying day and night and not lose heart.

It is not difficult to find examples of political, economic and social injustice in the wider world. Our television, newspapers and magazines are full of stories of inequality, deprivation and violence around the world. Yet it is not easy to assess the truth of these accounts. It is not easy to determine where blame lies. It is not easy to know how to act. We can feel impotent in the face of these assaults on human dignity.

The Great War for Civilisation is Robert Fisk's account of nearly three decades of reporting events in the Middle East. If we take it at face value, this book is a shocking account not only of the way people have been treated in that part of the world but also of the way in which we have been misinformed. I came away from that book feeling very angry. On the face of it we would appear to have very little influence over these events but that would be to miss some important opportunities. We can pray. We can work to remove stigma. We can speak out against prejudice. We can avoid making generalisations and more… (Fisk, 2006).

But perhaps more important still, we can campaign for the church to be at the forefront of movements for social justice. Traditionally, the church seems to have regarded the promotion of justice as quite separate from its mission to evangelise. This is part of the historical separation between the sacred and the secular. It is a division which is misleading and dangerous. Our sacred mission must include our care for the secular world for the enterprise to be worthy of the name 'mission'. Our Christian enterprise must embrace real concern for the human condition. And the human condition is not foreign to us. It is where we 'live and move and have our being'. It is where we encounter people. And it is where we meet God.

A recent edition of the *Church Times* carried an article in which the author stated, 'A sincere desire to remedy social evils is an integral part of authentic Christian living.' Yes! We can all agree with that. But he then went on to say, 'But these agendas must not be pursued at the expense of individuals' becoming more Christ like'. No! I'm sorry professor, I think you're wrong. It is precisely because we maintain this separation between the pursuit of personal piety and the quest for social justice that we fail to be convincing Christians. You were right the first time. The two must be fully integrated. Surely, the Christian message is that you cannot have the one without the other (Frame, 2007).

'Then the king will say to those at his right hand, 'Come, you that are blessed by my Father, inherit the kingdom prepared for you from the foundation of the world; for I was hungry and you gave me food, I was thirsty and you gave me something to drink, I was a stranger and you welcomed me, I was naked and you gave me clothing, I was sick and you took care of me, I was in prison and you visited me.' Then the righteous will answer him, 'Lord, when was it that we saw you hungry and gave you food, or thirsty and gave you something to drink? And when was it that we saw you a stranger and welcomed you, or naked and gave you clothing? And when was it that we saw you sick or in prison and visited you?' And the king will answer them, 'Truly I tell you, just as you did it to one of the least of these who are members of my family, you did it to me.'' (Matthew 25:34-40)

Generous Justice

This theme is taken up by Timothy Keller in his book *Generous Justice*. During his ministry he has met many people for whom their faith is about personal salvation rather than social justice. For some, 'doing justice' is inextricably linked with the loss of sound doctrine and spiritual dynamism'. He wants to suggest that:

> ...the Biblical gospel of Jesus necessarily and powerfully leads to a passion for justice in the world. A concern for justice in all aspects of life is neither an artificial add-on nor a contradiction to the message of the Bible (Keller, 2010:xiv).

Keller comes from an evangelical background and the gift of God's grace is central to his faith, but his understanding goes beyond the claim that this free gift is essentially a personal matter:

> Most people know that Jesus came to bring forgiveness and grace. Less well known is the biblical teaching that a true experience of the grace of Jesus Christ inevitably motivates a man or woman to seek justice in the world (Keller, 2010:ix).

One of the founders of the Social Gospel movement was Walter Rauschenbusch who was a pastor in the Hell's Kitchen area of New York City in the 1880s:

> His first-hand acquaintance with the terrible poverty of his neighbourhood led him to question traditional evangelism, which took pains to save people's souls but did nothing about the social systems locking them into poverty. Rauschenbusch began to minister to 'both soul and body', but in tandem with this shift in method came a shift in theology (Keller, 2010:xii).

He rejected many traditional doctrines and began to see salvation not just in personal terms but in social terms also. We have already met Jo Sobrino's recasting of the word 'salvation' in a similar vein.

Speaking Christian

One of the chapters in Marcus Borg's book, *Speaking Christian*, is concerned with how the word 'salvation' has become distorted from its biblical meaning by the 'heaven and hell framework' in current usage. In the Bible, salvation is less about our future life in heaven than about our present life on earth. It is about liberation from bondage, return from exile and rescue from peril. It is about how we achieve justice for those who suffer injustice and how we conquer violence with peace. But many of the issues that we think of as justice issues today – race, gender and human rights – had not yet arisen. So the Bible's passion for justice is focused on economic justice:

> The economic justice that is the Bible's passion concerns the basic necessities of life. In the Bible, they are land and food, the material basis of existence. Everybody should have enough, not as the product of charity, but as the result of the way the system is put together. The Bible knows that powerful and wealthy elites commonly structure the world in their own self-interest. Pharaoh and Herod and Caesar are still with us. From them we need to be saved (Borg, 2011:49).

For Borg, and for us, salvation is ultimately about transformation, a twofold transformation – of ourselves and of the world:

> I think most people yearn for this. We yearn for the transformation of our lives – for a fuller connection to what is, from liberation to all that keeps us in bondage, for sight, for wholeness, for the healing of the wounds of existence. And most of us yearn for a world that is a better place (Borg, 2011:54).

For this transformation to take place our concerns must be grounded in the human condition and in the world of the twenty-first century.

Courage

> O God, give us the serenity to accept what cannot be changed, courage to change what should be changed, and the wisdom to know the difference.
> Reinhold Niebuhr

Introduction

In *A New Dictionary of Christian Ethics* Roger Hazelton writes:

> The place of courage in the moral life has always been acknowledged even if variously understood and debated. Christian ethical reflection on the subject owes much to ancient Greek and Roman thought, especially Aristotle and the Stoics. As one of the cardinal virtues along with wisdom, justice, and temperance, courage was seen as necessary to all truly moral conduct, a mean struck between rashness and cowardice, a capability of human character to resist pain, danger, or adversity by enduring what cannot be changed and by changing what cannot be endured (Hazelton, 1967).

The Diving-Bell and the Butterfly

Jean-Dominique Bauby was a successful French businessman. He was editor-in-chief of the French *Elle* magazine and comfortably well-off with a wife and two young children. He was 45 years old and a very active man enjoying sport and other outdoor activities with his family. One day he is testing the latest BMW for the magazine. The company has provided him with the car for the day. As he is driving home he suddenly feels very ill. He pulls over to the side of the road. Help is called and he is rushed to hospital. He falls into a deep coma. He has had a stroke.

He was in a coma for three weeks, but it was several more weeks before he fully appreciated what had happened to him.

He had had a massive stroke which had left him paralysed from head to toe. He was unable to speak or move a muscle. Blinking his left eyelid was his only means of communication. His mind was fully intact but his body was useless. He was a prisoner in his own body. He was suffering from what is called 'locked-in syndrome'.

Gradually, he began to come to terms with his condition. He found a way to 'dictate' by blinking, using letters of the alphabet in a particular order. His alphabet started ESAI, with letters placed according to the frequency of use in the French Language. So he blinked once for E, twice for S, three times far A and so on. In this way he was eventually able to dictate quite fast. In due course he dictated a book, *The Diving-Bell and the Butterfly,* and it became a bestseller. A film was soon to follow (Bauby, 1998).

It is difficult for us to imagine what it must be like to suddenly lose all those faculties: to be suddenly unable to speak or communicate: to be suddenly unable to walk or move about. He seemed to have lost many of those things which we associate with being a person. The way we speak and what we say. The way we walk and the body language that we use. Some people even thought he had lost all claim to be a person. His friends overheard a conversation in a cafe. "Did you know that Bauby is now a total vegetable?" said one. "Yes, I heard, a complete vegetable", said another. The tone of voice left no doubt that Bauby now belonged to a vegetable stall and no longer to the human race. This was not only cruel, it was utter nonsense. Bauby was very much alive and his personality shines through the pages of this book.

Before his stroke, Jean Bauby was like most men of his generation and lived life to the full. After his stroke, he was no longer like most men of his generation but he continued to live life to the full. He was grossly handicapped by his inability to speak and to move and he could have given up if that was all there was to life. But he decided that there was more to life and he lived it. His changed circumstances focused his mind on those things which really mattered. He found the adjustment an enormous struggle but his courage and determination paid off. He was able to discover resources within himself that he never knew existed.

Sadly, Jean Bauby died on 9th March, 1997 but his legacy is this book which has inspired and continues to inspire. It was not written just for those who find themselves in hugely changed circumstances. It was written for all of us. It is a testament to great courage.

The Courage to Be

Few of us will experience the trauma of 'locked-in syndrome' but most of us suffer fear and anxiety at some point in our lives. This can sometimes be acute and debilitating amid the pace and pressures of the modern world. To deal with the stress we need to adopt strategies and to muster the courage to cope. The American theologian, Paul Tillich, wrote more than most on the subject of courage in the Christian context, particularly during periods of great disillusionment in the twentieth century. In his Introduction to Paul Tillich's book, *The Courage to Be*, Peter Gomes writes:

> Paul Tillich was one who, in the middle of the twentieth century, spoke convincingly to the crisis of spirit and mind that hovered over the religious life of thoughtful people. He provided a new theological vocabulary with which to address the profound disquietude provoked by modernity's confrontation with death and meaningless. Of all his many writings, none better captures the essence of Tillich's thought than *The Courage to Be*, published in 1952 (Tillich, 2000:xi).

Tillich's book is not an easy read, and in the first paragraph we are faced with a word that will be unfamiliar to many people – ontology. Ontology is that branch of philosophy that deals with the nature of being. We speak of human beings but ontology deals with the nature of all forms of being. In his opening paragraph, Tillich gives us his definition of courage:

> Courage is an ethical reality, but it is rooted in the whole breadth of human existence and ultimately in the structure of being itself. It must be considered ontologically in order to be understood ethically (Tillich, 2000:1).

So Tillich unites both meanings of the concept of courage, the ethical and the ontological and he summarises the meaning of each:

> Courage as a human act, as a matter of valuation, is an ethical concept. Courage as the universal and essential self-affirmation of one's being is an ontological concept. The courage to be is the ethical act in which man affirms his own being in spite of those elements of his existence which conflict with his essential self-affirmation (Tillich, 2000:3).

The courage to be is that of using the power of every aspect of our being right through to God, the 'ground of our being', to prevail over the threat of non-being and subsequent fear and anxiety. The only way to combat anxiety is to first convert it to fear for fear has an object that can be acted upon; anxiety only has the threat itself.

Tillich identifies three types of anxiety that we all face – anxiety of fate and death, anxiety of guilt and condemnation and anxiety of emptiness and meaninglessness. These three types of anxiety take on two forms – existential and pathological. Existential anxiety exists in all of us but if we are unable to deal with it becomes pathological anxiety.

In the face of these anxieties we seek to maintain the affirmation of our being by clinging to it in two ways. The first is to preserve our autonomy by holding on to anything which seems to provide support like historical traditions, personal convictions and emotional preferences. The second is to discard our autonomy, to retreat from freedom and to subject ourselves to authority which then takes over responsibility from us. Neither strategy works.

If we are unable to take this anxiety courageously upon ourselves then there are two options – despair and neurosis. We can avoid despair by escaping into neurosis:

> Neurosis is the way of avoiding non-being by avoiding being. In the neurotic state self-affirmation is not lacking; it can indeed be very strong and emphasized. But the self which is affirmed is a reduced one... He affirms something which is less than his essential or potential being. He surrenders part of his potentialities in order to save what is left (Tillich, 2000:66).

According to Tillich, it is not possible to remove our fears and anxieties but it is possible to tackle them and achieve the necessary balance. And this balance must be biological as well as psychological:

> Without the anticipating fear and the compelling anxiety no finite being would be able to exist. Courage, in this view, is the readiness to take upon oneself negatives, anticipated by fear, for the sake of a fuller positivity. Biological self-affirmation implies the acceptance of want, toil, insecurity, pain, possible destruction. Without this affirmation life could not be preserved or increased. The more vital strength a being has the more it is able to affirm itself in spite of the dangers announced by fear and anxiety. However, it would contradict their biological function if courage disregarded their warnings and prompted actions of a directly self-destructive character. Biological self-affirmation needs a balance between courage and fear (Tillich, 2000:78).

This need for balance between fear and courage is perhaps somewhat surprising and the notion that anxiety and fear are a necessary part of our being is perhaps frightening. We long for security but it is a fruitless search:

> The drive for security, perfection, and certitude is biologically necessary. But it becomes biologically destructive if the risk of insecurity, imperfection, and uncertainty is avoided... Life includes both fear and courage as elements of a life process in a changing but essentially established balance. As long as life has such a balance it is able to resist nonbeing (Tillich, 2000: 79).

In his book, *A New Christianity for a New World,* John Shelby Spong attacks those who offer a false certainty and a false sense of security:

> Security is so seductive, and insecurity so frightening. But security is always false, and insecurity is always real. No religion can make anyone secure, though it, like the drugs on which our society is so dependent, can give the illusion of security. True religion enables one to grasp life with the radical insecurity and to live it with courage (Spong, 2002:68).

Graceful Courage

In his book, *Graceful Courage,* Roger Hazelton explores the subject of courage 'in deliberately human terms':

> Hence courage has been termed a way of taking the human measure of one's world, a kind of virtue necessary to becoming human, a resilient steadfastness before life's hazards and setbacks. Neither physical energy nor spiritual inspiration alone accounts for its presence, as it arises in the middle zone between bare survival and devotion to superior,

> self-surpassing values. It vibrates within the tension set up by fear and faith. Its resources come from contrary directions although they meet at that mysterious juncture called 'the heart' (Hazelton, 1985:113).

He then asks the question, 'Why not simply leave the matter there?' His answer is 'No!':

> Does not courage by its very presence suggest a 'more-than' rather than a 'nothing-but' reading of our humanity itself? In other words, can courage even be conceived apart from the conviction that here humanity is overreaching itself, harnessing possibility to actuality, moving slowly but surely toward its own fulfillment? Such a belief has always been a salient feature of humanistic thought. However, as we ask whence comes this power to produce as well as to endure change, we are led to think of a source of energy resembling what religions call God (Hazelton, 1985:113).

For Hazelton, this energy is 'grace' a word which he defines as 'the sense of enabling and resourceful energy coming from a source as much beyond as within myself':

> Grace, then, delineates a common bond, even a common ground, between what is known to be human and what is believed to be divine. It is not an 'either/or' word for enforcing what Soren Kierkegaad declared to be 'the infinite qualitative distinction' between Creator and creature, but a 'both/and' word of intimate relationship (Hazelton, 1985:114).

Grace is, of course, a word that is widely used in Christian theology, but it is sometimes narrowly defined to imply that a 'divine injection' of grace somehow 'takes over' our humanity. But in Galatians, Paul's writing is more nuanced:

> ...and it is no longer I who live, but it is Christ who lives in me. And the life I live in the flesh, I live by faith in the Son of God (Galatians 2:20).

In other words, we are transformed by grace but retain our faculties as human beings. If we are not careful we can get tied up in the limitations of language but there seems little doubt that:

> Paul's 'paradox of grace' holds a significant truth. 'I' and 'not I' carry equal weight, each necessary to the meaning of the other. If one has to make a choice one must choose both (Hazelton, 1985:117).

These difficulties over the understanding of grace arise from the assumption that the divine and the human are quite separate entities with mutually exclusive meanings. This in turn arises from a traditional understanding about God:

> It should not come as a surprise that the word 'God' should have come to signify a cosmic overlord or super being whose supreme and sovereign power makes up for human deficiency by overriding and overruling our poor, pitiful pretense of freedom. From here it is but a short step to the belief that such a God is totally other, utterly unlike anything we know in ourselves or in our world. What we forget is that these claims made for God bear bitter fruit in a very precise sense of that word, based on the odd and really outrageous premise that if God does everything then human beings can do nothing except to let God have absolute control over their lives in the world. This view of an all-powerful deity, if followed through logically, would eliminate the need and motivation for courage (Hazelton, 1985:125).

We really must not allow this to happen.

'Courage is the greatest of all virtues'

In his book, *Courage: Eight Portraits,* Gordon Brown, the former Prime Minister, writes about the life and work of eight courageous men and women of the twentieth century – Edith Cavell, Dietrich Bonhoeffer, Raoul Wallenberg, Martin Luther King, Robert Kennedy, Nelson Mandela, Cicely Saunders and Aung San Suu Kyi. He is clearly inspired by these people and is fascinated by the qualities of courage that they possessed:

> The kind of courage that fascinated me went beyond physical bravery, though almost always it did involve that admirable quality. It was not just risk-taking, and definitely not risk-taking in a doubtful cause. Here was altruistic courage: sacrifice and determination for a higher purpose; the courage that endures and prevails, and eventually dignifies all humanity (Brown, 2007: 1).

In common usage, 'fascination' is a somewhat superficial word. Yet its use in this context has considerably more depth.

In his Conclusion to the book, Brown quotes Churchill who in turn is drawing on the words of Aristotle:

> What their lives and abiding influences demonstrate is that courage is, indeed, the greatest of all virtues. All of us value duty, honesty, kindness, humility, responsibility, integrity, but none of these can exist without courage. As Winston Churchill said, 'Courage is the first of human qualities because it is the quality which guarantees all others' (Brown, 2007: 236).

For many people Gordon Brown is a man of principle with a strong moral sense. He spoke of his 'moral compass' and of his parents being his great inspiration. His father was a Church of Scotland minister and he was no doubt influenced by his

Calvinist background. Edith Cavell was also 'a child of the manse' and he writes of her:

> Edith Cavell's life was not just the sum of chance and accident, but a purposeful resolve at each crossroads in her life. It was a search to give expression to her vocation to minister… Edith Cavell's duty was to humanity, and her legacy is its triumph (Brown, 2007:35).

Gordon Brown is passionate about the part played by courage in the welfare of humanity and, although as a politician he was at times neither popular nor successful, we would probably agree that his 'heart was in the right place':

> People of courage will always be loved, because they ennoble the human race to which they belong… They give us glimpses of the nobility of which humanity is capable. They raise our sights and challenge us to be all that we are capable of being. They answer the human hunger for meaning and invest in our human condition a value so great as to assure its pricelessness (Brown, 2007:237).

The implication is that these human qualities are not only moral qualities but spiritual qualities, and that in pursuing these human qualities men and women are on a path towards God. The gap between the human and the divine closes. The following quotation from Dietrich Bonhoeffer has already been used but it is particularly apt here:

> To be a Christian does not mean to be religious in any particular way, to cultivate some particular form of asceticism (as a sinner, a penitent or a saint), but to be a man. It is not some religious act which makes a Christian what he is, but participation in the suffering of God in the life of the world…

(Bonhoeffer, 1965:123).

It is interesting that another politician, John F Kennedy, wrote a similar book in 1955. In *Profiles in Courage,* he also writes about eight prominent political figures. Whatever we may sometimes say and think about politicians, for many of them, traditional virtues like courage still have an important place (Kennedy, 2013).

Jesus the Good Shepherd

It is not difficult to find other examples of people who can inspire and motivate us to be more courageous in our personal lives. But for David Cruz, and for us too, the greatest example is that of Jesus as the 'good shepherd' in the gospel of John:

> I am the good shepherd. The good shepherd lays down his life for the sheep. The hired hand, who is not the shepherd and does not own the sheep, sees the wolf coming and leaves the sheep and runs away – and the wolf snatches them and scatters them. The hired hand runs away because a hired hand does not care for the sheep (John 10:11).

In his commentary on John, *The Gospel of John,* William Barclays gives a vivid description of what life was like for the shepherd of Jesus' time:

> A real shepherd was born to his task. He was sent out with the flock as soon as he was old enough to go; the sheep became his friends and companions; and it became second nature to think of them before he thought of himself… His life was very hard. His staff was the weapon with which he defended himself... In Palestine the shepherd went in front and the sheep followed. The shepherd went first to see that the path was safe, and sometimes the sheep had to be encouraged to

> follow. The shepherd's task was not only constant but dangerous, for in addition, he had to guard the flock against wild animals… and robbers ready to steal the sheep. Constant vigilance, fearless courage, patient love for his flock, were the necessary characteristics of the shepherd (Barclay, 1965:53-62).

It is easy to see why Jesus adopts the image of the shepherd for it shows the kind of relationship that Jesus has with his followers and the kind of relationship he expects his followers to have with those whom they meet each day:

> It is easy to spot the good shepherd within us at work. For example, each and every time that we act upon our instincts to lay down our own lives for another person who is lonely, depressed, or fearful, the shepherd within us is at work. Each and every time that we summon the courage to stand up in defence of the poor, the abused, the oppressed, the shepherd within us is at work. And each and every time that we walk alongside another person who is suffering from the darkness of cancer, Alzheimer's, or another terminal illness, the shepherd within us is at work (Cruz, 2007:79).

The metaphor of the 'shepherd' is one of many powerful words that convey so much in the language of the Bible. We shall be looking at the role of myth, metaphor and symbol in a later chapter of this book but suffice to say at this stage that most of us seriously underestimate the importance of the non-literal elements of the biblical narrative.

Courage in the face of the storms of life

I well remember some years ago spending two days on a diving ship in the North Sea. In order to position itself exactly over the appropriate place for the dive, this ship was fitted with very powerful engines and very substantial stabilisers. They allowed the ship not only to move forwards and backwards but also from side to side! And when the ship was in position this same technology kept it there and in all weathers. The ship seemed quite impervious to the wind and waves lashing it from the outside. Inside we were in a different world of calm and quiet efficiency. Full-course meals were served every six hours around the clock for those on duty and they ate with hearty appetites.

Contrast this with the small motor boat that we hired on holiday more recently to reach inaccessible beaches on the Greek island of Ithaca. The weather was fine and the sea was calm and we settled down for a smooth trip along the coast. As we crossed the estuary the wind increased and the waves became stronger and the boat started to rock from side to side. It was not exactly frightening but we held on tight all the same. And we put on the rather inadequate life jackets just in case. We expected the engine to stop any moment. We felt very vulnerable.

In the gospels we read the story of Jesus and his disciples crossing the Sea of Galilee in a small boat. After a long and tiring day they leave the crowds behind and cross to the other side of the lake. Jesus settles down to sleep. A storm arises and the frightened disciples shake Jesus awake. He quells the storm; the wind ceases and there is a dead calm. Jesus then challenges the disciples about their faith (Mark 4:35-41).

It is a good story. It can obviously be seen to demonstrate the power of Jesus over the storm. It can also be seen as a demonstration of the disciples' lack of faith. But if we leave it there as an incident in the life of Jesus in first-century Palestine then we have lost some of its impact. This is a story that has much to say at all times and in all places. It has much to say about our response to the storms of life that we all experience.

We only have to read our newspapers or watch television to remind ourselves that we live in a world of storms. Some storms are naturally occurring, some man-made. Few weeks pass without reports of earthquakes, hurricanes and floods somewhere in the world. Few days pass without reports of abductions, robbery and murder. Storms occur too at a personal level. Divorce, redundancy, sickness, injury – the list goes on. What do the gospels tell us about the response of God to storms?

First, he does not prevent storms occurring. Jesus chose to quell the storm on the lake after it had happened. God does not remove the storms of life from our experience. They are part of life and although he does not wish them on us he allows them to happen. God does not shield us from any possible contact with the world around us as in the big ship in the North Sea. He allows us to be exposed to these forces as on the small boat bobbing about just offshore among the Greek islands.

Secondly, God enables us to conquer the storms. Jesus calmed the storm and it was his power not the disciples' that quelled it. The storms of life can be quelled but if we rely on our own resources then we are likely to find that we are not able to cope. We need the faith that the disciples lacked. We will not solve many of these problems of life by protecting ourselves with the trappings of modern civilisation like the big ship in the North Sea. We will only do so by facing up to the challenge as in the little boat.

Our Christian faith does not protect us from the storms of life but it does enable us to face them with courage and determination.

Temperance

> Ultimately, the only power to which man should aspire is that which he exercises over himself.
> Elie Wiesel

'You came to see a race today'

Anyone who has seen the film *Chariots of Fire* will remember Eric Liddell, the Christian athlete who would not run in the 100 metres at the 1924 Paris Olympic Games because the heats for the race were on the Sunday, but who went on to win gold in the 400 metres. In due course Liddell's faith took him to China as a missionary where he was to die of a brain tumour in a Japanese internment camp in 1945.

There is a moment in the film where, in a gentle and soft Scottish accent, Liddell talks to a group of spectators after a race:

> You came to see a race today. To see someone win. It happened to be me. But I want you to do more than just watch a race. I want you to take part in it. I want to compare faith to running in a race. It's hard. It requires concentration of will, energy of soul. You experience elation when the winner breaks the tape – especially if you've got a bet on it. But how long does that last? You go home. Maybe your dinner's burnt. Maybe you haven't got a job. So who am I to say, "Believe, have faith," in the face of life's realities? I would like to give you something more permanent, but I can only point the way. I have no formula for winning the race. Everyone runs in her own way, or his own way. And where does the power come from, to see the race to its end? From within (Liddell 1981).

Chariots of Fire is a moving film because it captures something of the character of Eric Liddell, but it is only a film and like all films it is subject to the artistic license of the director. Biographies of his life take us much closer to this extraordinary man, to the personal qualities that he displayed and the self-control that he exercised as he prepared himself for these grueling races and for the greater race that was to come.

In his book, *Eric H Liddell: Athlete and Missionary,* D P Thompson tells the story of Liddell's life and writes of the reaction in Scotland to the news of Liddell's death in 1945. He had touched the lives of many people and this tribute was one of many paid to him at his memorial service:

> The details of the last few years of his life are not yet known to us, but we can be certain that under the most severe of all trials, he exhibited just those qualities which he showed in his sporting life. His life was perhaps a short one; but his work, as he clearly saw it, and, as we believe divinely inspired, carried out away from the applause of the crowd, will remain an inspiration to many. In these days of exaggerated hero worship and publicity for sporting champions, Eric Liddell's example reminds us to put things in their proper perspective. Sport to him was sport – not the be-all and end-all – and success in it did not prevent him from picking out the things spiritual from the things temporal. He was an example which must have helped others to make a similar choice (Thompson, 1971:212).

In the late 1960s I was a House Tutor in Liddell House at Eltham College where Eric Liddell had been a pupil in the 1900s and I had been a pupil in the 1950s. The school was founded in 1842 as the School for the Sons of Missionaries and educated the sons of missionaries serving with the London Missionary Society and the Baptist Missionary Society for nearly a hundred and fifty years. A girls' school for missionaries' daughters had been founded in Walthamstow a few years previously. Members of these societies realised that in those days it was not easy to find schools in which parents could be confident that their sons and daughters would be adequately cared for during their long periods abroad. There is little doubt that in these unique circumstances where most of the pupils came from missionary backgrounds, Eltham College and Walthamstow Hall were major influences on the children in their care:

> For this very reason, you must make every effort to support your faith with goodness, and goodness with knowledge, and knowledge with self-control, and self-control with endurance, and endurance with godliness, and godliness with mutual affection, and mutual affection with love (2 Peter 1:5-7).

Temperance as self-control

In recent times, temperance has been closely associated with moderation, particularly in eating and drinking. However, in earlier thought its meaning was much richer. For Plato, temperance was one of the four cardinal virtues along with prudence, justice and courage. For him, it was 'one of the four hinges on which swings the gate of life'. Aristotle defined temperance as a mean between self-indulgence and insensibility. Drives and instincts should be held in the right balance and properly controlled by reason. As self-control, temperance is a core value in the Christian tradition.

In his book, *The Four Cardinal Virtues*, Josef Pieper looks more closely at the meaning of the Greek and Latin roots of the word 'temperance' and 'unpacks' the notion of temperance as 'self-control':

> A study of the linguistic meaning of the Greek term, *sophrosyne*, and of the Latin *temperantia* reveals a much wider range of significance. The original meaning of the Greek word embraces 'directing reason' in the widest sense. And the Latin stays close to this far-reaching significance. In 1 Corinthians

> 12.24 we read, *Deus temperavit corpus*. 'God has so arranged the body, giving the greatest honour to the inferior member, that there be no dissention within the body, but the members may have the same care for one another. If one member suffers, all suffer together with it; if one member is honoured all rejoice together with it'. The primary and essential meaning of *temperare*, therefore, is this: to dispose various parts into one unified and ordered whole (Pieper, 2007: 146).

Thomas Aquinas, who had much to say about the cardinal virtues, identifies a secondary meaning of temperance as 'serenity of spirit' which Pieper explains as follows:

> It is obvious that this proposition does not imply a purely subjective state of mental calm or the tranquil satisfaction which is the by-product of an unassuming, leisurely life in a narrow circle. Nor does it mean a mere absence of irritation, or dispassionate equanimity. All this need not go deeper than the surface of the intellectual and spiritual life. What is meant is the serenity that fills the inmost recesses of the human being, and is the seal and fruit of order. The purpose and goal of *temperantia* is man's inner order, from which alone this 'serenity of spirit' can flow forth. 'Temperance' signifies the realising of this order within oneself (Pieper, 2007: 146).

In a sense, the one meaning of temperance follows from the other, for if life is unified and well-ordered then a certain serenity pervades the spirit. Temperance is therefore perhaps best understood as 'self-order' rather than 'self-control'.

Temperance as self-preservation

Pieper claims that:

> *Temperantia* is distinguished from the other cardinal virtues by

> the fact that it refers exclusively to the active man himself. Prudence looks to all existent reality; justice to the fellow man; the man of fortitude relinquishes, in self-forgetfulness, his own possessions and his life. Temperance, on the other hand, aims at each man himself. Temperance implies that man should look to himself and his condition, that his vision and his will should be focussed on himself (Pieper, 2007: 147).

For Pieper, this leads to two possibilities:

> For man there are two modes of this turning toward the self: a selfless and a selfish one. Only the former makes for self-preservation; the latter is destructive. ...Temperance is selfless self-preservation. Intemperance is self-destruction. Intemperance is self-destruction through the selfish degradation of the powers which aim at self-preservation (Pieper, 2007: 148).

Selfless self-preservation is a strange notion and seems contradictory. Yet it expresses that tension which exists in all of us between those things that enhance our humanity and those things which aggravate it. And that tension exists because all of us have the potential to act both positively and negatively and at times we seem unable to exert the necessary self-control. As Paul puts it, 'For I do not do the good I want, but the evil I do not want is what I do' (Romans 7:19).

Paul attributes that weakness to sin and others will speak of original sin. Original sin as preached by Augustine and successive generations of the Christian Church is the doctrine that all inherit the sin of Adam whose blemish is passed on to succeding generations. But the notion of original sin does not really make sense if Adam was never an historical figure and man was never made perfect in the first place but is part of a process of evolution. The 'fall downwards' should perhaps be replaced by a 'fall upwards'. We all have the propensity for both good and evil through the choices that we make but there is perhaps some hope that we may move in the direction of perfection even if we never reach there.

A passage in the Apocrypha has something very pertinent to say in this context and the phrase 'the generative forces of the world are wholesome' is a powerful idea:

> Do not invite death by the error of your life, or bring on destruction by the works of your hands; because God did not make death, and he does not delight in the death of the living. For he created all things so that they might exist; the generative forces of the world are wholesome, and there is no destructive poison in them (The Wisdom of Solomon 1: 14).

Temperance and sensuality

It was Augustine's own experience of the natural urge to sensual pleasure that caused him to be so keenly aware of its particular dangers. And we all know from our own experience how powerful these urges can be. Pieper writes:

> The natural urge toward sensual enjoyment, manifested in delight in food and drink and sexual pleasure, is the echo and mirror of man's strongest natural forces of self-preservation. The basic forms of enjoyment correspond to those most primordial forces of being, which tend to preserve the individual man, as well as the whole race, in the existence for which he was created. But for the very reason that these forces are closely allied to the deepest human urge toward being, they exceed all other powers of mankind in their destructive violence once they degenerate into selfishness (Pieper, 2007: 150).

It is perhaps not surprising that so much attention has been paid to sexual pleasure because it is so powerful and potentially destructive. There is no doubt that sexuality has become increasingly prominent in the contemporary world. But there is perhaps another reason for this prominence which Pieper expresses as follows:

> ...a smouldering subterranean Manichaeism casts suspicion on everything pertaining to physical reproduction as being somehow impure, defiling, and beneath the true dignity of man (Pieper, 2007: 153).

Manichaeism originated in Persia in the third century and survived well into the Middle Ages. It reached its zenith in the fourth century and Augustine was one of its followers in his early years. Although he adandoned its teachings, he never quite shook off its influence and this is seen in his doctrine of original sin. Manichaeism is closely related to Gnosticism and is strongly dualist in nature. According to its teachings, there were originally two separate realms: a realm of spirit, goodness and light, and another realm of matter, evil and darkness. The human being is part of this unhappy mixture, the soul being imprisoned in the body. Salvation consists of liberating the spiritual from the material.

This notion that matter is somehow evil is refuted by Christians for whom matter is intrinsically good. At the end of the first account of creation in Genesis the author writes, 'And God saw everything that he had made, and indeed, it was very good' (Genesis 1:31). However, the notion that the material world is somehow inferior to the spiritual world persists and is one of the causes of the problems of sexuality and gender in contemporary debate. Some Christians seem unable to fully embrace humanity despite the incarnation. One of my former teachers called this 'platonic drag' for it is in Plato's teachings that these ideas originate.

For Aquinas it is self-evident 'that sexual powers are not a necessary evil but really a good' and he 'says incisively that there is something divine in human seed'. Pieper writes:

> It is equally self-evident to Thomas's thinking that, like eating and drinking the fulfillment of the natural sexual urge and its accompanying pleasure are good and not in the least sinful assuming, of course, that order and moderation are preserved (Pieper, 2007: 154).

It is worth reminding ourselves of some of the other ways in which temperance should and should not express itself.

Temperance as humility

Humility is often misunderstood. We think that humility has something to do with holding back, 'of constant self-accusation, of disparagement of one's being and doing, of cringing inferiority feelings'. The reverse is probably nearer the truth. One of the goods in which man naturally seeks fulfillment of his being is excellence:

> The vitue of temperance, insofar as it relates this natural urge to the order of reason, is called humility. The ground of humility is man's estimation of himself according to truth. And that is almost all there is to it (Pieper, 2007:189).

The pursuit of excellence is part of the natural urge to fulfil our potential in whatever way we can. High-mindedness or the striving of the mind for great things is a worthy aspect of a temperate life:

> Nothing lights the way to a proper understanding of humility than this: humility and high-mindedness not only are not mutually exclusive, but actually are neighbours and akin; and

> both are equally opposed to either pride or pusillanimity (Pieper, 2007:189).

It is worth expanding on what Aquinas and Pieper mean by high-mindedness:

> Fearless frankness is the hallmark of high-mindedness; nothing is further from it than to suppress truth from fear. Flattery and disimulation are equally removed from the high-minded. The high-minded man does not complain; for his heart is impervious to external evil. High-mindedness implies an unshakable firmness of hope, an actually challenging assurance, and the perfect peace of a fearless heart. The high-minded man bows neither to confusion of the soul, nor to any man, nor to fate – but to God alone. A humility too weak and too narrow to be able to bear the tension of cohabitation with high-mindedness is not true humility (Pieper, 2007:190).

The term 'humility' comes from the Latin word *humilitas*, a noun related to the adjective *humilis*, which may be translated as 'humble', but also as 'grounded', 'from the earth', or 'low', since it derives in turns from *humus* (earth). The word 'grounded' seems to embrace many aspects of temperance and not just humility. An electrical power source is often connected to the 'ground' to dissipate a power surge. Perhaps that says it all!

"I'm a very umble person"

At the start of Charles Dickens' novel, David Copperfield, Uriah Heep is a young clerk in the law firm of Mr Wickfield. Dickens relates Copperfield's first words to Heep. "I suppose you are a great lawyer?" he says. "Me, Master Copperfield?" says Uriah "Oh no! I'm a very umble person." "I am well aware that I am the umblest person going. My mother is likewise a very umble person. We live in an umble abode, Master Copperfied, but have much to be thankful for. My father's former calling was also very umble…", and so it goes on. Despite his protestations of humility, we soon discover that Uriah Heep is a scheming and selfish individual. As the story unfolds, he slowly undermines his employer, is eventually arrested for fraud and is thrown into prison. He has the pretence of humility but nothing more (Pierce 1878: 319).

In the fourteenth chapter of the gospel according to Luke we hear the parable about the seats of honour at a wedding banquet. You will recall the words of Jesus:

> When you are invited by someone to a wedding banquet, do not sit down at the place of honour, in case someone more distinguished than you has been invited by your host; and the host who invited both of you may come and say to you, 'Give this person your place,' and then in disgrace you would take the lowest place. But when you are invited, go and sit down at the lowest place, so that when your host comes, he may say to you, 'Friend, move up higher'; then you will be honoured in the presence of all who sit at the table with you. For all who exalt themselves will be humbled, and those who humble themselves will be exalted (Luke 14:8-14).

But there is something slightly puzzling about this parable. On the face of it Jesus is showing us how to get ahead in life by pretending to be humble just like Uriah Heep in Dickens' novel. Go to the lowliest place so that you can achieve the highest place later. But that is not what this parable is all about. We know that simply taking a lower seat so that we will not be shamed if someone better comes along is not an act of real humility at all. We know better than to equate true humility with the act of humbling ourselves outwardly, especially if we do so with the express hope of being promoted later. No, the pretence of humility is not humility at all. So what then is this parable really about? Well, it is not so much a parable about what humility is, as it is a parable about how we can make room in ourselves for humility to come about. Jesus is showing us how we can open ourselves in order that we might be granted humility. It is a very subtle distinction. Humility is one of those strange virtues that is very hard to actively put into practice. You can't really work at being humble, strive for humility, or actively cultivate a humble spirit. It's not something you can control. It is not something we can determine to become. It is something that comes upon us if we make a space within ourselves for humility to take root.

The choices that we face as we approach life itself are actually very much like the choices a wedding guest faces as he or she approaches a banqueting table. We can approach each event or situation looking for what we can get out of it for ourselves, or we can look for what we can give to it for the sake of others. If we go in selfishly, we will always strive for the best place, the highest place, the place that makes us feel important, worthy, and respected, or the place from which we can see that we will reap the most advantage, which may mean taking the lower seat with the hope of advancement.

If, on the other hand, we approach life selflessly and in an attitude of unconditional love then we have made space in our lives for true humility. And advancement may or may not come as a result. Humility is indeed about knowing our place. And exaltation is thrown in, free of charge. Exaltation comes by invitation only, and the humble are those who never forget it.

Simone Weil, the great French philosopher and mystic, describes humility as 'the freely accepted movement towards the bottom'. For her, the heart of Christianity is the consent to be last, the willing acceptance of 'the lowest place'. It is a huge challenge.

The Temperance Movement

At some times and in some places temperance has had a very

specific meaning related to the use of alcohol. For some people, the obligation of temperance in the use of alcohol means moderation, for others total abstinence.

In his article, *Temperance in the Use of Alcohol* in *A new Dictionary of Christian Ethics*, the prominent Methodist, Kenneth Greet, writes that 'the history of the temperance movement and its many organisations during the nineteenth century is full of interest':

> Among other things, the temperance movement helped to channel religious energies into party politics, particularly as several Protestant groups such as the Methodists and the Baptists opposed alcohol… (but) the opposition to alcohol was not only religious and moral; for example, in the USA it included such factors as suspicion of industrial cities and immigrants. The main debate in the temperance movement was between those who believed that the only way to attack the drink evil was through education or 'moral suasion' and those who espoused the cause of legal prohibition (Greet, 1967:619).

Both aspects of the temperance movement have registered success and failure. Prohibition was attempted in the USA but ultimately without success although it did alert the public to the dangers of alcohol and the need for some legislative control. In the UK there are now severe penalties for those who drive under the influence of drink, but:

> …temperance in the use of alcohol has declined as a live political issue. Attempts to isolate the drink problem from other social questions have increasingly been seen as unprofitable. Many temperance organisations have now extended their brief, especially to take account of the menace of other types of drug addiction (Greet, 1967:619).

The temperance movement and other 'ginger groups' have had a significant impact because they have highlighted particular aspects of our national life and led directly or indirectly to change. It is good that people are prepared to fight for these causes even if they sometimes get it wrong. Passion is a worthy Christian virtue.

Faith

> To have faith is to meet the world with the conviction that in spite of all its ambiguities and its downright evils, there can be discerned in it the reality of love and a ground of hope.
> John Macquarrie, *Paths in Spirituality.*

The 'theological' virtues

As we have already seen, Thomas Aquinas adds to the four cardinal virtues – wisdom, justice, courage and temperance – the three theological virtues – faith, hope and love. For Aquinas, the cardinal virtues can be acquired by men and women themselves; the theological virtues are gifts from God.

Recovering the meaning of faith

We have already met Marcus Borg's book, *Speaking Christian,* in which he shows how many of the 'big' words in Christianity have 'acquired meanings that are serious distortions of their biblical and traditional meanings'. The word 'faith' is no exception.

By examining a range of dictionary definitions, Borg shows that there are basically two such understandings in common usage. 'Faith' is either identified with 'belief' or it is used as a synonym for 'religion'. But neither of these meanings is what 'faith' meant in pre-modern Christianity:

> The ancient meanings are expressed by the Latin words *fidelitas* and *fiducia* and their Greek equivalents. *Fidelitas* means 'fidelity' or 'faithfulness' …In our relationship with God, faith as fidelity does not mean simply not going after other gods, but commitment, loyalty, allegiance, and attentiveness to our relationship with God, as known especially in Jesus. *Fiducia* means 'trust'. Faith in God is more than commitment. It is also about deep trust in God. Here, the opposite of faith is not infidelity but 'mistrust', that is,

'anxiety' (Borg, 2011:121).

Faith as fidelity and trust is very different from faith as believing a set of statements to be true, which is what belief usually means in common usage. The fact that the original meaning of belief was not the assent to a set of propositions but the living of a way of life is further evidence of the confusion that lies at the heart of our theological language:

> Faith as faithfulness to God and trust in God is the product of a deeper and deeper centering in God. Faithfulness leads us to pay attention to our relationship with God and through such attention we become even more deeply centered in God. Trust is the fruit of that deeper centering. It grows as we center more and more in God (Borg, 2011:122).

Borg's metaphor of faith as 'deeply centring in God' is similar to Paul Tillich's metaphor of God as the 'ground of our being' and of faith as the state of being 'ultimately concerned'.

Borg argues that faith understood as 'believing in a set of proposition' can lead to anxiety if we understand our convictions in the context of what he calls 'heaven and hell' Christianity:

> If we believe there is a final judgement in which we are sent to either heaven or hell, how could we not be anxious? Have I believed strongly enough or behaved rightly enough. But faith as faithfulness and trust eliminates that anxiety and frees us for transformation in this life (Borg, 2011: 122).

And it is transformation in this life which should be the focus and goal of our humanity.

Faith as 'ultimate concern'

Writing in the 1950s, Paul Tillich also had problems with the definition of faith. In the introduction to his book, *Dynamics of Faith,* he writes:

> There is hardly a word in the religious language, both theological and popular, which is subject to more misunderstandings, distortions and questionable definitions than the word 'faith'. It belongs to those terms which need healing before they can be used for the healing of men. Today the term 'faith' is more productive of disease than of health. It confuses, misleads, creates alternatively scepticism and fanaticism, intellectual resistance and emotional surrender, rejection of genuine religion and subjection to substitutes (Tillich, 2001:xxi).

Tillich's solution to the problem is to reinterpret the word 'faith' and 'to remove the confusing and distorting connotations'. For Tillich, 'faith' is the state of being 'ultimately concerned':

> Man, like every living being, is concerned about many things, above all about those which condition his very existence, such as food and shelter. But man, in contrast to other living beings, has spiritual concerns – cognitive, aesthetic, social, and political. Some of them are urgent, often extremely urgent, and each of them as well as the vital concerns can claim ultimacy for a human life or the life of a social group. If it claims ultimacy it demands the total surrender of him who accepts this claim (Tillich, 2001:1).

Tillich illustrates this unconditional demand by reference to examples of extreme nationalism in recent history. If the nation is our ultimate concern then the nation demands total allegiance and the nation becomes a god. Hitler's Third Reich is a tragic example. Tillich illustrates the promise of total fulfilment by reference to the religion of the Old Testament where the ultimate concern of pious Jews is not the nation but God. 'You shall love the Lord your God with all your heart, and with all your soul, and with all your might' (Deuteronomy 6:5).

In our contemporary world, it is the concern for success, social standing and economic power which for many is their ultimate concern. This concern demands unconditional surrender to the material world, to the preoccupation with self and to market forces. It promises fulfilment of one's being in every aspect of one's personality. But the price of this fulfilment is the breakdown of human relations and personal integrity. When fulfilled, the promise of this faith proves to be empty.

Faith as ultimate concern is an act of the total personality and includes all its elements – cognitive, emotional and volitional. It is not just one aspect of that personality but transcends each individual aspect as well as their totality. Faith goes to the very depths of our being. It is in this sense that our ultimate concern can be the ground of that being, God.

But faith is not certainty. The relationship between the finite being that is man and the infinite Being that is God means that there must always be uncertainty. Faith is a risky undertaking and requires courage:

> If faith is understood as belief that something is true, doubt is incompatible with the act of faith. If faith is understood as being ultimately concerned, doubt is a necessary element in it. It is a consequence of the risk of faith (Tillich, 2001: 21).

This is why it is the questions than we ask that are more important than any answers that we may give. There is a certain finality in answers which precludes any doubt; there is no such finality in questions. Jesus invaraiably answered questions with another question.

The distortions which have arisen in the understanding of faith have arisen ironically from our definition of faith as being ultimately concerned and as a centred act of the whole personality. If one of the functions of the personality is completely identified with faith then that faith is distorted:

> The most ordinary misinterpretation of faith is to consider it an act of knowledge that has a low degree of evidence but is supported by religious authority. Something more or less probable or improbable is affirmed in spite of the insufficiency of its theoretrical substantiation. If this is meant then one is speaking of *belief* rather than faith (Tillich, 2001: 36).

Faith is not belief. Faith should not be used in connection with knowledge, whether it is knowledge on the basis of evidence, or whether it is on the basis of trust in authorities.

In Tillich's definition, faith is not the same thing as trust but trust is clearly an important element in faith. Trust is also more accessible to us because it is in common usage in a way that faith is not. For most of us, faith is essentially a religious term and is used sparingly. Trust is in more frequent use although it deserves more attention. It is therefore a good place to start, particularly as trust in God is, in Tillich's terms, very close to what he understands by faith. For Borg, trust is one aspect of faith.

Is trust in God just an acceptable risk?

Ever since the site of the wreck of the Titanic was discovered some years ago, there has been renewed interest in the circumstances of the sinking of this luxury liner in the North Atlantic in 1912. There has been renewed interest in the materials of which the ship was built and there has been speculation that the steel hull was too brittle. There has been discussion about the route taken by the ship and about why it sailed so far north. Every aspect of the ship and every aspect of that voyage has been examined in detail. Inevitably, a multi-million pound movie has now been made and the tragedy of the sinking of the Titanic has been brought into even sharper focus by what has been described as a very realistic and moving film.

Those who sailed in that ship were confident that they were experiencing a magnificent example of what was then modern technology. It was built to the highest standards and was embarking on its maiden voyage completely risk-free. They probably gave little thought to their safety, but if they did they were soon completely reassured. 'This ship is unsinkable' they were told. If they had been given some idea of the possible risks, had they been known at the time, they would probably still have been willing to go. They would have decided that this was a risk worth taking. As we might say, 'This was an acceptable risk?'

Martin Luther, that great figure of the German Reformation, described the person without faith as like someone who has to cross the sea, but is so frightened of the journey that he will not trust the ship. According to Luther, faith in this context is not simply about believing that the ship exists; it is about stepping into it and entrusting ourselves to it. The 'ship of faith' is a familiar image, and in many ways our spiritual journey is like a voyage at sea.

We shall never know if the Titanic deserved the trust that those passengers placed in it and was just the victim of devastating circumstances. We shall never know if it sank because of some basic defect in the ship itself or some negligence in those who were responsible for the journey. What we do know is that the passengers placed in that ship a kind of trust and for whatever reason that trust was misplaced.

In the world of the twenty-first century, we have sometimes become obsessed with risk, and constantly want reassurance that an activity is risk-free. In matters of faith, those who want such reassurance or want the reassurance of a 'risk analysis' are going to be disappointed. They must gain reassurance in some other way. The trust we place in God is born of a deep conviction of the integrity and reliability of God that is much more than the assessment of an 'acceptable risk'.

And what about trusting each other?

In his New Year message, broadcast on 1st January, 2006, the Archbishop of Canterbury, Rowan Williams, called for a renewed sense of trust in a world fearful of terrorism. He was in New York on 11th September, 2001 and shared the experience of all those who witnessed the attacks on the twin towers.

Trust is at the heart of our relationships with each other, and it is difficult to see how we could live a normal life without some measure of basic trust. As we go about our business each day we rely on those around us to behave in predictable ways. We trust that car drivers will obey the rules of the road as we engage with them at junctions and crossings. We trust that teachers will act responsibly in educating and caring for our children. We trust that doctors will diagnose and treat us to the best of their ability. Sometimes, of course, our trust is misplaced, but that is the exception rather than the rule.

At one remove from the routine of our daily lives, we place our trust in a whole host of agencies and individuals who more indirectly affect our lives. We trust those who lead us and act on our behalf. We trust the government and its agencies. We trust the political and judicial systems. We trust local government and its institutions. Or do we? Increasingly, it seems that we don't. In his message, Rowan Williams, called for a renewed sense of trust in a world fearful of terrorism.

Williams speaks of the increasing lack of trust in leaders, including clergy. 'Trust is so important – yet more and more the talk is of a lack of trust: in politics, in business, in public life – from policemen to vicars.'

On a global scale, he said that the way the world's economy was run had also contributed to a feeling 'that the powerful cannot be trusted in a world where too many feel they have nothing to lose'. And with the continuing threat of terrorism, it was hardly surprising that people found trust hard. 'We don't know where the enemy is – and it is an enemy who is skilful and merciless and willing to risk everything.'

He added that although it was easy to grumble at the security constraints and checks 'part of us knows just why we move in this atmosphere of suspicion... Once you see the dreadful results of terrorism at close quarters, you can begin to appreciate why everyone comes to be viewed with a degree of mistrust.'

However, he went on to challenge people about what message they were promoting. 'Am I making the world a place where trust makes sense?' And deeper still, 'Am I confident that even in my failings and my betrayals I am loved and trusted?' He described a person of faith as someone who is not necessarily full of a particular kind of religious certainty 'but a person who has become trustworthy because they know that God is to be trusted and that God had trusted, loved and forgiven them' (Williams, 2006).

The breakdown of trust

Some years ago I spent two weeks doing Jury Service at St Albans Crown Court. Working on a jury can be a stressful and draining experience particularly if the case involves strained or broken relationships. On a jury you see life in the raw. You see what happens when trust between people breaks down completely. And you begin to realise in a new way how important that trust between us actually is. The trust between business partners engaged in a common enterprise, the trust between friends sharing the same interests, the trust between members of a family, the trust between husband and wife, the trust between parent and child.

All our relationships of whatever kind depend on trust. The formal contract between employer and employees is only the framework. If there is not at least some measure of trust then the welfare of everyone involved is at risk. The trust between friends breaks down if one or other defaults on an agreement. The marriage between two people should be the public expression of something deep within their relationship. If that relationship is not bound by trust then it is unlikely to survive. Trust is the 'cement' that holds human relationships together.

In recent years there have been spectacular breakdowns of trust in our national and international life. The banking crisis which erupted in 2008 and which nearly paralysed the world economy was in large part the result of a failure of moral integrity amongst those who had traditionally enjoyed the trust of their clients and the wider public. The days of the slogan 'my word is my bond' had long past but nothing had been put in its place. Regulation on its own could not have prevented this disaster; only a culture change would have been adequate to the task. The public has now lost trust in banking professionals and it will be some time before that trust is restored.

Trust in politicians has also been severely tested by the revelations of irresponsible, if not criminal, behaviour in the handling of expense allowances by some members of parliament. It was particularly depressing to listen to some politicians lamely attempting to justify their actions and the unwillingness of others to admit that they had been wrong. The claim that 'an error of judgement' had been made was too often the response. This attempt to blur the distinction between 'right' and 'wrong' is very worrying.

Trust in members of the police force has also been weakened by the behaviour of some individual police officers. It may be that only a small minority of police officers are involved but the whole movement has been tainted by suspicions, allegations and prosecutions. Trust is a fragile thing which can so easily be destroyed. The tragedy is that too many of those involved seem oblivious to the implications of what has happened.

Perhaps the most serious breakdown of trust in recent years

has arisen as a result of child sex abuse by priests, particularly within the Roman Catholic Church. The fact that this abuse was often covered up by the hierarchy of the church makes it particularly shocking. Furthermore, such coverups were often justified by placing the interests of the church as an institution above the interests of the children as people and this hugely magnifies the offence. A recent report from the United Nations includes this paragraph:

> The committee is particularly concerned that in dealing with allegations of child sexual abuse, the Holy See has consistently placed preservation of the reputation of the Church and protection of the perpetrators above children's best interests, as observed by several national commissions of inquiry (Mickens, 2014).

In all these crimes against children in our churches the humanity of those who suffer is totally ignored. Children are treated as a means to an end and not as an end in themselves. And it is not just in cases of child abuse that this occurs and it is not just in the interests of the church as an institution that this is perpetrated. It happens when the interests of a particular set of theological propositions are at stake. That includes the pursuit of youngsters in the hope that some will be 'converted'. It happens whenever people are treated as a means to an end in any aspect of church life. The claim of this book is that human beings must always be treated as an end in themselves. Trust is not possible in any other circumstances.

Faith and Reason

Finally, something needs to be said in connection with current debates about 'faith' and 'reason'. These two paths to religious truth have been in tension for more than two thousand years but in recent decades the debate has become more virulent, not least because of the writings of those who are sometimes described as the 'militant atheists' of our time, two of whom are Richard Dawkins and Christopher Hitchins. Their most popular books are, respectively, *The God Delusion* (Dawkins, 2006) and *God is Not Great* (Hitchins, 2007).

Historically, there have been two categories of views regarding the relationship between faith and reason. Rationalism holds that truth should be determined by reason rather than faith. Fideism holds that faith is necessary, and that beliefs may be held without evidence or reason, or even in conflict with evidence and reason. Richard Dawkins and Christopher Hitchins are rationalists, that is, they reject faith altogether. In his witty but challenging study, *Reason, Faith, and Revolution,* Terry Eagleton writes that many people:

> …are aware that without reason we are sunk, but that reason, even so, is not in the end what is most fundamental about us. Richard Dawkins claims with grandiloquent folly that religious faith dispenses with reason altogether, which wasn't true even of the dimwitted authoritarian clerics who knocked me around at grammar school. Without reason, we perish; but reason does not go all the way down. It is not wall to wall (Eagleton, 2009:109).

Those last phrases say it all. We know intuitively that reason does not cover all the ground. The truths conveyed by many of the themes in this book cannot be revealed without something that goes well beyond reason. Rationalists and fideists separate faith and reason. The Christian Churches have generally taught that faith and reason can and must work together. This was certainly the theme of the encyclical letter, *Fides et Ratio* (Faith and Reason), issued by Pope John Paul II in 1998, and of Pope Benedict XVI's address to the UK Parliament in 2010:

> The Church remains profoundly convinced that faith and reason 'mutually support each other'; each influences the other, as they offer to each other a purifying critique and a stimulus to pursue the search for deeper understanding (John Paul II, 1998).

In his book, Eagleton ruthlessly pursues Richard Dawkins and Christopher Hitchens (who together he calls Ditchkins) in the way in which they misrepresent both faith and reason:

> There is probably no greater evidence of Ditchkins's theological illiteracy than the fact that he appears to subscribe to what one might call the Yeti view of belief in God. I mean by this the view that God is the sort of entity for which… the evidence we have so far is radically ambiguous, not to say downright dubious; and because we cannot thus demonstrate God's existence in the reasonably straightforward way we can demonstrate the existence of necrophilia or Michael Jackson, we have to put up instead with something less than certainty, known as faith (Eagleton, 2009:110).

He goes on to point out that God is not an entity in the world and that faith in God is not about the assent to a statement that God exists but the living of a life in relationship with him. In other words faith is performative rather than propositional. But there is a kind of certainty in faith:

> For Christianity, faith is traditionally regarded as a question of certainty, not of plausibility, intelligent guesswork, or speculation… Faith, as the author of the *Epistle to the Hebrews* observes, is 'the assurance of things hoped for, the conviction of things unseen'. The virtue of hope for Christianity equally involves a kind of certainty; it is a matter of an assured trust, not of keeping one's fingers crossed. Whatever else may

> divide science and religion, it is not for the theologian the issue of certainty (Eagleton, 2009:112).

But, the relationship between faith and reason is misrepresented as much by fideists as by rationalists. Christian fundamentalists are generally fideists:

> The fundamentalist is like the kind of neurotic who can't trust that he is loved, but in an infantile spirit demands some irrefragable proof of the fact. He is not really a *believer* at all. Fundamentalists are faithless… In a world of extreme uncertainty, only copper-bottomed, incontrovertible truths promulgated by God himself can be trusted (Eagleton, 2009:114).

Hence fundamentalists must claim that the Bible is the inerrant word of God since otherwise they would be left floundering as they cannot cope with uncertainty. The debate continues.

Hope

> The ability to hope is the greatest gift that God could make to man.
> Carlo Carretto, *Summoned by Love*

The Triumph of Hope

Nelson Mandela was educated in a Methodist missionary school and it is clear that those early years within a Christian community made a profound impression on him. Although in his long life he may not have said much about his religious faith as such, he did say a great deal about those human aspirations which were clearly an essential part of that faith. And one of those aspirations was 'hope'.

Mandela's autobiography *Long Walk to Freedom* (Mandela, 2009) has been published in two parts, the second of which is called *Triumph of Hope*. It is worth noting that Desmond Tutu also wrote a book called *Hope and Suffering* (Tutu, 1983) about the same struggle for equality in South Africa. Barak Obama's book *The Audacity of Hope* (Obama, 2007) on the struggle in America is in a similar vein. Hope has therefore been a major theme in the campaign for human rights.

Parts of Mandela's book were written secretly during his long years as a prisoner on Robben Island. It was written on scraps of paper that were smuggled out to his friends on the mainland and later compiled into the book. I have been to Robben Island and have stood in Mandela's cell. Although nothing can compare to the experience of these men, it is possible to understand something of the context within which this book was written by visiting that desolate spot. And it is a desolate spot. It is a barren island of scrub and stone. It is the kind of place that could so easily lead a prisoner to despair. And that was the intention. Everything was done to break Mandela's spirit. Yet he was somehow able to rise above it all. He never gave up.

Apart from families who could visit only once every six months, the only other people Mandela could meet were priests. In a letter to the Archbishop of Cape Town, Mandela wrote of his appreciation of the ministry of one particular priest, Fr Hughes, 'What he said not only enriched the spirit, even more, it left me full of hope'. You can see that hope in his face in the few photographs that we have from that time. You can certainly see it in his writing in which that hope shines through. As someone has said of his book, 'It burns with the luminosity of faith in the invincible nature of human hope'. As Mandela said himself in the book:

> I am fundamentally an optimist. Whether that comes from nature or nurture, I cannot say. Part of being optimistic is keeping one's head pointed toward the sun, one's feet moving forward. There were many dark moments when my faith in humanity was sorely tested, but I would not and could not give myself up to despair. That way lays defeat and death (Mandela, 2009).

In coming into the world Jesus brought hope to the people of Palestine at a time when they suffered under the occupation of a foreign power. And down through the ages he has come again and again to people in their distress. And he comes again in our own time to those who need him most. And he will continue to come. The traditional way in which we express this hope is through our expectation of the second coming of Jesus at some point in the future. But if we become too preoccupied with a future event then we can become blind to the present realities. Jesus is not constrained to time and place. He comes in the now of the past, he comes in the now of the present and he comes in the now of the future. It is not so much that Jesus did come or will come, but that he does come. And he comes primarily through us.

And it is in that sense that Jesus brings hope to us. He comes to us in the glimpses that we see of him in the people we meet each day. He comes in the inspirational people who cross our path. He comes to us in the great characters of our time. He comes in people like Nelson Mandela.

Hope springs eternal

The journalist, Melanie Reid, broke her neck and back falling from a horse in April 2010. She spent 12 months in rehab and is now tetraplegic. She works for *The Times* and traces her progress each week in *Spinal Column,* a regular column in the Saturday magazine. In a recent extract from *Spinal Column* she tells the following story:

> Annette Greenhalgh is one of my inspirations. In middle age, she fell off her horse drag-hunting and injured the spinal cord in her neck grievously, leaving her a tetraplegic. Some months later she managed the symbolic stagger out of hospital using a Zimmer, but her hands were largely useless and her body a frozen, aching purgatory. She couldn't control her functions or feel her limbs or where she was putting her feet. She could so easily have given up and chosen life in a wheelchair.
>
> Instead, she threw the works at it. After all, she had a friend who, after five years in a wheelchair, had begun to walk again. She possessed the discipline, spirit and resources to put together a daily programme of physiotherapy, interspersed with an afternoon nap. She did hydrotherapy and gym, different physiotherapy and osteopathy for different days. She was stretched, kneaded and exhorted, driven constantly to pain and nursed back by Nurofen and wine. She relearnt how to move, enduring the periods when no neurological progress happened, inching forward over the months.
>
> After a while her bladder and bowels began to work again. After three years she was on crutches; after four on sticks. By five years, amazingly, she recovered proprioception in her

> limbs – she now gets feedback from her legs and feet to tell her where they are. The latter have shrunk back to normal size. Now, approaching six years post-accident, she can push a supermarket trolley around the store without stopping for a rest, and walk unaided at home.
>
> ...Recently – wonderfully – she wrote to tell me that her clawed hands have started to unfurl as a result of much work on her arms. That's what makes a day euphoric for me. Every bulletin from her speaks of new hope, but warns of patience. "We have to redevelop and retrain the system and it takes a long, long time," she advises. "Take it steady. Your body needs to wake up slowly and with huge consideration. Remember, this is a delicate and long-term project. Improving day on day is impossible. Don't go there" (Reid, 2013).

The Christian hope

Hope has been an essential ingredient in the Christian tradition and its orthodox understanding is well expressed in the Preface to Brian Hebblethwaite's book, *The Christian Hope:*

> Christian faith in the love of God carries with it, necessarily, hope for the future of humankind, both as individuals and as the human community, and hope for the future of creation as a whole. Christianity is one of the chief exponents in the history of religions of the view that human beings and the universe, as God's good creation, have an eternal destiny, that history has a transcendent goal in the divine intention, and that in the end God's creative purpose will be finally realised (Hebblethwaite, 2010:vii).

In his book, Hebblethwaite traces the development of the theology of hope from the world of biblical times to the modern period, emphasising the tension that exists throughout between hope for the present and hope for the future. He distinguishes between hope in a Kingdom of God to be realised here on earth, and the ultimate Christian hope of a Kingdom of God that can only be realised in eternity.

In the nineteenth century there was a tendency for Liberal Protestantism to play down the ultimate Christian hope and to equate the Kingdom of God with the perfect community towards which humanity, under God, was progressing. In the twentieth century this tendency was reinforced by the movement we call Liberation Theology which focused on the need for social justice and human dignity particularly under the oppressive regimes of South America. Although some liberation theologians had distinct Marxist tendencies, the movement itself was fundamentally Christian, although certainly radical.

In his book, *A Theology of Human Hope,* Rubem Alves, himself a liberation theologian, attempts to break free from the stale tension between the present and future hope of humankind and argues for the complete 'death and rebirth of the inherited paradigm of Western theological thinking'(Alves, 1971: x). Hebblethwaite comments:

> Alves writes of the history and politics of freedom and of the way in which both Christians and humanists should work together to create a new future. Hope, says Alves, has to be the language of the possible. It inspires work for the realisation of real historical possibilities. But, whereas humanism has nothing but human resources to pit against the structures of domination that again and again frustrate people's hopes. Christianity knows that human liberation is the business of a power transcending history and creating possibilities beyond purely human calculation (Hebblethwaite, 2010: 186).

It would have been more accurate to describe the contrast as between 'secular humanism' and 'Christian humanism' in this piece, as the common denominator is the 'human' perspective, and it is the human perspective that is the focus of this book.

The right to hope

One of those mentioned in Hebblethwaite's book and who has contributed significantly to the debate is the American theologian Paul Tillich. In a sermon preached in 1965, entitled *The Right to Hope,* Paul Tillich asks a question:

> Nobody can live without hope, even if it were only for the smallest things which give some satisfaction even under the worst of conditions, even in poverty, sickness, and social failure. Without hope, the tension of our life toward the future would vanish, and with it, life itself. We would end in despair, a word that originally meant 'without hope', or in deadly indifference. Therefore I want to ask this question today: Do we have a right to hope? (Tillich,1965).

Tillich points out that hope is a major theme in the Bible. Men and women of the Old Testament struggled to maintain hope in the face of one catastrophe after another. Hope often turned to despair. There is the despair of Job as 'the waters wear away the stones; the torrents wash away the soil of the earth; so you (God) destroy the hope of mortals' (Job 14: 19). In the New Testament there is the desolation of the two friends on the road to Emmaus after the crucifixion of Jesus. 'But we had hoped that he was the one to redeem Israel' (Luke 24:21). And there is the anguish of the early church as it fights with hopelessness as the expectation of the early return of Christ is not fulfilled.

Gradually the hope for an imminent return of Christ was replaced by the hope for eternal life in Christ. But even this hope became complicated by debates about the meaning of 'eternity'. At the same time, the world view of many Christians was changing:

> ...the hope for the individual for participation in eternal life was more and more undercut by the present understanding of our world through science and philosophy. Imaginations of a heavenly place above and a hell below became symbols for the state of our inner life. The expectation of a simple continuation of life after death vanished in view of a sober acceptance of the seriousness of death and a deeper understanding by theology of the difference between eternity and endless time (Tillich,1965).

But there is always a reason for hope in the routine of daily life, namely, the seed-like presence of that which is hoped for. We see it literally in the seeds sown in gardens as they give hope for the flowering and the fruit. We see it in the child as we hope for its growth and maturity into adulthood. We see it in the hope for the nurturing of love in relationships. But it is hope, not certainty.

Hope implies waiting and waiting implies patience. 'Be still before the Lord, and wait patiently for him.' (Psalm 37:7). But this must be an active not a passive waiting particularly as it refers to the hope we have within ourselves of our own development.

> He who waits in laziness, passively, prevents the coming of what he is waiting for. He who waits in quiet tension, open for what he may encounter, works for its coming... Such openness is highest activity; it is the driving force which leads us toward the growth of something new in us. And the struggle between hope and despair in our waiting is a symptom that the new has already taken hold of us (Tillich, 1965).

This waiting in hope is not easy for individuals or for mankind as a whole. The hope of progress towards a better world was shattered by events of the twentieth century but hope for transformation of societies has not died:

> There will be victories as well as defeats in these struggles. There will be progress and regressions. But every victory, every particular progress from injustice to more justice, from suffering to more happiness, from hostility to more peace, from separation to more unity anywhere in mankind, is a manifestation of the eternal in time and space. It is, in the language of the men of the Old and New Testaments, the coming of the Kingdom of God. For the Kingdom of God does not come in one dramatic event sometime in the future, It is coming here and now in every act of love, in every manifestation of truth, in every moment of joy, in every experience of the holy (Tillich,1965).

For Tillich, the answer to the question 'Do we have a right to hope?' is emphatically, Yes! We have both a right and a duty to hope despite the uncertainty of what the mystery of 'eternity' might mean.

The Eternal Now is the title of a book of Tillich's sermons, one of which he explores the notion of 'life after death':

> Many people hope for a continuation of this life after death. They expect an endless future in which they may achieve or possess what has been denied them in this life. This is a prevalent attitude about the future, and also a very simple one. It denies that there *is* an end. It refuses to accept that we are creatures, that we come from the eternal ground of time and return to the eternal ground of time and have received a limited span of time as *our* time. It replaces eternity by endless future. But endless future is without a final aim; it repeats itself and could well be described as an image of hell. This is not the Christian way of dealing with the end. The Christian

> message says that the eternal stands above past and future. "I am the Alpha and the Omega, the beginning and the end" (Revelation 1:8). The Christian message acknowledges that time runs towards an end, and that we move towards the end of that time which is our time. Many people – but not the Bible – speak loosely of the "hereafter" or of the "life after death". Even in our liturgies eternity is translated by "world without end." But the world, by its very nature, is that which comes to an end. If we want to speak in truth without foolish, wishful thinking, we should speak about the eternal that is neither timelessness nor endless time. The mystery of the future is answered in the eternal of which we may speak in images taken from time. But if we forget that the images are images, we fall into absurdities and self-deceptions. There is no time *after* time, but there is eternity *above* time (Tillich, 1963:105-6).

The traditional Christian hope for the future is not only associated with the hope of life after death but also with hope for the return of Jesus who will inaugurate a new order. Richard Pomeroy writes in his book, *Paul Tillich: A Theology for the 21st Century:*

> The apostles originally expected that the second coming of Christ would occur immediately following his earthly ministry, and certainly during their lifetimes. With the second coming, a new eon would begin in which evil would be abolished. This expectation was not fulfilled and the nature of the world and its estrangement from God continued. This became a major issue in the early days of the church and among Jesus' apostles The apostles, through the resurrection (Easter), and a life transforming experience when the Divine Spirit descended upon them (Pentecost), gained a new understanding of what the 'new eon' meant. Rather than an

> immediate second coming of Christ and the abolishment of sin, the 'new eon' would appear in the lives of individual persons as a New Being, transforming one's life in a manner similar to the apostle's transformation at Pentecost. The hope of humanity for a 'new eon' has been fully realised in Jesus as the Christ, who is the ultimate ideal (Pomeroy, 2002:22).

For Tillich, these issues can only be understood by elevating the temporal into the eternal. We cannot apply temporal words to eternal issues. Temporally, our individual lives will come to an end and the world will come to an end at a time dictated by the scientific laws that govern the universe, and that will be that. Eternally, it makes no sense to speak of an end for throughout our lives we are taken up to a greater or lesser extent into eternity according to the extent to which we have embraced the ultimate meaning of eternity which is love. Eschatology, or the theology of the last things – Death, Judgement, Heaven and Hell – is not about future events but about present realities.

A covenant of hope

History was being made as the first African-American president in US history took the oath of office on 20th January, 2009. The huge number of people who travelled to Washington demonstrated that this was no ordinary inauguration. The eagerness on their faces showed and he did not disappoint.

Barak Obama was doing many things when he delivered his address. He was looking back on the past and on the successes and failures of the previous administration. He was looking to the future and outlining his plans for change. But he was also doing something else. In his contribution to *Credo* in *The Times* on Saturday 24th January, 2009, the former Chief Rabbi, Jonathan Sacks, reminds us that what he was doing 'was something almost unintelligible in terms of British political culture yet central to that of the US. He was, and knew he was, renewing the covenant.'

(Sacks, 2009)

In Europe we sometimes speak of the social contract that exists between citizens of the state. The Founding Fathers of America thought in terms of a different idea which goes back to:

> ...the moment at Mount Sinai when the Israelites bound themselves by sacred covenant to become one nation under God, a phrase that became part of the American pledge of allegiance. They thought not of the social contract that creates a state, but of the social covenant that creates a society. A social contract is about power; a social covenant is about collective responsibility. A social contract is about governments and laws. A social covenant is about the shared ideals of its citizens... (Sacks, 2009).

History will determine if the aspirations of covenant outlined in Barak Obama's inauguration address were realised in practice. Certainly, expectations were raised.

The language of a biblical covenant is not new to us in Britain but it is rarely used in respect of a social covenant between us. But despite our different culture we have a similar Judeo-Christian heritage to the USA. Perhaps both Christians and Jews should be sharing this notion of covenant with others. It would be a powerful reminder to us of the things that bind us together as it is to the people of the USA.

Barack Obama called his book, subtitled *Thoughts on Reclaiming the American Dream, The Audacity of Hope.* There really is something audacious about the virtue of hope.

New Hope

Some time ago on television there was a reconstruction of an event that had taken place some months before. A workman who had been digging a deep but narrow trench in the road had fallen in. He had become wedged and was unable to pull himself free.

The more he struggled the more dangerous it became as the walls of the trench started to collapse on him. After some time, the emergency services were able to stabilise the sides of the trench and lift him free. When interviewed later, the workman admitted that as the hours passed in the trench he had begun to lose hope that he might ever be freed. However, the men and women of the emergency services were there when he needed them and their constant encouragement gave him new hope.

We are regularly and rightly reminded of the events of September 11th, 2001 in New York. We have seen again the vivid images on our television screens and re-read the graphic accounts in our newspapers. We have heard more about the way those most closely involved are still dealing with this tragedy in their lives. For many thousands of families coming to terms with the loss of a husband, wife, son or daughter this has been a harrowing time. We remember images of those going through the painful experience of hoping that their loved ones might yet have survived. We have been reminded of the pictures of the posters all over New York as families waited and hoped. We know also that many others have met these people at their point of need and given them something to hold on to for the future – a kind of hope.

The loss of hope is a devastating experience. Some of the saddest words in the Bible are those spoken by two of Jesus' followers as they discuss his death on the road to Emmaus. An unknown traveller then joins them and they reflect on the death of their friend. 'We had hoped that he was the one to set Israel free' (Luke 24:21). They were aware of reports that Jesus had been raised from the dead but they were not convinced. Later, as they ate a meal together, their unknown companion reveals himself as Jesus. They are overjoyed and rush back to Jerusalem to tell the other disciples. Jesus had met them at their point of need and changed their despair into hope. Jesus still meets us at our point of need and gives us hope even in the most traumatic circumstances.

New Hope (formerly Watford New Hope Trust) exists to serve homeless and vulnerably-housed people by providing accommodation and opportunities to rebuild damaged lives. It was founded on Christian principles but supports people regardless of faith. As its name implies, New Hope gives hope to those on the margins of society, many of whom are close to despair. It has provided food and shelter, companionship and support, to thousands of men and women over the years. It meets people at their point of need and gives them hope.

The Bishop of St Albans' *Harvest for the Hungry* Appeal is a regular feature of the calendar in this part of the world. One of the most encouraging aspects of recent times is the way in which governments, agencies and individuals have responded to the humanitarian tragedies that regularly unfold around the world. Relief organisations are spearheading relief and constantly meeting people at their point of need and changing their despair into hope.

The Calling of a Cuckoo

The Calling of a Cuckoo is the title of a book by David Jenkins, a rather controversial Bishop of Durham from 1984 to 1994. In this book he traces his journey through the turbulent ten years of his bishopric. He tells us of the circumstances of some of his more controversial remarks. He explains the background to these remarks and the impact that they had on those listening. And with the benefit of hindsight he tries to identify the causes of some of the more forceful criticism that he received. In almost every case it is the backward looking perspective of many of his critics that troubles him most (Jenkins, 2003).

The rescue of the men from the San Jose mine deep in the Atacama Desert of Northern Chile in October 2010 was a remarkable event. Boreholes were drilled through the rock to reach the men some 2300 feet below ground. They were then winched up through the shaft to a rapturous welcome above. It was an outstanding technological achievement. Through newspapers and television the world watched and waited, and were able to follow the progress of the rescue attempt from its early stages to its successful conclusion. We felt for the families waiting at the pithead for news of their loved ones. We were impressed by their capacity for hope sustained by their deep religious faith. We rejoiced with them as the first miners were brought to the surface.

Only a month later, the people of Greymouth in New Zealand also had hope for their loved ones trapped in the Pike River Mine following a massive underground explosion. But the outcome for them was very different. All the miners are assumed to have perished in a second massive underground explosion. Both mining communities clung on to hope for it is a very powerful human emotion. The fact that in one case that hope was realised and that in the other that hope was dashed does not diminish its power. But hope is not certainty and in human affairs we cannot know what the outcome will be.

The hope that is offered by Jesus is also a human hope and our part in that enterprise is to do all that we can to realise the hope that so many have in our world today. There were things that could be done to realise the hopes of the Chilean people and those efforts were successful. There was not much that could be done to help realise the hopes of the New Zealanders because the natural forces were so strong. But there is still much that we can do to realise the hopes of many in the bleakness of their otherwise hopeless world. What is so often lacking is the will.

If you are wondering why David Jenkins called his book *The Calling of a Cuckoo,* the title comes from a remark made about him by Margaret Thatcher speaking to Conservative activists in 1985. "After all", she said, "it wouldn't be spring, would it, without the voice of the occasional cuckoo!" David Jenkins is no cuckoo!

Hope has a face

In his book *The Human Face of God*, David Cruz encourages us to see the face of Jesus in the people around us. He writes:

> Just as we can unexpectedly recognise a familiar face in a crowd, it can be said of the human face of God that while it is often partially hidden and obscured, it is also waiting to be recognised and rediscovered in the faces of ordinary people and ordinary moments (Cruz, 2007: ix).

In the chapter entitled *Hope Has a Fac*e, Cruz writes about the way the spiritual writer Father Henri Nouwen inspired many of his readers to be people of hope. Nouwen was a Dutch Roman Catholic priest who left a highly acclaimed academic career to share his life with people with mental disabilities as pastor of l'Arche Daybreak Community in Toronto, Canada:

> Even a casual reading of any of his books on spirituality allows his readers to feel more hopeful about the most trying of circumstances. I once heard Nouwen describe what it was like to care for the severely mentally challenged in a home for the disabled. It struck me as remarkable that someone so brilliant and intellectually gifted could exude such hope and joy when describing the simple acts of kindness extended to those who could hardly speak. Nouwen not only wrote about hope, he gave hope to those often considered hopeless (Cruz, 2007:86).

Cruz identifies two distinguishing characteristics that messengers of hope like Father Nouwen share in common:

> The first is that messengers of hope look beyond the present moment. To look beyond the present moment is the capacity to refuse to languish in the struggles, disappointments,

> setbacks, and failures of daily life as if they will last forever. Rather, a messenger of hope looks beyond the present moment to a brighter day to come... A second distinguishing characteristic shared by persons who are messengers of hope is that of maintaining a healthy perspective in the face of difficulties or struggles. The capacity to maintain this more positive perspective is especially helpful when things simply do not go according to plan (Cruz, 2007:88).

Hope is a quality that transcends the routine and mundane. It is a quality that gives new vigour to life and living. It is a quality that lifts the human spirit. It is a quality which has aspirations of the eternal. Hope is clearly of God. The theologian, Hans Kung, writes in his book, *On Being a Christian*:

> He is a God who does not make empty promises for the hereafter nor trivialize the present darkness, futility and meaninglessness, but who himself in the midst of darkness, futility and meaninglessness invites us to the venture of hope (Kung, 1978).

Love

> Love… is the supreme badge of any true Christianity, and the traits of the beatitudes in a person's life are a surer evidence that he belongs to Christ's family, than is the fact that he holds current opinions on obscure questions of belief.
> Rufus M. Jones, *Spiritual Reformers in 16th and 17th centuries.*

Loving wastefully

In the twelfth chapter of the gospel according to John, Jesus joins his friends for a meal. Lazarus is alive again and his sisters play out their accustomed roles. Martha serves the meal and Mary sits at Jesus' feet. Then, as if on impulse, Mary suddenly darts to the other side of the room to collect something. She comes back and anoints the feet of Jesus with expensive oil. And the house immediately fills with the fragrance of the perfume. It catches everyone by surprise. It seems outrageous. It seems over the top. But that's the point. Brothers don't get raised from the dead every day!

Mary's action was shocking to those around her for a number of reasons. First, she went against the cultural traditions of the day. Women were not supposed to be the centre of attention in the presence of men for this was a patriarchal society. Women were not expected to touch a man in this way. And most certainly respectable women did not let their hair down in public. Mary's act of extravagant giving seems to have been uncalculated and spontaneous. It was a sign of love and gratitude to Jesus for what he had done for her family. Like Mary, sometimes our hearts are in the right places and we do the right thing out of love. At other times we hold back out of fear of what others might think because we have violated some culturally conditioned tradition.

Mary's action was also shocking because of its extravagance. John tells us that it was 'a pound of costly perfume made of pure nard'. Then we're told of Judas' complaint that the perfume could have been sold for three hundred denarii and the money given to the poor. Three hundred denarii was close to one year's wage for a labourer at the time. Thus Mary's gift was certainly extravagant. Moreover, perhaps the perfume had been put on one side for the burial anointing of family members. In any event, this complaint of Judas is a classic one. Too often we look at life only in terms of monetary value. This blinds us to the proper place for extravagant giving motivated by love. Love is not love if it nicely counts the cost. Albert Schweitzer once said, "If there is something you own that you can't give away, then you don't own it, it owns you." Mary's extravagant giving goes above and beyond a price tag – indeed it's priceless.

But let us dwell on this extravagance for a moment and examine the symbolism of the story; for John is full of signs and symbols and he gives us powerful direction. He tells us that 'the house was filled with the fragrance of the perfume'. For John this is symbolic of the beauty and sweetness of all acts done extravagantly and motivated by love. John's readers including us can be inspired to go and do likewise. For it is possible for us even in our weakness to undertake acts which take us above and beyond the ordinary and the mundane. Extravagance is not out of place in this story. And extravagance is not out of place in our story. For Jesus was extravagant in his love for us. We should be extravagant in our love for him and for those around us. John Shelby Spong calls such actions 'loving wastefully' (Spong, 2002:72).

There was once a young American couple, Stella and John They were very poor but very much in love. And each had one unique possession. Stella's hair was her glory. When she let it down it almost served her as a robe. John had a gold watch which had come to him from his father and which was his pride and joy. It was the day before Christmas, and Stella had exactly one dollar eighty-seven cents to buy John a present. She did the only thing she could do. She went out and sold her hair for twenty dollars. And with the proceeds she bought a platinum fob for John's precious watch. John came home late that night. And when he saw Stella's shorn head he stopped as if stupefied. It was not that he did not like it or love her any more. She was lovelier than ever. But... Slowly he handed her his gift. His gift was a set of expensive tortoiseshell combs with jewelled edges for her hair. And he had sold his gold watch to buy them for her. Each had given the other all he or she had to give. Real love cannot think of any other way to give.

'I love, therefore I am'

We are all familiar with the phrase attributed to the philosopher Rene Descartes, 'I think, therefore I am'. Descartes started off as a sceptic. That is, he began to doubt everything, even his own existence. But then he realised that he could be sure of his own existence because he could think about it. Thinking therefore became the test of existence. Hence, that memorable phrase. But we want to go further. Mere existence is not enough. We want to live life to the full. 'I love, therefore I am' expresses the fact that it is only by loving that we can know that we live. Thinking may be the test of existence but loving is the test of life. In his book, *Christian Love*, Bernard Brady writes:

> I love, therefore I am. Loving seems entirely natural and being loved seems wonderfully good. When we love great things or when we love greatly, we feel most alive. We make friends. We marry. We live in families. We feel a connection, however distant, with others. We work. We dedicate ourselves to ideals. We love, therefore we are (Brady, 2003:vii).

In *Love, Power, Justice*, Paul Tillich claims that the difficulties associated with understanding the meaning of the word 'love' can only be resolved by reference to the way that love is rooted in the nature of 'being itself'. Difficulties become insuperable, for example, if love is understood simply as an emotion because such a definition is not large enough to contain the full meaning of love. The nature of 'being itself' is what the theologians call an ontological question. Tillich is not always easy to understand, but bear with him. He puts it this way:

> Life is being in actuality and love is the moving power of life. In these two sentences the ontological nature of love is expressed. They say that being is not actual without the love which drives everything that is towards everything else that is. In man's experience of love the nature of life becomes manifest (Tillich, 197125).

As Brady expands on this theme he reminds us that, however we understand the meaning of love, the way God understands it is demonstrated clearly and unequivocally in Jesus Christ. We can do no other than follow him:

> Loving and existence are dramatically and emphatically tied together for the Christian. At least they ought to be. Christian faith attests to a God described as love, and holds that God demands that we love. God models love particularly and most intensely through the life, teachings, and death of Jesus. By nature we love; by faith we must love (Brady, 2003:vii).

'Four loves' or one

"When *I* use a word," Humpty Dumpty said, in rather a scornful tone, "it means just what I choose it to mean—neither more nor less." "The question is," said Alice, "whether you *can* make words mean so many different things." And the answer is that we can and we do. The word 'love' is a case in point. We use it in a multitude of different ways.

In his book, *The Four Loves,* C S Lewis distinguishes between the four words used for 'love' in the Greek language – *storge* or affection, *phileo* or friendship, *eros* or romantic love, and *agape* or charity. The first three are the 'natural loves' with which we are all familiar. The last is the specifically Christian virtue of unconditional love and at its finest is what we understand as 'divine love'. The back cover introduction to the book reads as follows:

> Lewis sees how each merges into another, how one can even become another, without losing sight of the necessary and real differentiation between them. He knows the peculiar values of each without supposing any to be all in all or self-sufficient; and he discerns too the deceptions and distortions which can render the first three, the natural loves, dangerous without the sweetening grace of charity, the divine love which must be the sum and goal of all (Lewis, 1965).

So, these distinctions are important not least because the word 'love' has been confused and corrupted in common usage in modern times. But it is not necessary to expand at length on these distinctions because what matters is not what divides these words one from another but what unites them. As Paul Tillich points out in *Love, Power and Justice,* if love is rooted in 'being' then it is essentially one:

> The ontology of love leads to the basic assertion that love is one. This contradicts the main trend in recent discussions of the nature of love. They were useful in so far as they directed the attention to the different qualities of love. But they were and are misleading in so far as they consider the differences of quality as differences of types. The error was not that one distinguished the qualities of love. The error was that one did not start with an understanding of love as one (Tillich, 1971: 28).

Love is rooted in God and the different forms of love flow from that central source and manifest themselves in a multitude of different ways. But because love is rooted in God, love is also that which brings things together:

> Love is the drive towards the unity of the separated. Reunion presupposes separation of that which belongs essentially together... Love manifests its greatest power where it overcomes the greatest separation... It is the fulfilment and the triumph of love that it is able to reunite the most radically separated beings, namely individual persons (Tillich, 1971:25-6).

The understanding that love brings people together is a strong message for our times. We live in a world in which the forces that drive people apart sometimes seem overwhelming. The increasing numbers of couples who divorce are sometimes driven apart by the stresses of modern living. Some are unable or unwilling to accept the demands of a loving relationship. Perhaps their love for each other is without depth or resilience and they fall at the first hurdle. Perhaps their love is conditional and when those conditions are broken the marriage fails. That is why the message of unconditional love is so important.

The virtue of unconditional love – *agape*

In classical Greek, the meaning of *agape* was fairly broad, but its use in the Bible and in subsequent Christian writings is far more specific:

> Reflection on the life Jesus lived, on the words he preached, and on the act of his death provides, for the Christian, the meaning of *agape* (Brady, 2003: 54).

Towards the end of his book, Brady summaries what he believes are the characteristics of that love – affective, affirming, responsive, unitive and steadfast.

Agape is affective or emotional love. The affective element arises because love is a 'stirring of the heart'. In the New Testament we see the affections of Jesus. He was moved to tears when his friend died. When he encountered suffering or poverty he was moved to help:

> Without the soul being stirred, without emotion, there is no agape. When the soul is stirred by agape it is, to use Thomas' analogy, like a furnace; it radiates and loves all around it. The stronger the fire, the deeper the love, the more able it is to love others (Brady, 2003: 267).

Agape affirms the other. It affirms the basic human dignity and uniqueness of the other person. It says 'yes' to the other and to the self. In the New Testament there are many stories of Jesus reaching out to those whom he meets whatever their background and disposition:

> Unless we love people for who they are in both their uniqueness and their humanness, we do not truly love. Turn that statement around: We do not want to be loved merely because we are a person (no one wants to be generically loved) nor do we want to be loved because of a particular characteristic or physical trait (what if my full head of dark hair is no longer full or dark). We want to be loved in our totality (Brady, 2003:268).

Agape is responsive to the other. Love is an active response directed at the well-being of the other. It is participation in the promotion of the other's flourishing. It is the service of others in self-giving and self-sacrifice. Brady calls it 'self-subordination'. Jesus said:

> ...whoever wishes to become great among you must be your servant, and whoever wishes to be first among you must be slave to all. For the Son of Man came not to be served but to serve, and to give his life a ransom for many (Mark 10: 43-45).

Agape unites. It is in the very nature of love to bring people together. Tillich describes love as 'the drive towards the reunion of the separated'; this theme runs through the Bible as the people sin and break their relationships with God only in time to renew their covenant. Jesus is the focus for unity:

> If there is any encouragement in Christ, any consolation in love, any sharing in the Spirit, any compassion and sympathy, make my joy complete: be of the same mind, having the same love, being in full accord and of one mind (Philippians 2: 1-3).

Agape is steadfast. God's love endures even in the face of human unfaithfulness. In Psalm 136 the phrase 'for his steadfast love endures for ever' is repeated as a kind of refrain at the end of each verse. The love of Jesus never wavered.

Martin Luther King captures this essential element of love in this powerful message to his opponents from one of his sermons originally written in jail:

> We shall match your capacity to inflict suffering by our capacity to endure suffering. We shall meet your physical force with soul force. Do to us what you will, and we shall continue to love you... Throw us in jail and we shall still love you. Bomb our homes and threaten our children, and we shall still love you. Send your hooded perpetrators of violence into our community at the midnight hour and beat us and leave us half dead, and we shall still love you (King, 1957).

Love of God

The love of God is expressed in many New Testament texts but is dramatically summarised in *The First Letter of John:*

> Beloved, let us love one another, because love is from God; everyone who loves is born of God and knows God. Whoever does not love does not know God, for God is love. God's love was revealed among us in this way: God sent his only Son into the world so that we might live through him (1 John 4:7-9).

Jesus often describes the love of God through parables. In Luke he tells three stories about God's love. The first is about a man who loses one of his one hundred sheep and goes out to find it. The second is about a woman who loses one of her ten silver pieces and diligently searches to find it. The final story is the parable of the Prodigal Son and is about a father who 'loses' a son and is perhaps the most dramatic of all. The picture of the father running to the younger son and kissing him before he can give the prepared speech of repentance is a telling description of God's love:

> So he set off and went to his father. But while he was still far off, his father saw him and was filled with compassion; he ran and put his arms around him and kissed him (Luke 15:20).

But Paul has perhaps the most passionate expression of God's love in the New Testament. In the Letter to the Romans he writes:

> For I am convinced that neither death, nor life, not angels, nor rulers, not things present, nor things to come, not powers, nor height, nor depth, nor anything else in all creation, will be able to separate us from the love of God in Christ Jesus our Lord (Romans 8:38-39).

It is important to note that in the expression 'God is love', the New Testament comes closest to telling us about the 'being' of God.

Love of neighbour

The New Testament also has a lot to say about love of neighbour but the theme is most dramatically expressed in the parable of the Good Samaritan:

> "Which one of these three, do you think, was a neighbour to the man who fell into the hands of the robbers?" He said, "The one who showed him mercy." Jesus said to him, "Go and do likewise" (Luke 10: 36-37).

The people listening to this parable might well have defined 'neighbour' as a friend or member of their own community. Jesus makes it clear that our neighbour is not limited to the person who lives next door or to an acquaintance but refers to anyone in need. And by choosing the neighbour in this parable from outside the community Jesus reinforces the point.

Another story from the same gospel also captures essential elements of neighbourly love. Jesus has been invited to the house of Simon, a Pharisee, but he does not receive the traditional gestures of welcome. During the meal a woman arrives and takes centre stage. This woman is described as a sinner and may well have been a prostitute but she proceeds to kiss the feet of Jesus and anoint them with ointment. It is a dramatic gesture in which the woman meets the need of Jesus for relief from sore feet and Jesus meets the need of the woman for forgiveness:

> Then turning towards the woman, he said to Simon, "Do you see this woman? I entered your house, you gave me no water for my feet, but she has bathed my feet with her tears and dried them with her hair. You gave me no kiss, but from the

> time I came in she has not stopped kissing my feet. You did not anoint my head with oil, but she has anointed my feet with ointment. Therefore, I tell you, her sins, which were many, have been forgiven; hence she has shown great love. But the one to whom little is forgiven, loves little". Then he said to her, "Your sins are forgiven" (Luke 7: 44-48).

It is not clear whether the woman was forgiven because she loved much or whether she loved much because she had already been forgiven. Regardless of which came first the story shows her heaping love on Jesus and his generous response. Love is reciprocated.

In a story reminiscent of this story, Jesus illustrates his love for his disciples as he washes their feet in John's account of the Last Supper:

> After he had washed their feet, had put on his robe, and had returned to the table, he said to them, "Do you know what I have done to you? You call me Teacher and Lord – and you are right, for that is what I am. So if I, your Lord and Teacher, have washed your feet, you also ought to wash one another's feet. For I have set you an example, that you also should do as I have done to you" (John 13: 12-15).

The litmus test of our love for others is the quality of our service to others. In Luke's account of the Last Supper, the disciples get into an argument about which one of them is the greatest. Jesus' answer is clear:

> The kings of the Gentiles lord it over them; and those in authority over them are called benefactors. But not so with you; rather the greatest among you must become like the youngest, and the leader like one who serves. For who is greater, the one who is at table or the one who serves? Is it not

> the one at the table? But I am among you as one who serves (Luke 22: 25-27).

"I am among you as one who serves", says it all!

Love of self

Surprisingly, apart from the Great Commandment itself, there is nothing in the New Testament specifically about love of self. However, we can draw some general conclusions about self-love from the tone of other references. Bernard Brady quotes from Garth Hallett's book *Christian Neighbor Love* (Hallett, 1989):

> Garth Hallett convincingly argues that the most appropriate phrase to describe relationship between love of self and neighbour love in the New Testament is 'self-subordination'. Self subordination means that "one should give independent consideration of one's own benefit, but only on the condition that maximum benefits to others is first assured." "Overall", he writes, "it seems that when there is no question of conflict with God's call or others' good, the New Testament has no quarrel with benefit to self" (Brady, 2003: 270).

More specifically, we never see Jesus putting his own interests before the interests of others in his ministry. In reading the gospels, Hallett writes, we do not hear Jesus:

> ...serving his own good in a way unrelated to others' good: not when he rested by the well, nor when he drank his host's wine, nor when he accepted their invitation to dine, nor when he rode into Jerusalem instead of entering on foot. However, neither do we find him denying his own good in a way unrelated to others' good (Brady, 2003: 270).

The ancient Jews had hundreds of commandments. Sometimes a

teacher would be asked to summarise the law in the time he could stand on one leg. Jesus is asked such a question and his answer is very clear. Love is the core of the law. Love of God, love of neighbour and a proper love of self. Love of God? Yes! Love of neighbour? Yes! Love of ourselves? But what is a proper love of self?

Anthropology, sociology and psychology, and the other human sciences, have contributed much to our understanding of the human condition in the last hundred years or so. The insights of psychology, in particular, have increased understanding of our intellectual and emotional selves enormously. We now know much more about what it means to have a healthy mind as well as a healthy body. And a good deal of this has to do with how we think of ourselves, our self-esteem.

Depression is widespread in our society and is one of the most debilitating illnesses of our age. For a long time it was not taken seriously by professionals and many people had to struggle on without treatment. Now things have improved and mental illness is properly recognised. Depression may not always be about a lack of self-esteem but I guess that it often is. And one of the things we have learnt from professionals is that a lack of self-esteem can be very disabling. Those who work in this field will tell you that low self-esteem can cripple a person's ability to form relationships. In other words, if we are unable to value ourselves we are unlikely to be able to value other people.

And this is sometimes compounded by religious teaching that tells us that there is something basically bad within us that needs to be rooted out before we are worthy of further progress. I hope that we do not understand any concept of original sin in that way. Because if we believe that we are basically bad inside then we cannot be at home there. And if we are not at home with ourselves then we are not comfortable in bringing others into our lives. And if we are unable to bring people into our lives then we cannot love them. Loving others is about vulnerability and generosity. It does not come easily.

Loving ourselves is about being ourselves and not someone else. Youngsters find this particularly difficult but it's not just a problem for them. There is pressure on all of us to conform to an image rather than to build an identity. So we are tempted to wear masks. And to use different masks for different situations. One for home, one for school or work, and another with friends. And its stressful for the mask must not be allowed to slip. We try to look confident about work when we are actually frightened of failure. We pretend to be confident about relationships but actually need a confidant and someone to talk to. And it's hard to prevent the mask from slipping: to be able to convince all the people, all the time, that the mask is us and that we are in control. We think that we will only be accepted if we are perfect. We forget that God made us and accepts us in our imperfection.

Loving ourselves then is about developing our humanity to the full. It is only by being fully human that we can fulfil the commandments of Jesus. Jesus was fully human and we aspire to be like him. So let us celebrate our humanity as we celebrate his. As human beings, we certainly have faults and there are times when we are very unlikeable people. But unlovable? Never!

How does love of self relate to love of neighbour and love of God? It is enough to understand that it is not possible to have the one without the others if love is to be in all its fullness. For some people these three aspects will remain distinct; for others they conflate into one. For those who understand God as 'a being' then the distinction may be important. For those who understand God as 'being itself' then the distinction may be meaningless. For the essence of being is love.

Love in a world of need

It should not be necessary to argue that engagement in God's love includes engagement with a world in its variety of need. There are pressing economic, political, social and personal needs that demand to be addressed. But there are Christians in our day who still do not make this connection. Even if they make the connection, issues of human dignity and social justice, for example, are not given the priority they deserve.

For some people, primary issues get put to one side as secondary issues loom much larger. Homosexuality is a case in point. People have seen texts in the Bible that seem to condemn homosexuality and they think that they can then speak with biblical authority. But this is not how the Bible works. These texts, and indeed all texts, do not stand on their own and cannot be taken at face value. They need to be interpreted and they need to be taken in the context of the Bible as a whole. And the Bible as a whole does not condemn homosexuality. In fact it barely addresses it. It has more important things to do.

We really do face an urgent need to recast the Bible for our own time. After decades and indeed centuries of work by scholars, we still treat the Bible as if every word were somehow dictated by God. We forget that it was written by a variety of human authors over a long period of time. There are contradictions and inconsistencies and the text is not uniformly reliable. There is, of course, literal truth in the Bible. But we miss other kinds of truth that we find in the stories, poetry and wisdom of the Bible if we always assume a literal reading. We need to see the Bible as a rich and varied source of revelation. And we need to see it as a whole.

In the Old Testament there are ten commandments and more than six hundred laws governing the way lives were to be lived. In the New Testament there is one commandment and one law. 'A new commandment I give unto you, that ye love one another; as I have loved you' (John 13:34). Everything follows from that. Jesus is not interested in the minutiae of individual laws about this and that. His concern is for our overall disposition and if that is right there is a good chance that everything else will follow.

If we have truly understood the nature of that commandment,

and our disposition is right, then love for God, ourselves and others will be an integral whole. If not, then we shall join those for whom individual issues loom large, become detached and easily distorted. There really is only one commandment.

Persons in Relation

The implication of this commandment as an integral whole is that individual persons are not fully persons except in relationship with each other and with God.

Persons in Relation is the second book published from the Scottish philosopher John Macmurray's 1953-54 Gifford Lectures under the title *The Form of the Personal.* The first volume, *The Self as Agent*, 'was concerned to exhibit the primacy of the practical in human experience, and the need to transfer the centre of gravity in philosophy from thought to action'. The second volume, *Persons in Relation*, was concerned to end:

> …the solitariness of the thinking self, sets man firmly in the world which he knows, and so restores him to his proper existence as a community of persons in relation. It is the purpose of this book to show how the personal relation of persons is constitutive of personal existence; that there can be no man until there are at least two men in communication. Our main effort, therefore, must be directed towards determining the formal characters of personal relationship (Macmurray, 1995:12,17).

As Frank Kirkpatrick points out in his Introduction, Macmurray is not making some obscure philosophical point but is attempting to 'spell out the nature of what he often called 'friendship' or 'fellowship'':

> It involved such things as mutuality, love, heterocentrism, compassion, and sharing. It was, ultimately, constituted by the

> sheer delight of simply being with and for other persons. In making that claim Macmurray captures something much closer to a Biblical and Christian view than one can find in the areligious references of political and moral philosophy. While not a conventional believer, Macmurray remained profoundly religious and always sought to place his notion of community in the context of a Biblical view of God's intention to create community through divine acts that sought human cooperation in the world (Macmurray, 1995: xxi).

From a theological perspective, the notion that we are only truly ourselves in relationship has its origins in the Doctrine of the Trinity. This reminds us that the three aspects of God – Father, Son and Spirit – are only active in relationship with each other.

Goodness

Goodness is a special kind of truth and beauty. It is truth and beauty in human behaviour.
Harry Allen Overstreet, *The Enduring Quest.*

The 'classical' virtues

The so called 'classical virtues' of goodness, truth and beauty are yet another way in which particular virtues have been gathered together. The background is both pagan and religious and we find references to these virtues in the writings of all the major religions and philosophies. A high point arrived when the philosophers of Athens – Socrates, Plato and Aristotle – laid out explicitly their own definitions of truth, beauty and goodness and what it means to lead lives guided by these virtues. A low point was reached in the twentieth century when dictators – Stalin, Mao and Hitler – imposed their own version of what was true, beautiful and good and demanded conformity. Between these points there has been vigorous debate about what these words might actually mean.

The Golden Rule

The book, *Cheshire,* by Richard Morris is a biography of Leonard Cheshire (Morris, 2000). It is the story of a man whose war career brought him the highest military distinction. It is the story of a man who is now remembered more for his peacetime work of compassion. His pioneering work to provide recognition and support for the disabled led to a movement which now supports care homes in many countries throughout the world. It is clear that a strong Christian faith motivated him. But what made his contribution so distinctive and his legacy so immense? The clue may lie in some words from the gospel according to Matthew: 'In everything do to others as you would them do to you' (Matthew 7:12).

This is Matthew's account of the way Jesus expressed what has now become known as 'the golden rule'. This principle, at least in its negative form, was stated long before the time of Jesus, and arises quite independently of Jesus in other traditions. In the writings of Judaism we read 'What is hateful to yourself, do to no other'. The same rule arises in non-Christian traditions. Confucius instructed his followers: 'What you do not want done to yourself, do not do to others'. And there are many other examples. But all except the saying of Jesus have one thing in common – they are all expressed in the negative form. Do not do...!

Some have seen the negative statement of the golden rule as more powerful because, they say, 'it is more realistic, and goes to the heart of the problem'. Some have seen little significance in the distinction because the two versions amount to the same thing. Others consider the positive form to be more forceful because it 'makes greater demands on the altruism of its hearers'. John Chrysostom, that great Archbishop of Constantinople, compares the two versions in this way. The negative version, he says, requires a 'departure from evil' while the positive version demands 'the exercise of virtue'.

In some ways, the negative form of the rule is not a religious rule at all. When we are told that we must refrain from doing to others that which we would not wish them to do to us, what are we actually saying? We are making a common-sense statement without which normal social intercourse would be impossible. Life would be intolerable if we could not assume that others would conform to this rule. So, it is more of a legal statement than a religious one. And it is relatively easy to follow. We could follow it simply by inaction. But a way of life which consists in doing nothing would amount to very little indeed.

On the other hand, the positive form of the rule demands something of us. When we are told that we must actively do to others what we would have them do to us, we are invoking an entirely new principle. It is one thing to say that I must not do anything to hurt or injure people. The law can compel us to do that. It is quite another thing to say that I must go out of my way to help and support people. Only love can compel us to do that. So an appeal to law and an appeal to love is one way in which we can distinguish between these two versions of the golden rule.

Take a very simple analogy. If a man has a motor car, the law can compel him to drive in such a way that he does not injure anybody else on the road. Furthermore, if he infringes that law, he can be punished in the courts. The law has been imposed. It comes from outside. But no law can compel this man to drive in such a way that he or she is prepared to allow a medical emergency vehicle to pass or to stop and help someone in distress. No law is infringed if he fails to stop. But something from within us tells us that he has nonetheless failed.

It is perfectly straightforward to live our lives according to the negative form of the golden rule. Most of us would find relatively little difficulty in disciplining ourselves to avoid hurting people. Just obeying the law would be simple and uncomplicated. But is that the kind of life that Jesus meant us to live. Somehow, I don't think so. It seems to me that his purpose is very different. In restating the golden rule in its positive form, Jesus shows us that the Christian life is about 'going out of our way'. But it goes further. As someone has said, these words of Jesus 'are not just to provide a rule of thumb for interpersonal relations, they are intended to shatter the radical self-centredness that obscures our awareness of the rights and needs of others.'

Leonard Cheshire achieved what he did because he went 'out of his way'. When he first met Arthur who had been injured in the war and had nowhere to go, he realised that unless somebody went out of their way to care for Arthur he would receive little support. Night and day he took care of him – washing him, feeding him, sheltering him – until Arthur's death. And it was this experience that was the spur which urged him on to look after many thousands of others over the years. It was an attitude of mind, it was an act of faith and it was positive action that led Cheshire to found the care homes that bear his name – now known as Leonard Cheshire Disability.

Leonard Cheshire died in 1992 aged 75. Some years later, his brother Christopher wrote, 'I don't follow how he did all that. If you find out, let me know.' I feel sure that many will have replied, 'Yes, I know!

But the golden rule can be framed within a sharper distinction, what some describe as 'the battle between good and evil'.

The battle between good and evil

The battle between good and evil is a constant theme in the Bible. Indeed it has been a constant theme throughout history both in fact and in fiction. History is full of war and the 'threat of war'. Literature and art are full of illustrations of conflict between the forces of good and the forces of evil. Sometimes those forces reflect what some believe to be a cosmic conflict between God and Satan. Sometimes these forces are identified with particular human beings and the battles between good and evil men. Sometimes these forces are identified with the battle within each of us between our worthier and baser motives. Christians all agree that good is ultimately personified in Jesus. Christians do not all agree that evil is personified in Satan; but all agree that both good and evil are powerful forces whichever way we care to describe them.

One of the themes of the 'travel narrative' in Luke is the growing opposition that Jesus encounters on his way. In one incident, Jesus is accused of being in league with the devil and of performing exorcisms by black magic. He answers this complicated charge by accepting the reality and power of Satan but claiming that God represents the only power capable of breaking Satan's grip. Satan was a very real presence to the people of

Jesus' time. The battle between good and evil was a constant theme and it was seen as a relatively straightforward contest. Everyone was either black or white.

The Name of the Rose, by Umberto Eco, which is about monastic orders and religious movements in the Middle Ages, is a very 'dark' book. Readers are left with the overwhelming impression that people of the Middle Ages were obsessed with the battle between good and evil in a way that is quite different to times a thousand years earlier. This battle was being waged both in the open and in secret and the forces for good and evil seemed to constantly change sides. At times the whole of society seemed to be corrupt; at other times the forces for good seemed to achieve the upper hand. The battle between good and evil was very real but it was certainly not simple. Everything was an uncertain shade of grey.

In our own time we are confronted by the same battle between good and evil but in yet another form. There are some who see the 'war against terrorism' as simply a battle between the good of western democracy and the evil of Islamic fundamentalism. And as such they believe it is perfectly reasonable for one side to take pre-emptive action against the other side which might be planning the next terrorist attack. Others believe that this is certainly a battle between good and evil but that good and evil are on the opposite sides. Western democracy is evil and Islamic fundamentalism is good. Yet others believe that there is good and evil in all men and women and on both sides.

The conflict between good and evil is not simple, and those who offer simplistic solutions are dangerous and irresponsible. The conflict between good and evil is also not cloaked with secrecy or somehow not our responsibility to resolve. The conflict between good and evil is very much our responsibility. Our challenge is to recognise the good and to recognise the evil wherever it might be and to make the appropriate response.

But goodness is not something to be pursued only by

individuals; it has an important social dimension. 'The common good' is increasingly seen as a powerful way of expressing this dimension.

The Common Good

The notion of 'the common good' is a major aspect of Roman Catholic Social Teaching. In the book *Christian Ethics,* edited by Bernard Hoose, Charles Curran writes:

> The Christian tradition in general and the Roman Catholic approach in particular have emphasised the importance of the 'common good'. Human beings are not just isolated individuals but are social beings called to live together in civic and political community. The common good refers to shared or public values and interests which ultimately redound to the good of all members of the community. Such an understanding of society is opposed to individualism which sees society as the sum total of individuals and also to collectivism which denies the legitimate needs and rights of individuals who are submerged in the collectivity (Curran, 1998: 81).

The doctrine of the 'common good' in Roman Catholicism is not only a unique body of teaching, which is unparalled in other parts of the Christian Church, but also an approach which deserves much wider dissemination. Its contemporary understanding is summarised in the document, *Gaudium et Spes* (Joy and Hope), which arose from the Second Vatican Council. Fortunately, the notion of the 'common good' has become more prominent in national debate in recent years following the Prime Minister's 'big society' initiative, and by an increased concern for social justice and human dignity amongst the public at large.

But, any notion of the common good depends on a shared understanding of the requirements of social justice and human rights. These shared understandings must extend to economic, political and religious realms and beyond, and much of this shared understanding clearly exists. However, difficulties arise with claims of absolute norms of justice and rights in a given community because the world has changed and unless these norms are re-examined and recast in the light of these changes then they will lose credibility. This does not amount to wholesale rejection of fundamental principles but it does mean honest examination. Liberation and Feminist theologies are not the only new movements which have challenged the *status quo.*

Today we are much more conscious of the pluralism and diversity in society and with an increased emphasis on individualism it is harder to recognise and agree on the common good of all. Yet, without some understanding of norms of justice and fundamental human rights there can be no stable society. In the turmoil of recent decades and in particular in the so called 'Arab Spring' we can see all too clearly what can happen when there is a sense of a shared destiny and equally what can happen if that understanding is lost. In our own country, the absence of shared values in many aspects of our national life in recent years has led to serious consequences. We desperately need to reset our moral compass. One of those who has championed both the individual and the collective good is Desmond Tutu, the former Archbishop of Cape Town.

Made for Goodness

Desmond Tutu was born in the Transvaal in 1931 but his family moved to Johannesburg when he was twelve. There he met Trevor Huddleston, who was a parish priest in the black slum of Sophiatown, and was to have a major influence on his life. "One day," said Tutu, "I was standing in the street with my mother when a white man in a priest's clothing walked past. As he passed us he took off his hat to my mother. I couldn't believe my eyes – a white man who greeted a black working class woman!"

In 1960 Tutu was ordained a priest following in the footsteps of his mentor Trevor Huddleston. He retired as Archbishop of Cape Town in 1996.

Throughout his adult life Desmond Tutu was fully engaged not only in his work as a priest but also in the struggle for human rights for the black population of South Africa. After the fall of apartheid he chaired the Truth and Reconciliation Commission which was responsible for bringing together those who had suffered and those who had caused that suffering in a true spirit of reconciliation. Nelson Mandela and Desmond Tutu are regarded as pivotal figures in the peaceful transfer of power from white minority to black majority rule in South Africa. Nelson Mandela died in December 2013 but both men continue to be held in high esteem. Both received many international awards including the Nobel Peace Prize.

Desmond Tutu is recognised everywhere for the depth of his spirituality, the exuberance of his personality and his simple joy in living. In 2010, together with his daughter Mpho, he wrote, *Made for Goodness,* a book in which he seeks to answer the question, "What do I see in the heart of humanity and in the sweep of history that confirms my conviction that goodness will triumph?" He starts from a very clear premise:

> We are fundamentally good. When you come to think of it, that's who we are at our core. Why else do we get so outraged by wrong? When we hear of any egregious act, we are appalled. Isn't that an incredible assertion about us? Evil and wrong are aberrations. If wrong were the norm, it wouldn't be news. Our newscasts wouldn't lead with the latest acts of murder or mayhem, because they would be ordinary. But murder and mayhem are not the norm. The norm is goodness (Tutu and Tutu 2010: 5).

In order to emphasise the point, Tutu reminds us of those

qualities in people that we find attractive. There are superficial qualities to which we are momentarily drawn but there are also more profound qualities to which we are draw at a much deeper level:

> You can see from the people we truly admire that we are attracted to goodness. We do not revere people who are successful. We might envy them and wish that their money were transferred to our bank account. But the people we revere are not necessarily successful, they are something else. They are good (Tutu & Tutu, 2010:5).

And to illustrate the point he recalls Mother Teresa, Mahatma Gandhi and Martin Luther King. They were respected and revered not for their successes, although they certainly had them, but for their goodness. And he pays tribute to his friend:

> In our own time Nelson Mandela commands the same kind of admiration. He walks into any place, and people are transfixed – not because he is mighty and macho, but because he is gracious and good (Tutu & Tutu, 2010:5).

But he goes on to say that we misunderstand what this goodness means if we believe that we must strive for goodness and that 'our perfection is the price we imagine we must pay for the love of God':

> So we strive endlessly to 'be good' or to 'do good' instead of realising that we are good. We don't have to struggle and strive to overcome an innate tendency to do what is bad or wrong. In everything we do we can fulfil the purpose for which we were made and rejoice in our inherent goodness. In short, we can stop 'being good' and simply live from our goodness (Tutu and Tutu, 2010:23).

Our goodness comes from God because goodness is of God. We share in his goodness in the same way as we can share in his creativity and in his beauty, and in all those other attributes with which we are concerned in this book. Each of these qualities reveals a different aspect of God. The more we make them our own, the fuller we become as human beings and the closer we come to God.

But what about evil? What about sin? Evil is clearly a part of our world and Desmond Tutu is more qualified than most to testify to the ability of men and women to perpetuate evil:

> At the core of our being is goodness. This is not to deny the reality of sin. Sin is real. Depravity and cruelty are real. Evil exists. But sin, cruelty, and evil are not our essential nature. They are aberrations. What is normative is goodness. Wrongness runs against the grain of creation. Evil is so contrary to our nature that we must construct justifications to allow ourselves to do what we know to be wrong or cruel. We concoct a justification or we claim that we are powerless to affect change (Tutu & Tutu, 2010:194).

But this claim seems to go against the traditional emphasis in Western Christianity on 'sin'. In the chapter on Humanity we have already met the views of John Shelby Spong, the former Bishop of Newark, where he shows how damaging traditional theology has been and how negative a view of humanity it has given us. I repeat:

> It is time, I am convinced, to move Christianity beyond that historically inaccurate and psychologically damaging definition of humanity that has resulted in a constant denigration of human life as helpless, depraved, sinful, and in need of divine rescue. The suggestion made by so much of the Christian theology of the past that every baby is born with the

> stain of original sin distorting his or her goodness is abhorrent to me. I now regard the traditional Christian interpretation of the account of the fall of humanity, told in the narrative of the Garden of Eden, as the ultimate example of distorted negative thinking (Spong, 2002:149).

In one of a series of lectures to undergraduates at Cambridge University in 2004, J S Whale writes of one way of re-evaluating this doctrine in the modern world:

> Eden is on no map, and Adam's fall fits no historical calendar. Moses is not nearer the Fall than we are, because he lived three thousand years before our time. The Fall refers not to some datable aboriginal calamity in the historic past of humanity, but to a dimension of human experience which is always present – namely, that we who have been created for fellowship with God repudiate it continually; and that the whole of mankind does this along with us. Every man is his own 'Adam', and all men are solidarily 'Adam'. Thus, Paradise before the Fall, the *status perfectionis,* is not a period of history, but our 'memory' of a divinely intended quality of life, given to us along with our consciousness of guilt (Sykes, 2002: 407).

In this passage, the author reinforces the danger of maintaining historical approaches to the Genesis narratives which make no sense in the modern world; having said that, there are those who have moved on to more mature understandings of these matters. Unfortunately, there are many others who are locked into traditional understandings which are ingrained in our psyche and still dominate our liturgy.

The message of Desmond Tutu is that humanity flourishes most successfully when we place the emphasis on good rather than evil although we accept that both exist and both can be equally powerful. The legacy of The Truth and Reconciliation

Commission is powerful testimony to this truth.

Goodness Reframed

In a final section, it is worth reflecting on the ways in which 'goodness' is in danger of being compromised by the changes taking place in our national and international life.

In his book, *Truth, Beauty and Goodness Reframed,* Howard Gardner identifies two 'novel forces' which have complicated the status of 'the good' in recent years:

> Particularly among the young, postmodern modes of thought have come to permeate the ways in which we think about human affairs. Even more dramatically, our entire conception of 'the good' is being continually and radically altered by the digital media (Gardner, 2011:94).

So far as postmodern modes of thought are concerned, Gardner's research shows some disturbing trends:

> Americans increasingly assert their right to formulate their own moral principles and are surprisingly reluctant to pass judgement on the morality of their peers. Still another trend is equally disturbing: Young Americans seem to lack an ethical compass that governs their own behaviour (Gardner, 2011:98).

And he adds:

> While the postmodern critique has had its positive aspects, it leads to an unacceptable normless situation, a classic example of anomie, whereby young people – and people who are not so young – are reluctant to judge *any* behaviour, action, or attitude as immoral, unethical, just plain wrong. Where anything goes, nothing will endure (Gardner, 2011:99).

So far as digital media is concerned, it 'poses fundamental new challenges to our conception of 'the good.'' Consider an individual's sense of identity:

> Youth have long engaged in various moves to determine who they are, how to present themselves, what kinds of personal and professional commitments to make. This state of affairs, quite normal, can lead to reasonable and wise decisions. The new digital media, however, provide innumerable opportunities to generate multiple selves online through games and networks (Gardner, 2011:100).

Gardner comments:

> Ethical issues arise when youth misrepresent themselves in ways that could do harm to others, to family or friends – providing information that is misleading or hurtful, without taking responsibility for the effects of these self- or family portrayals (Gardner, 2011:100).

Having said all this, Gardner is optimistic:

> Every society, and, indeed, every individual, has some sense of what it means to be good, and some thoughts about how to achieve the good. As we learn more about different religions, belief systems, and cultural practices, we come to appreciate that our sense of good may not be the same as that held by other persons or other cohorts, in other places and at other times. And as societies become more complex, we need delineations of the good with respect to specific professions and varieties of citizenship. So we may or may not succeed in arriving at a consensual view of the good. But the search for the good, and the hope that some kind of workable consensus might arise remain essential (Gardner, 2011:190).

Truth

> Truth is given, not to be contemplated, but to be done. Life is an action – not a thought.
> F W Robertson *Sermons.*

Biblical truth

It seems appropriate to start our examination of the second of the 'classical virtues' by considering biblical truth, and for two reasons. First, the Bible is clearly a primary source of what we might mean by truth. Second, any discussion of biblical truth raises difficult issues of interpretation.

When Pontius Pilate interrogated Jesus before his crucifixion, Jesus proclaimed that "Everyone who belongs to the truth listens to my voice". To this, Pilate replied "What is truth?" Although we have no record of any reply by Jesus, Christians affirm that Pilate was staring Truth in the face, for Jesus had earlier said to Thomas, "I am the way, and the truth, and the life".

What is truth? Ever since that question was first asked of Jesus, people have been quick to provide an answer. And they have been very confident that their answer is the only answer. Some will say truth lies in the scriptures. Others will claim that truth lies in the tradition of the church. Yet others will argue that truth lies in our ability to reason things out for ourselves. Or that we can only be sure of the truth that lies in our own individual experiences. Or truth lies in the person of the pope, the bishop or the priest. Or it lies in the martyrs or the saints. Or the truth lies in the words of this man or woman or that. So many claim that they know where to find the truth.

The trouble with those who claim to know the truth or where to find it is that they are often unwilling to accommodate those with a different point of view. This is particularly true of those who claim that the Bible is the whole truth and nothing but the truth. They claim that no interpretation is needed to access this truth and they dismiss any attempt at biblical criticism. They claim to know a truth that is the same for all who read the Bible from whatever direction they approach it. They claim something really remarkable.

But their claim is demonstrably false. Even if you believe that God somehow dictated the Bible to the scribes who wrote it, you cannot get away from the fact that amongst a number of like-minded people you will encounter an equal number of different opinions of what the truth actually is. For those who believe that the Bible did not come to us in this way and that it was the work of inspired but fallible men (and women?), the Bible becomes even more complex and in need of interpretation. Quite apart from the numerous inconsistencies within it, it was quite clearly written at a time and in a place that is so different from our own that we must surely pause before applying the norms of that time and place to ourselves. We do not have the same attitude to family life, to the role of women, to the place of slaves, and so it goes on. And yet we continue to read the Bible uncritically. It is as if work of biblical scholars had never existed.

The Bible contains an infinite variety of truth. The Bible undoubtedly contains history, but it also contains wisdom, poetry, prophecy, apocalyptic and a lot more. It contains the perspectives of individuals and groups in a multitude of different times and places. And we need the widest range of interpretations in order to do it justice. We need 'a kaleidoscope of interpretations' which include not just the commentaries that we would expect to see but also the work of George Herbert and William Blake. And we need to take imaginative writers seriously as commentators even where they are not easily assimilated into orthodox piety. Blake, after all, was notorious for being a 'one-man church'. Creative imagination is a good thing and we need more of it in our approach to the Bible.

But how do we understand truth in the routine of daily life. How far can we get by just using our common sense?

Truth as common sense

In our early years, we do not need to be told what is true and what is not true. From the first days after birth, our senses tell us what the world is like and what it is not like. A newborn baby can grasp her mother's hand and know the truth that it is actually there. That same baby can hear the door close and know the truth that her father is home. The child senses truths about the world through hearing, sight, touch, smell and taste well before it is able to use language. In due course those truths are articulated in language where truth finds its natural home.

In his book, *Truth, Beauty and Goodness Reframed,* Howard Gardner writes:

> Our conception of truth arises initially from common sense, with an emphasis both on *common* and on *sense*. We rely in the first instance on our senses and, in the second instance, on what is commonly sensed – that is, what is seen or heard or smelled not just by us but by other representative members of the community, particularly those who are considered knowledgeable. And for much of life, that is enough (Gardner, 2011:21).

But common sense is notoriously unreliable:

> Alas, common sense cannot get us very far. Misinformation or disinformation can spread rapidly through a community – becoming, in a sardonic phrase made famous by economist John Kenneth Galbraith, 'the conventional wisdom'. After all, despite the evidence of our senses, the earth is not flat, the sun does not revolve around the earth, time and space are not absolute, human beings were not created on the sixth day – the list of one-time widely acknowledged truths now rejected is endless (Gardner, 2011:21-22).

There are also more subtle ways in which 'common sense' can be tainted. We are easily manipulated and swayed against the evidence of our own senses. Those who have served in a jury know how easy it is to be persuaded by the majority view despite firm convictions to the contrary. You enter the jury room firmly convinced of the defendant's innocence; you leave equally firmly convinced of his guilt. The motives of those who have convinced you of a contrary view may well be suspect.

Nevertheless, it is through our senses that we do experience truth, and not just our senses but the senses of all those in communities both past and present. We enjoy a rich legacy of truth:

> The sphere of human knowledge represents a communal trek, over many centuries and many terrains, to place our senses of truth on firmer footing... In the search for truth our greatest allies are the scholarly disciplines and the professional crafts – in short, areas of expertise that have developed and deepened over the centuries. Each discipline and craft explores a different sphere of reality and each attempts to establish truths – the truths of knowledge, the truths of practice (Gardner, 2011:23).

But it is important to remember that not all statements can be accurately described as either true or false. Many statements simply cannot be tested and their veracity is unknown. Some may be true in some circumstances but not others. Others may be true at one time or place but untrue at another. Quite frequently statements are foolish or simply do not make sense. So:

> Not a single truth any more, but a plurality of truths, each appropriate to its realm, each fallible, but each subject to continuing refinement and improvement. Never perhaps reaching the Promised Land of Pure Ultimate Truth, but over

> the centuries moving steadily in the right direction. In that limited but real sense, we can see that we have a truer picture – more properly, truer pictures – of the world than those who came before us, but also that we can never assume we have arrived at the ultimate destination: Our successors may well come to possess truer versions still (Gardner, 2011:37).

Since philosophers first raised the issue there has been a vigorous debate about the nature of truth. Is truth something absolute and fixed or is it relative and contingent?

Truth as 'absolute' or 'relative'

In his book, *Truth: A Guide for the Perplexed,* the philosopher Simon Blackburn describes the attitudes adopted by protagonists in the debate and outlines the nature of the debate itself:

> When we are absolutists we stand on truth. We like plain, unvarnished objective fact, and we like it open, transparent, and unfiltered. We may not like it everywhere, so we may feel like confining truth to some area: scientific truth, but not aesthetic truth or moral truth, for example. But somewhere the absolute truth can be found. And as well as truth, absolutists cherish its handmaidens: reason, which enables us to find it or certify it, and objectivity, which is the cardinal virtue of reasoning (Blackburn, 2006: xv).

All very neat and tidy but:

> Relativists mock these ideals. They see nothing anywhere that is plain, unvarnished, objective, open, transparent or unfiltered. They debunk and deny. They insist upon the universal presence of happenstance, brute contingencies of nature or culture or language or experience, that shape the way we see things. Nietzsche said 'There are no facts, only interpreta-

> tions'. That will do as a relativist slogan, and in many people's eyes Nietzsche is a high priest of relativism (Blackburn, 2006:xv).

At times the debate has been fierce and so far as religious truth is concerned, the leaders of the Roman Catholic Church have been quite clear where they stand. During the Pope's visit to the United Kingdom in 2010 he spoke of the 'dictatorship of relativism', a phrase that he first used at the Conclave at which he was elected Pope in 2005. In this more recent speech he claims that a 'dictatorship of relativism threatens to obscure the unchanging truth about man's nature, his destiny and his ultimate good'.

The Roman Catholic Church is not alone amongst conservative groups both within Christianity and elsewhere who claim that they, and they alone, have the truth and that this truth is unchanging. This uncompromising stand is a particular feature of the modern religious landscape but it has been around for centuries. The Inquisition wreaked havoc in the Middle Ages as does the Taliban in more recent times. There have always been institutions and groups who are prepared to impose their will by force. These represent extremes but they were and are none the less real.

It is tempting to suggest that all claims to absolute truth are attempts by those who have power to control those who do not and to use the fear of violence or damnation as weapons in a war against dissent. Historically, there is certainly some truth in this but in modern times this is too simplistic. Many of those who defend this point of view have real integrity and very real concerns about the alternatives. However, they also often have a religious world view that is woefully outdated and which almost forces them to take this stand.

Religious truth is usually stated in propositions and most branches of Christianity have statements of faith which contain an outline of what adherents believe and which are expected to be accepted by all who claim allegiance. The earliest document of faith and order in the church is the so called *Didache* or *The Teaching of the Twelve Apostles* which dates from the first century. The *Nicene Creed* which is widely used in Christian liturgy to this day arose from the Council of Nicea in AD 325. It is used as a profession of faith and its purpose is to act as a benchmark of orthodoxy in most branches of the Christian church. Some groups go much further. Those churches affiliated to the Evangelical Alliance, for example, are required to accept an eleven-point *Basis of Faith*. And this list is prefaced by the comment 'All our members agree that the statements below are true'.

But in many of these debates we confuse the word 'truth' with something which can best be expressed by the word 'factuality'.

'Truth' confused with 'factuality'

In his book *Speaking Christian*, Marcus Borg reminds us that one of the reasons why 'Christian language has become a problem for millions today is the modern church's embrace of literalism as the most faithful way for understanding its key terms and language'.

Much to the surprise of many people, this understanding of Christian language is recent, the product of the past few centuries. During the medieval period theologians came to distinguish four different 'senses' of scripture – literal, allegorical, anagogical and moral. By the 'literal' sense they meant the original meaning – which, confusingly, might itself include allegory, as in Paul's interpretation of the story of Sarah and Hagar in Galatians 4, or metaphor, as in Jesus' saying 'I am the good shepherd'. The 'allegorical' sense was the discovery of a Christian message within a passage whose original meaning did not seem to have anything to do with it: thus, for instance, Abraham's sending of his servant to find a bride for his son

(Genesis 24) could be read as an allegory of God sending the gospel to find a bride (i.e. the church) for his son (i.e. Jesus Christ). The 'anagogical' sense was a way of discovering in the text a picture of the future life: perhaps the best-known example of this would be the use of Psalms which speak of going up to Jerusalem as a way of referring to the Christian's destination in the heavenly city. ('Anagogical' means 'leading upwards', i.e. lifting up the mind and heart to contemplate the things above, as in Colossians 3.1-2.) The 'moral' sense was a way of discovering lessons on how to behave hidden within texts which were not straightforwardly teaching such a thing.

At the Reformation, the slogan *sola scriptura* (only scripture) was part of a protest against medieval corruption both in the Church and in interpretation of the Bible. The Reformers insisted that scripture contained all that was necessary for salvation. And they set scripture against the tradition of the church. They recovered the literal sense against the lush growth of the three other senses. But the word 'literal' did not mean for them what it means for us today. The 'literal' sense means the 'sense of the letter'; and if the 'letter' – the actual words used by the writers – is metaphorical, so be it. The 'literal' sense was the sense that the first writers intended. We need to note that to invoke 'the literal meaning of scripture' could only be valid if it meant, not 'literal' as opposed to metaphorical, but 'literal' as opposed to the other three senses. So Luther was not in the same camp as many of today's fundamentalists, despite what they may claim:

> The factual inerrancy of the Bible was first explicitly affirmed just over three centuries ago in the second half of the 1600s in a book of Protestant theology. The claim was a reaction to the Enlightenment, that period of Western cultural history that began not long before with the birth of modern science – with figures like Copernicus in the 1500s, Galileo in the early 1600s and Newton later in the century… The Enlightenment has

> decisively shaped contemporary thinking. For many in our time it has led to an identification of truth with factuality. The effects upon the understanding of language are far-reaching, because according to this view either statements are factually true or they aren't true at all (Borg, 2011:24-25).

The confusion of 'truth' with 'factuality' has profound implications:

> The impact of literalism on Christian language makes the Bible and Christianity incredible for many. It is a major reason why young people have little or no interest in Christianity. Though some are enthusiastic members of churches that proclaim biblical inerrancy and literalism, the majority find these ideas literally unbelievable. They cannot see how one particular religion is the only true religion or that its language must be interpreted literally and absolutely. But literalism is not only a problem that needs to be addressed for the sake of outsiders. It also very much affects insiders; for Christians, it narrows, reduces, flattens, and ultimately distorts the meanings of the Bible and Christianity (Borg, 2011:26).

The problem with the word 'truth' as with many other words which we use in religious discourse is that all are subject to the limitations of language.

Truth as 'language' or 'life'

To claim that propositional statements are 'true' is to give language a status that it cannot possibly have if only because all such statements mean different things to different people. Accepting 'the divine inspiration and supreme authority of the Old and New Testament Scriptures, which are the written Word of God' is a statement that is open to a multitude of interpretations. To claim that such propositional statements are our best attempt to put into words what we believe to be true is much nearer the mark. Wittgenstein, that great philosopher of language, rejected the idea that language has a direct connection to reality and argued that concepts do not need to be so clearly defined to be meaningful.

Wittgenstein argued that if you want to understand something, it is not enough to understand the meaning of words and the way they logically fit together. Rather, it is important to look at how those words are used. He speaks of language as a 'form of life' in which we play 'language games' which, like all games, operate by rules and structures. As a 'language game', religious language is understood in terms of the part that it plays in people's lives. It helps us to understand ourselves and relate to others who play the same game. It expresses attitudes and intuitions about the world and the place of humankind within it.

It follows that no doctrinal statements can contain absolute truth because of the necessary limitations of language itself. Such statements can point towards truth but a multitude of interpretations will necessarily get in the way of truth itself. Some interpretations will converge on similar understandings; others will diverge so much that they are barely recognisable as coming from the same source. That means that although there may be such a thing as absolute truth for us as individuals there can be no agreement with others because such agreement must be mediated by language. Truth as expressed through language must therefore necessarily be relative.

The same is true when truth is mediated through art, music or literature. We can agree that a painting conveys truth but not that it is true. We are quite content with the notion that the painting reveals a multitude of different truths about the world in a multitude of different ways to a multitude of different people. Such a notion does not detract from the value of the painting; it merely acknowledges the limitations of the artistic medium of paint. Indeed we value great pictures, music or literature precisely because they convey great truth enhanced by the rich diversity of responses to them. The 'buzz' that can be experienced in the crowded galleries of great exhibitions is testament to that fact.

We need to discard the notion that truth is some kind of impenetrable edifice and to agree with Ann Lewin that truth is more 'camp' than 'castle' as expressed in her poem from *Candles and Kingfishers* (Lewin, 1997).

Truth as 'camp' not 'castle'

The inhabitants of medieval fortresses tended to treat everyone who approached the gates as an enemy. For some people their understanding of the truth is just such a barrier in their relationships with other people. They are right and everyone else is wrong. They have closed minds.

But there is another understanding of truth which replaces the fortress by the camp. A camp generally provides no barrier to those who wish to enter or leave. All are free to come and go as they please. Strangers who approach the camp are given refreshment and rest. They share experiences of their journey and go away invigorated by this exchange with their hosts. And their hosts are enriched by what they have learnt from their guests. In a similar way, those who live their lives without barriers are enormously enriched by the contacts they make with others. Although they have their own beliefs and convictions, they are prepared to listen to others. They have open minds.

So, the claim that absolute truth can be conveyed by language is thoroughly unsound and the further claim that any particular statement can somehow encapsulate the essence of belief is equally unreasonable.

Belief as 'action' not 'words'

This would not be so serious if we had not accorded so much weight to creedal statements of faith. As it is, they have become a litmus test of faith and groups have become exclusive because of their unwillingness to embrace those who are unwilling to 'tick the boxes'. This problem is compounded by the fact that the original meaning of 'belief' was not the assent to a series of theoretical propositions but the commitment to a practical way of life.

In her book, *The Case for God,* the religious historian Karen Armstrong, reflects on this changed use of the word 'belief' within Christianity.:

> Belief no longer means 'trust, commitment and engagement' but has become an intellectual assent to a somewhat dubious proposition. Religious leaders often spend more time enforcing doctrinal conformity than devising spiritual exercises that will make these official 'beliefs' a living reality in the daily lives of the faithful. Instead of using scripture to help people to move forward and embrace new attitudes, people quote ancient scriptural texts to prevent any such progress (Armstrong, 2009:311-12).

She draws a parallel with Islam:

> The Qur'an has no interest in belief; indeed, this concept is quite alien to Islam. Theological speculation that results in the formation of abstruse doctrines is dismissed as *zannah,* self-indulgent guesswork about matters that nobody can prove one way or the other but which makes people quarrelsome and stupidly sectarian. Like any religion or *philosophia,* Islam is a way of life. The fundamental message of the Qur'an was not a doctrine but an ethical summons to practically expressed compassion: it is wrong to build a private fortune and good to share your wealth fairly and create a just society where poor and vulnerable people are treated with respect (Armstrong, 2009:101).

We may have serious reservations about some aspects of Islam, but its followers seem to have understood something fundamental about belief, namely that it is a way of life.

"Kill them all: God will know his own"

So, it is said, the monk Arnold Amaury, leader of the Albigensian Crusade, addressed his troops as they prepared to storm the town of Béziers, in South-West France, on the morning of 22nd July, 1209. The soldiers took their leader at his word and massacred everyone – men, women and children – and by the end of the day more than twenty thousand people were dead.

This crusade was launched by Pope Innocent III and was directed at the Cathars. They were an heretical group that was growing fast, particularly in the Languedoc region of Southern France. Among other things, the Cathars believed in dualism. Relying on the interpretation of particular biblical texts and on a trend present in Roman Catholicism itself, they believed that the material world in which beings were corruptible, mortal and imperfect, could not be the work of God, but only that of the Devil. The Old Testament demiurge God was considered by them as the Evil One, and only the New Testament was the work of the good God. In considering the material world as the work of the Devil, they were part of a tradition in philosophy that goes back to Plato and infiltrated Christianity at an early stage. I have already mentioned that an eminent teacher of mine once called it 'platonic drag', and it is still with us. Traces of it exist even within the Church of England, and are not unrelated to our present crises over the ordination and consecration of women, and the acceptance of gays and lesbians amongst us. Our 'hang-ups' over sexuality have some of their roots here.

The Cathars were not alone; they shared their beliefs with groups in other parts of Europe – Waldensians in Italy, Bogomils in Bulgaria etc. – who were likewise vigorously pursued by the Catholic Church. When eventually the Crusade ran out of steam, the Holy Inquisition took over the task and many thousands were burnt at the stake. You may have been to South-West France and visited many of the sites associated with the Cathars. To look at the castles perched on top of hilltops and to contemplate the sufferings of these people as they were hunted down and killed is a salutary reminder that Christian fanatics have a lot to answer for. The final stronghold of the Cathars was Montségur and as two hundred of their leaders were led to their deaths on a huge pyre at the foot of the mountain, so this movement was effectively wiped out.

Following terrorist outrages around the world we are very aware that there are fanatics in our midst. There are those within all religious traditions who continue to promote violence in the cause of their version of 'the truth'. Christians no longer burn other Christians but in some parts of the world they get very close. We need to reassure ourselves that we all have some glimpse of 'the truth'. At the same time, we need to remind ourselves that none of us has a monopoly of that truth.

Beauty

> Every bit of beauty in this world, the beauty of man, of nature, of a work of art, is a partial transfiguration of this world, a creative break-through to another,
> Nicolas Berdyaev *Christian Existentialism.*

God as Beauty

God as beauty perhaps seems strange. Yet we often associate the beauties of the natural world with the works of God. We stand in awe of mountains and valleys, rivers and trees, flowers and fields. They raise our spirits and seem to point to something above and beyond. We associate the beauties of man's creativity with the inspiration of God. We are deeply moved by music, art, poetry and literature all of which we describe as gifts from God. We wonder at the beauty of how mathematics, science and engineering are constructed and attribute that to God. We speak of the beauty of the human form. We even refer to the beauty of a well-shaped phrase or a finely tuned argument. And so it goes on... Yet, what exactly is beauty?

What is beauty?

In his book, *Art and the Beauty of God,* the former Bishop of Oxford, Richard Harries, tells the story of visiting one of his former parishioners in hospital:

> Her body was so wasted away she hardly made a bump under the bedclothes. She was nearly blind. After the initial greetings were over she suddenly said, "Tell me Father, what *is* beauty?" That this question was in the forefront of her mind as she approached death is remarkable. It was an important question for her. And it is an important question for us (Harries 1996:19).

There have been many attempts to define beauty but all have been somewhat inadequate because of the impossibility of describing beauty in mere words. Yet it is possible to say something in words about the character of beauty or the attributes of something which is beautiful. For Thomas Aquinas 'wholeness, harmony and radiance' were the defining characteristics of what is beautiful. Others wanted to extend the definition to include 'symmetry and measure'. It is easy to see how a painting can demonstrate these qualities:

> ...but every work of art has wholeness and harmony of one kind or another. Poetry makes use of metre, rhythm and rhyme; a novel has a beginning, a middle and an end and a host of subtle interconnections, parallels, echoes and contrasts in the text; and so on (Harries, 1996:22).

This view that there are certain defining characteristics of beauty is in sharp contrast to the one so widely held in the modern world that 'beauty is in the eye of the beholder'; that beauty is entirely a matter of personal taste and there is nothing independent about it. The very fact that we can discuss a work of art with those whose views are different from our own indicates that the judgement of what is beautiful has both objective and subjective elements. It is also true that these judgements are historically and culturally conditioned. What is beautiful for some at a particular time and in a particular place will not be for others in different circumstances. And sadly for some:

> ...the emphasis on wholeness, harmony and radiance will point to what is pretty rather than what is beautiful. However, beautiful works of art often include that which is disturbing and ugly, dark and disruptive. They can express violence, evoke sorrow and depict the sordid. There is a world of difference between superficial prettifying and genuine beauty.

> There is also radiance, though this needs to be interpreted more widely than physical light. It includes illumination of all kinds, intellectual, moral and spiritual. Works of art not only satisfy the senses, they bring insight and challenge (Harries, 1996:22).

The word beauty is used most obviously about aspects of the physical world but it is also used about the spiritual world. We can speak of the beauty of a landscape but we can also speak about the beauty of a person:

> Indeed it is the central thrust of Plato, Plotinus, Augustine and others that we should seek the higher beauty. We should move on from an appreciation of the beauty of the body to the beauty of the soul, from the beauty of the earth to the beauty of the intelligible world. All this is a prelude to discerning the source and standard of beauty, in beauty itself, as a Platonist would say, or in God as a Christian would put it (Harries, 1996:26).

Beauty as a real value

In the Preface to his book, *Beauty: A Very Short Introduction*, the philosopher Roger Scruton makes the point that 'beauty concerns matters of taste, and maybe taste has no rational foundation' Since it is in the nature of tastes to differ, there is no reason why one person's taste should be superior to another's. This relativism has led some people to dismiss judgements of beauty as purely 'subjective'. The implication is that beauty is not worthy of study particularly when it would appear to have no rational foundation. But Scruton argues that:

> ...such sceptical thoughts about beauty are unjustified. Beauty is a real and universal value, one anchored in our rational nature, and the sense of beauty has an indispensable

> part to play in shaping the human world'. (Scruton 2011: xi).

Scruton's claim that 'beauty is anchored in our rational nature' suggests that the judgement of beauty is not like other judgements. He expresses it in the form of a paradox:

> The judgement of beauty makes a claim about its object, and can be supported by reasons for its claim. But the reasons do not compel the judgement, and can be rejected without contradiction. So are they reasons or aren't they? (Scruton 2011:7).

The point is that although our judgements of beauty are entirely subjective, they are often supported by critical reasoning which focuses entirely on the character of the object. We can give reasons why we judge something to be beautiful. It may be that we like the brushwork in a Lucian Freud painting or the structure of a Beethoven quartet. But our judgement that these are beautiful is not subject to reason.

There is a tradition, according to Scruton, which has its origins in the work of Plato, that:

> ...beauty is an ultimate value that should be pursued for its own sake, and for the pursuit of which no further reason need be given. Beauty should therefore be compared to truth and goodness, one member of a trio of ultimate values which justify our rational inclinations. (But) to say as much is to overlook the subversive nature of beauty. Someone charmed by a myth may be tempted to believe it: and in this case beauty is the enemy of truth... A man attracted to a woman may be tempted to condone her vices: and in this case beauty is the enemy of goodness. Goodness and truth never compete, we assume, and the pursuit of the one is always compatible with the other. The pursuit of beauty, however, is far more questionable (Scruton 2011: 2-3).

The notion that 'beauty is an ultimate value' was absorbed into Christian theological thinking by Thomas Aquinas. He claims that:

> ...truth, beauty and goodness are transcendentals – features of reality possessed by all things, since they are aspects of being, ways in which the supreme gift of being is made manifest to the understanding (Scruton 2011: 2-3).

For Aquinas, these transcendentals were attributes of God. Scruton does not argue with this tradition but points out the difficulties and chooses to put these theological points to one side in what for him is a philosophical argument.

This is, however, an important argument in the context of this book. For, although, we might not want to say that that everything beautiful is of God, we might want to say that everything of God is beautiful. Therefore, despite the difficulties, we would wish to pursue further this close association between beauty and God. If we understand God as 'the ground of our being' or as 'Being itself', then beauty becomes an aspect of both being and Being. It is no coincidence then that Malcolm Muggeridge called his classical account of Mother Teresa's journey into compassion, *Something Beautiful for God* (Muggeridge 1971).

Our awareness of beauty

A more mystical approach is explored in John O'Donohue's book, *Divine Beauty,* where he seeks to 'awaken our awareness of beauty':

> In Greek, the word for 'the beautiful' is *to kalon.* It is related to the word *kalein* which includes the notion of 'call'. When we experience beauty, we feel called. The beautiful stirs passion and urgency in us and calls us forth... into the warmth and wonder of an eternal embrace. It unites us again with the

> neglected and forgotten grandeur of life (O'Donohue 2003: 23).

In a short review of the book, the *Sunday Times* critic writes, 'O'Donohue stops us in our tracks, reminding us that we might be alive for reasons other than productivity and consumption.'

O'Donohue calls to mind the beauty of the natural world in the poetic and evocative language that is so characteristic of the book. I make no apology for quoting extensively from it:

> The beauty of the Earth is the first beauty. Millions of years before us the earth lived in wild elegance. Landscape is the first-born of creation. Sculpted with huge patience over millennia, landscape has enormous diversity of shape, presence and memory. There is poignancy in beholding the beauty of landscape: often it feels as though it has been waiting for centuries for the recognition and witness of the human eye (O'Donohue 2003: 42).

He approaches the beauty of sound and music in a similar vein:

> Faced with the strangeness and silence of the earth, one of the most beautiful human creations has been music. The creation of exquisite music is one of the glories of the human imagination. Indeed, if we had done little else, music would remain our incredible gift to creation for there is no other sound on earth to compare with the beauty and depth of music. It has an eternal resonance... In contrast to most other forms of art, music alters your experience of time (O'Donohue 2003:70).

Sir Thomas Beecham memorably said of Frederick Delius that 'he had an extraordinary kinship with nature and an extraordinary sense of the beauty of sound'.

O'Donohue contrasts the faculties of intellect and imagination in their approach to beauty:

> The mind tends to see things in a singularly simple, divided way: there is good and bad, ugly and beautiful. The imagination, in contrast, extends a greater hospitality to whatever is awkward, paradoxical or contradictory... It has patience with contradiction because there it glimpses new possibilities. And the imagination is the great friend of possibility... In a sense, this is what beauty is: possibility that enlarges and delights the heart (O'Donohue 2003: 148).

The divine imagination

In the Western world we have become obsessed with those attributes of God that we think we can 'pin down'. We speak of the 'divine intellect' in ways that suggest that we know the mind of God. We speak of what we think is the 'divine will' with astonishing arrogance. We even presume to know how God feels about things! Yet the breathtaking examples of diversity in the world suggest something which we have completely ignored – the 'divine imagination'. And the divine imagination is not something that can be 'pinned down'.

The divine imagination opens up a completely new perspective for it is the source of the creativity of God in all its richness and diversity:

> Everything that is – every tree, bird, star, stone and wave – existed first as a dream in the mind of the divine artist. Indeed the world is the mirror of the divine imagination and to decipher the depths of the world is to gain deep insights into the heart of God. The traces of the divine imagination are everywhere... The divine imagination has infused the things of the world with secret depths... The more we give ourselves to experience and strive for expression, the deeper it opens before us (O'Donohue 2003:151).

In divine terms, at the deepest level creativity is:

> ...holiness. To create is to further the dream and desire of the creator. When the world was created, it was not a one-off, finished event. Creation is a huge beginning, not a finished end. Made in the image of the divine imagination, human creativity helps to add to creation. The unfinished is an invitation to our imagination. This is what happens in experience: the unfinished reaches towards us in order to come to form and expression. Expression is also how we develop and grow. The human self is not a finished thing, it is constantly unfolding. Experience is then essentially creative. Everything we feel, think and do... expresses and unfolds the dream of God (O'Donohue 2003: 152).

In human terms, imagination:

> ...offers wholesomeness: heart and head, feeling and thought come into balance. To follow the mind alone inevitably leads to an isolated and lonesome life. When we follow the heart alone, it can lead to sentimentality and the marshlands of blurred emotion. An awakened imagination brings the warmth and tenderness of affection into the life of thought; and it brings clarity and light of thought to the flow of feelings. This is how a great piece of literature claims us. We enter into the life of a character. Our empathy and our minds are engaged by the depth and complexity of the character's heart and by the quest of his mind for vision and meaning (O'Donohue 2003:156).

Sadly, the human imagination is neglected in the hustle and bustle of our daily lives and is much neglected in our churches. So much of our discourse is narrow or shallow. So much of our conversation lacks breadth and depth. We have limited vision because we are tethered to that which we can 'pin down'. We are wary of approaching things at a different or unfamiliar angle. Yet if developing our imagination is one of the ways in which we become more human, it is something that needs our attention for in becoming more human we come closer to God.

The beauty of God

'God is Beauty' is the title of the last chapter of O'Donohue's book:

> To participate in beauty is to come into the presence of the Holy… Whenever we awaken beauty we are helping to make God present in the world. The beauty of God is reachable for everyone and can be awakened in all dimensions of our experience… The two longings deepest in your heart – the longing to love and to be loved – are not merely psychological needs; at a more profound level, they are the stirring of God within you. Your capacity to care is God; it is your beauty… Our love for our friends and family, our concern for the world and for the earth, our compassion for the pain and desperation of others are not simply the product of an 'unselfish gene' within us, they issue from that strain of God in us that prizes above everything the kindness, the compassion and the beauty that love brings. Anywhere: in prayer, family, front line, hospital, brothel or prison, anywhere care comes alive, God is present (O'Donohue 2003: 235).

In a collection of letters and essays entitled *Waiting on God,* Simone Weil writes that:

> '…the beauty of the world is almost absent from the Christian tradition' yet 'a sense of beauty, although mutilated, distorted and soiled, remains rooted in the heart of man as a powerful incentive. It is present in all the preoccupations of secular life.

> If it were made true and pure it would sweep all secular life in a body to the feet of God, it would make the total incarnation of the faith possible' (Weil 1959: 116,118).

In his biography of Simone Weil, David Anderson writes:

> As we contemplate this beauty, this order of the world, we are led into a state of self-renunciation. We no longer see ourselves as the centre of the world, we give up our 'false divinity', we renounce our ambition to 'command', we abandon the illusion that we can create our own reality. In short we become detached from our 'personality', our selfish ego, and that is the meaning of love' (Anderson 1971: 67).

In his book, *Art and the Beauty of God,* Richard Harries draws on the thoughts of the poet Wilfred Owen and agrees with him that the concept of beauty has been neglected in the Christian tradition. He writes:

> People have found the Christian faith too narrow in its sympathies, inimical to the feelings and stifling to the imagination. In short, it has seemed to afford them no aesthetic philosophy. By this Owen meant no place for beauty, whether in the arts or in nature. This is a disaster. For without an affirmation of beauty there can in the end be no faith and no God worth our love (Harries, 1996:1).

Yet it is clear that in the world at large there is an increasing awareness and experience of the spiritual dimension of the arts. It follows for Harries that:

> If a religious perspective on life is to carry conviction it has to account for the powerful spiritual impact which the arts, in all forms, have on people. Christianity needs to have a proper

place both for the arts and for beauty (Harries, 1996:2).

We know beauty

In his article, *Grace and Radiance,* in *The Tablet* of November 2012, Daniel O'Leary recalls a pastoral visit to a hospital ward.

> Across the ward, a man is struggling. His body is writhing on the chair near the bed. His right leg, arthritic and misshapen, is kicking against the cubicle curtain. Sweat edges down the furrows of his grim face. I want to help him but I myself am anxiously recuperating. Taut and strained with the intense effort, he makes one last concentrated twist. And before a passing nurse can assist him, he utters a hoarse growl of triumph. The battle is over. Calm now, he proudly begins the long and complicated manoeuvre of buttoning up his cardigan – the cardigan that Dan had just managed to put on.
>
> Why do I still remember Dan's small victory when I have already forgotten the world records of the recent Olympic champions? It has to do, I think, with a certain simplicity, a concentration, a determination on Dan's part. It was neither contrived nor attention-seeking. It was utterly honest; it was total and it was real. It was, I now believe, beautiful (O'Leary, 2012).

Mystery

> We have lost the mystical sense, and what is religion without mysticism?
> Henri Frédéric Amiel, *Amiel's Journal*

Taking us 'beyond ourselves'

We turn now from themes which concern the character of the human person to themes which take us beyond ourselves. Mystery, Creativity, Imagination and Freedom remind us that our humanity is not entirely contained within tangible human experience but extends to those things which are much less easy to describe.

'The Mysteries'

Some time ago I went to see a performance of *The Mysteries*. This was a London West End production that made an unusual impact. It is a story in the manner of the Medieval English mystery plays – the Chester cycle in particular. It is told in four languages of South Africa but its greatest impact lies elsewhere. It is not in the words but in the music, the drama and the dance. It is full of images, of symbolism. It stretches the imagination. It confronts the mystery. It is a story in which the bare bones of biblical narratives become something quite different. Watching it, we become less concerned with what actually happened than with what it all might actually mean. And towards the end, we are confronted with the greatest mystery of them all – the Resurrection.

Myth and mythology

The Concise Oxford English Dictionary describes myth as, 'A traditional narrative usually involving supernatural or imaginary persons and often embodying popular ideas on natural or social phenomena'. It also describes a myth as, 'A widely held but false notion'; the former definition represents the original meaning of myth; the latter definition reflects its corruption in common usage. Some clarification is, therefore, necessary.

In her book, *A Short History of Myth,* part of *The Myths* series published by Canongate, Karen Armstrong describes mythology as 'designed to help us cope with the problematic human predicament. It helped people find their place in the world and their true orientation'. She goes on to show that from earliest times men and women have created myths about their forefathers 'that are not historical but help to explain current attitudes about our environment, neighbours and customs'. In the same way, 'we want to know where we are going, so we have devised stories that speak of a posthumous existence'. Furthermore, 'we want to explain those sublime moments, when we seem to be transported beyond our ordinary concerns.' So, the language of myth helps us to make sense of the past, present and future (Armstrong, 2005: 6).

In common usage, however, the word 'myth' is used to describe something that is not true. Public figures caught up in scandal will say that the accusations against them are a 'myth' and that nothing actually happened. 'When we hear of seas miraculously parting to let a favoured people escape from their enemies, we dismiss these stories as incredible and demonstrably untrue'. Since the Enlightenment, 'we have developed a scientific view of history; we are concerned above all with what actually happened'. But that is relatively recent. 'In the premodern world, when people wrote about the past they were more concerned with what an event had meant'. Mythology is then 'an art form that points beyond history to what is timeless in human existence, helping us to get beyond the chaotic flux of random events, and glimpse the core of reality' (Armstrong 2005: 7).

Mythos and Logos

In an article in *The Times,* entitled *Summer Solstice,* the author Jeanette Winterson discusses the place of myth in the modern world. She claims that 'our ancestors were more comfortable than we are with metaphor and poetic truth'. She goes on:

> The spectacular success of the Age of Enlightenment and all that has followed, has consigned *mythos* – poetic truth, to the dust and ashes at the back of the hearth, as the very poor relation of *logos* – rational truth (Winterson, 2006a).

She argues that 'we need the poetry and the myth back in our everyday lives, and art can provide that'. She illustrates her point with Shakespeare's *Midsummer Night's Dream,* together with Tippet's opera *The Midsummer Marriage* and Britten's version of *A Midsummer Night's Dream,* both of which focus on the mysterious drama of a solstice marriage:

> Shakespeare… was onto something with his crazy tale of love-potions and sprites, mistaken identities and talking walls, donkey-headed sex objects, and amorous fairies. Rational, it is not, marvellous, it is, and by taking us right outside the world of the known into the unquantifiable world of the unknown, Shakespeare can ask difficult questions about the nature of attraction, and remind us that whatever we do, maverick and wayward forces play more of a part in our choices than we like to think (Winterson, 2006a).

In her contribution to *The Myths* series, Jeanette Winterson expands our imagination by retelling the story of Atlas and Heracles in a book she calls *Weight.* In the introduction she writes:

> *Weight* moves far away from the simple story of Atlas's

> punishment and his temporary relief when Heracles takes the world off his shoulders. I wanted to explore loneliness, isolation, responsibility, burden and freedom too, because my version has a very particular end not found elsewhere. Of course I wrote it out of my own situation. There is no other way (Winterson, 2006b: xviii).

She sums up her approach to the stories in the series. 'The Myth series is a marvellous way of telling stories – re-telling stories for their own sakes, and finding in them permanent truths about human nature'. She goes on:

> All we can do is keep telling the stories, hoping that someone will hear. Hoping that in the noisy echoing nightmare of endlessly breaking news and celebrity gossip, other voices might be heard, speaking of the life of the mind and the soul's journey (Winterson, 2006b: xx).

Karen Armstrong is equally persuasive:

> Our modern alienation from myth is unprecedented. In the pre-modern world, mythology was indispensable. It not only helped people make sense of their lives but also revealed regions of the human mind that would otherwise have remained inaccessible. It was an early form of psychology... When Freud and Jung began to chart the modern quest for the soul, they instinctively turned to classical mythology to explain their insights, and gave the old myths new interpretation (Armstrong, 2005:10).

This reference to Freud and Jung reminds us that the human sciences of psychology, sociology and anthropology have a real contribution to make to our understanding of the human condition and our religious sentiment. Unfortunately, there is a feeling amongst many psychologists that, because religious faith cannot easily be approached with the traditional tools of scientific enquiry, it is not worthy of study. Equally, there is a feeling amongst many religious people that, because they believe spiritual forces act independently of other psychic forces, they are not accessible to these disciplines. Both positions are untenable.

Myth and Mystery

In our modern alienation from myth we have lost the ability to embrace mystery. In our preoccupation with the rational we have become obsessed with certitude. We are uncomfortable with the unknown and with the ambiguous. We feel insecure when confronted with language which cannot be reduced to the unequivocal. We feel vulnerable. We are fearful. But that need not be so. Uncertainty is not something to be feared but something to be recognised as an integral part of our spirituality. True spirituality is something that is dynamic and which evolves. It is not something that is static and unchanging.

Part of the difficulty lies in the notion that somehow what we believe rather than how we live is the ultimate test of our faith. Originally, the word 'belief' was associated with commitment and practical living not with the assent to a series of abstract theological propositions. And if faith is about life then it is bound to involve uncertainty for that is the nature of the journey. We cannot know what life has to offer and we cannot prepare ourselves for that life with an inflexible template. Our modern use of the word 'belief' is thoroughly unsatisfactory. In the book, *Living the Questions,* Marcus Borg is quoted as follows:

> When you think about it, faith as belief is relatively impotent… You can believe all the right things and still be miserable, or still be in bondage, still be untransformed. So the emphasis upon belief is, I think, modern and mistaken. It's

> also very divisive – once people start thinking that being a Christian is about believing the right things, then anybody's list of what the right things are to believe becomes a kind of litmus test as to who's really a good Christian and who's not (Felton & Procter-Murphy, 2012:221).

The creeds and other professions of faith provide an important framework but have become a straightjacket. And that straightjacket is alienating many who simply cannot assent to bold statements of this kind. The solution is not to continue to insist that the creeds must be taken at face value or to discard them in favour of something else. The answer is to see the creeds in a different way. They provide a gateway to the divine which despite the limitations of the written and spoken word provide a powerful focus. In the same way as art, music and literature are open to a multitude of interpretations, so those who are open to the mystery of the faith will offer a multitude of interpretations of the divine through the creeds. Gordon Kaufman, the American theologian has said:

> We may find a certain security in believing that 'our' way is the only way. This is a natural part of any cultic religious experience. Far greater faith is required, however, to seek and trust that which you accept as infinite, beyond your comprehension, and subject to change. Today, this just may be the challenge of an educated and thinking Christian – to retain a faith in the face of mystery (Felton & Procter-Murphy, 2012:220).

Rudolph Otto is just one in a long line of those who have attempted to describe the indescribable. In his book, *The Idea of the Holy,* he used the word 'numinous' to describe the awe inspiring 'other'. But this attempt to offer a vocabulary that suggests something just beyond that which we can grasp or describe has limited value. It suggests that such things can be grasped intellectually. Ultimately, of course, they can only be experienced (Otto, 1968).

The Mystics

Dag Hammarskjöld was United Nations Secretary General from 1953 to 1961. He was universally known and admired in his lifetime for his unstinting work for peace. But it was only after his death in 1961 that it became clear that he had an equally active inner life. His journal was discovered and published in 1964 as *Markings*. It has been an inspiration to many ever since. Hammarskjöld was a modern mystic.

In his Foreword to *Markings,* W H Auden writes:

> 'Markings was not intended to be read simply as a work of literature. It is also... an account of the attempt by a professional man of action to unite in one life the *via activa* and the *via comtemplativa.* Most of the famous mystics were members of one contemplative order or another... but they did not think of taking part in the affairs of this world as their function' but for Hammarskjöld, 'the road to holiness necessarily passes through the world of action' (Hammarskjold, 2006: xx-xxi).

Christianity claims a number of giants of mysticism whose works continue to inspire – Hildegard of Bingen, Julian of Norwich, Thomas Merton and Evelyn Underhill, to name just a few. All these mystics have attempted to experience the divine as directly as possible and have seen no need for mediation from priests or other interpreters. They have sought freedom from dependency on authoritarian religious experience. They have therefore been a challenge to the church which has too often seen them as a threat.

In her book, *Mysticism,* originally published in 1911, Evelyn Underhill gives a detailed account of the history of mysticism and of the personalities of those whom we call mystics. She shows that 'the great periods of mystical activity tend to correspond with the great periods of artistic, material and intellectual civilisation'. She goes on:

> As a rule they come immediately after, and seem to complete such periods: those outbursts of vitality in which man makes fresh conquests over his universe apparently producing, as their last stage, a type of heroic character which extends these victories to the spiritual sphere. When science, politics, literature, and the arts have risen to their height and produced their greatest works, the mystic comes to the front; snatches the torch, and carries it on (Underhill, 2009).

Underhill identifies 'three great waves of mystical activity'. They correspond to the close of the Classical, the Mediaeval, and the Renaissance periods: reaching their highest points in the third, fourteenth and seventeenth centuries. Although the fourteenth century was perhaps the highest peak in the development of mysticism, there have been significant developments in our own time. At the beginning of the twentieth century there was a revival of interest in mysticism with the work of W R Inge, Baron von Hugel and Evelyn Underhill herself.

Underhill claims that the mystics not only carry the torch on but that only the mystic can complete our knowledge of ultimate truth:

> Of all those forms of life and thought with which humanity has fed its craving for truth, mysticism alone postulates, and in the persons of its great initiates proves, not only the existence of the Absolute, but also this link: this possibility of knowing, finally of attaining it. It denies that possible knowledge is to be limited (a) to sense impressions, (b) to any process of intellection, (c) to the unfolding of the content of

> normal consciousness. Such diagrams of experience, it says, are hopelessly incomplete. The mystics find the basis of their method not in logic but in life… (Underhill, 2009).

In the commentary to *Living the Question: Embracing Mystery*, the authors write:

> Embracing mystery involves unlearning that which has come to be conventional wisdom. It entails honouring that which can be sensed but not described, felt but not quantified. That said, there can be no doubt that there are indeed mystics among us. When we embrace mystery, strive to emulate Jesus' deep experience of the Divine, and live at peace with the unknowable, we may be among them (Felton & Procter-Murphy, 2012:224).

A universal spirituality

Mystics can be found in every faith tradition. In his book, *The Mystic Heart*, Wayne Teasdale argues that mysticism is the source of all religious sentiment:

> For thousands of years before the dawn of the world religions as social organisations working their way through history, the mystical life thrived. This mystical tradition, which underpins all genuine faith, is the living source of religion itself. It is the attempt to possess the inner reality of the spiritual life, with its mystical, or direct, access to the divine. Each great religion has similar origin: the spiritual awakening of its founders to God, the divine, the absolute, the spirit, Tao, boundless awareness (Teasdale, 2001: 10).

Moreover, he argues that this spirituality has the power to transform our common life:

> Spirituality serves as our greatest single resource for changing our centuries-old tradition of violence and division. Spirituality is profoundly transformative when it inspires in us the attitude of surrender to the mystery in which 'we live, and move, and have our being' …We need to understand, to really grasp at an elemental level, that the definitive revolution is the spiritual awakening of humankind (Teasdale, 2001: 12).

Teasdale then goes on to outline the need for an 'interspirituality' that will overcome barriers between faiths and that will pave the way for a universal mysticism. He sees the emergence of an 'interspiritual age' in which there will be a 'dawn of a new consciousness and a radically fresh approach to our life as a human family in a fragile world'.

He sees encouraging signs of a mutual appreciation of spirituality amongst those of faith but recognises that there is still a very long way to go. There is still an inadequate appreciation of the pivotal role of spirituality amongst those who claim allegiance to particular religious traditions. There is still widespread suspicion, prejudice and ignorance of 'other' faith traditions. There are still those who claim an exclusive 'hotline' to God.

There is also a sense in which institutional religion has overwhelmed individual spirituality. There is little time or space within traditional liturgical practices for silence and for contemplation:

> Most Christian churches barely mention the mystical life, keeping the focus of prayer on the level of worship and devotion. The same is true in much of the Jewish and Islamic traditions… The religious life of the faithful is decided on the corporate, devotional level, while the contemplative and mystical are neglected (Teasdale, 2001: 11).

'Thin' places

Celtic spirituality is a form of Christian devotion which has been practised in Ireland and Scotland since the fifth century A.D. In recent years, there has been a revival of interest in Celtic spirituality, partly because of the popularity of Celtic religious art, and partly because of the wide influence of the Iona Community, a Christian community on the Scottish island of Iona. The phrase 'thin places' comes from this spirituality and refers to places where the boundary between the sacred and the secular, is especially thin.

While our culture tends to compartmentalise the sacred and secular, describing some special places and times as holy and others as quite different, the divine has a way of sneaking into our consciousness at the most unexpected times and of narrowing the gap between the two. A thin place is where the veil that separates the sacred from the secular is so thin that one is able to catch a glimpse of the mystery beyond. A thin place is where we experience the distance between us and the divine evaporating.

Most people have had experience of these thin places. In many spiritualities, the simplest of life's necessities are lifted up and permeated with something 'more'. For Christians, the common elements of bread and wine become the sacraments or means of grace in the Eucharist. We are all aware of how profoundly the spirit can work even in the most mundane of circumstances.

Some groups have embraced the world and imbued it with mystery in a way that is special. Quakers and Franciscans are just two examples of world views that see all life as sacred. For Quakers, this arises from a belief that there is an 'inner light' of the divine in all of us. For Franciscans, it arises from the commitment to the living of life as a sacrament. Both reject the division between sacred and secular.

Embracing mystery

At the beginning of a chapter entitled *The Promised Land of the Spiritual Journey,* Teasdale quotes the eminent scientist Albert Einstein:

> The most beautiful and profound emotion we can experience is the sensation of the mystical. It is the sower of all true science. He (or she) to whom this emotion is a stranger, who can no longer wonder and stand rapt in awe, is as good as dead (Teasdale, 2001:211).

This is a remarkable statement because it comes from arguably the greatest scientist of the twentieth century. Even in science, the most rational of enterprises, mystery has its place. In recent years, images from the Hubble Space Telescope have changed the way scientists see the universe and 'mystery' is no longer a 'dirty word'.

But there are those within the scientific community who would define their enterprise in much narrower terms. There are also, of course those within the religious community who take an equally narrow view. If we insist with the fundamentalists of science that only rational approaches to the world have any integrity, or if we insist with the fundamentalists of religion that only revelation has credibility then we have abandoned our humanity. In both cases we impose a straightjacket on our understanding in the face of all our experience that the human enterprise is much richer than any single narrow approach can adequately reflect. The essential point is that we must not shackle ourselves to anything that narrows our vision but allow ourselves to be free to explore whatever seems to point in the direction of whatever we hold to be the things of real value. Otherwise things may simply pass us by.

For those with religious inclinations, that centre of value will be expressed in terms of something 'other', what Rudolf Otto called, in his book, *The Idea of the Holy*, the 'numinous' or 'a non-rational, non-sensory experience or feeling whose primary and immediate object is outside the self'. For Christians that 'other' will be God, whether God be understood as 'the supreme being' or 'the ground of all being'. God did not create us to be bound but to be free. Only that which supports that freedom is worthy of the human condition (Otto, 1968).

'Bible black'

When Dylan Thomas's play *Under Milk Wood* was first performed in 1954, it caused quite a stir. It was controversial because of some of the material it contained but it also caught the public imagination because of its powerful use of metaphor. Those who know the piece will recall the image of the 'fishing boat-bobbing sea'. They will also recall the images of the starless 'Bible-black' night and its association with childhood images of the family Bible – not only black, but great, heavy, oppressive and awesome. Black is one of the most frequently used metaphors in the play and produces a dazzling range of images of night. In his use of metaphor, Dylan Thomas wanted to engage the imagination, and that is exactly what he achieved.

But it is not the metaphor of the Bible itself but the metaphors contained within the Bible that are most engaging. For the Bible is full of metaphors and the powerful use of metaphor by the various authors of the Bible act as a foil to those who would claim that the Bible is only to be understood literally. Yet when we speak of metaphor in this context we immediately come under suspicion. For surely a metaphor is simply an embellishment, a rhetorical flourish, a linguistic device or a way of pulling the wool over the eyes of the reader or listener we seek to impress. The dismissive phrase 'a mere metaphor' is indicative of this attitude. Argument rages over whether particular metaphors are simply ornaments to existing thoughts and words or are actually creative and part of what those words are trying to say. Dylan

Thomas's metaphors were much more than mere embellishment. And the metaphors in the Bible are very far from being just ornamental. The parables contain some of the finest examples of metaphor around, and by way of illustration we can explore aspects of two parables in the gospel according to Mark that might otherwise escape our notice.

Consider two of the Parables of the Kingdom – the parable of The Mustard Seed, and the parable of The Seed Growing Secretly (Mark 4: 30-32, Mark 4: 26-29). In each of these parables there is a crossover between the realistic world of first-century Palestine to the metaphoric world of the Kingdom of God. In the one parable, the Kingdom is like neither the pinhead-sized mustard seed nor the great tree which grows from it, but like the mysterious way in which the one grows from the other. In the other parable, the routine ordinariness of the life of the farmer who would sleep and rise night and day is contrasted with the mysterious secret work going on meanwhile under the soil. Work which transforms the seed planted months ago into a rich field of corn. In both parables there is a contrast between the familiar, that which is part of everyday life, and the mystery underlying it. The metaphoric mode of the parable suggests that as we go about our daily lives miraculous things are happening 'in the fields' all around us. Things on which our prosperity; indeed our very survival depends. This is a very powerful thought.

But beneath the surface of these parables there is not just mystery but movement. The Kingdom not only works mysteriously but dynamically. There is nothing static about the Kingdom of God. There is a dynamic at work beneath the surface which moves situations and people forward. If the seed becomes a tree, or the bare field becomes a harvest, something is making that happen. This metaphoric mode suggests that as we go about the routine of our daily lives things should be moving and changing around us and within us. It is often said that we cannot stand still, we can only go forwards or backwards. That too is a very powerful thought.

So mystery and movement are themes that form part of a broader and deeper understanding of these parables. The metaphors of these parables enable us to go beyond the mere words by engaging our imagination. And what is true of the parables is true of the Bible as a whole. Yet we become so concerned with what has actually happened that we too easily miss these underlying currents. Imagination is one of the most important tools that we can use in our approach to the Bible as we shall see in a later chapter.

Creativity

Creativity requires the courage to let go of certainties.
Eric Fromm

The awesome project of creation.

From the creation stories in Genesis to the apocalyptic writings in Revelation we see glimpses of the creative power of the one we call God; mountains and rivers, grassland and forest, plants and animals. And at the pinnacle of that creation are men and women just like us. 'And God saw everything that he had made, and, indeed, it was very good' (Genesis 1:31).

In reading these biblical passages we sometimes get bogged down with detail and miss the larger picture. Both Genesis and Revelation passages are particular genres of biblical writing. They are not intended to convey historical detail but to paint pictures. They have as much to say to our imagination as to our intellect. Words on their own are simply not enough to convey the wonder of creation. Only by stimulating our imagination can we begin, and then only begin, to comprehend what it is all about.

And if we look at the biblical message as a whole, we realise that the creative process is not something that God keeps to himself. It is something that he wants to share with us. Woven into the biblical narrative is the human vocation to be God's agents; to bring order out of chaos and to bring joy to the natural world and to each other. But in order to do this we must engage with the world and with each other. And only the right kind of engagement will do – the creative kind. That is, love.

Our treatment of the natural world is the subject of much debate at the present time and climate change is now at the top of the international agenda. Reports from the International Panel on Climate Change have made even the American government sit up and listen. As a leading article in *New Scientist* puts it:

> Three hundred government-appointed delegates from 113 countries were last week unanimous in agreeing what most climate scientists have believed for years: that the world is warming fast and that humans are almost certainly to blame (Pearce, 2007).

But not only governments have been accused of inaction. In a television programme called 'God is Green' the presenter asks the question, 'Why do the world's major religions have little to say on climate change?' It is a good question!

And then there is the sea. The American travel writer Paul Theroux expressed bewilderment at English people, in cars or on beaches, sitting looking at the sea. 'Why the puzzle?', Tom Wright, Bishop of Durham asks:

> Like a Wagner opera, operating at levels of symbol and drama which touch the nerves other communications cannot reach, the sea reminds us of forces within and around us that have the potential both for horrible destruction and for spectacular beauty. The sea offers its own daily liturgy of chaos and creation, judgment and salvation; like all good liturgy, it draws us into its rhythm (Wright, 2012:171).

And the Bible insists, of course, that the sea is also God's creation. It is not an alien force or a rival deity. But it is hugely symbolic for the people of Jesus' time and for us. It is symbolic of all the dark forces that operate in the world and in our lives. And onto this sea Jesus embarks with his disciples and their small boat. And that, itself, is hugely symbolic. Tom Wright again:

> Jesus asleep as the sea rages around him: why (so far as I can discover) has no great artist painted that scene? It combines Jesus' serenity in the face of threatening chaos, his sharing the lot of those engulfed by it, and God's rainbow promise that the

> mighty waters shall not have the last word (Wright, 2012:50).

So what do we make of our part in this mighty work of creation? For a former colleague of mine, and a noted theologian, the creative instinct in men and women is the essential element in their Christian identity. Towards the end of his life, and at the end of his yet unpublished autobiography, he wrote 'one last thought' and I quote:

> We are most truly ourselves when we are least aware of ourselves in an act of creating. Time and space disappear and we are caught up for a moment into eternity (Wallace-Hadrill, 1990).

The concept of creativity

Most ancient cultures lacked the concept of creativity, seeing art as a form of discovery and not creation. The notion of creativity probably originated in Western culture through Christianity and the biblical story of creation given in Genesis. In the Judaeo-Christian tradition, creativity was the sole province of God. Humans were not considered to have the ability to create something new except as an expression of God's work. It was during the Renaissance that creativity was first seen, not as a conduit for the divine, but from the abilities of 'great men'. But Renaissance creativity was not universally at odds with religion. The shift was gradual and would not become immediately apparent until the Enlightenment.

In his book, *Being Human*, John De Gruchy explains that:

> ...at one level Renaissance humanism was a recovery of classical paganism, but it was also a critique of bad religion in the interests of a better one, one that valued rather than repressed human dignity, beauty and potentiality. Much of the creative energy and output of the Renaissance painters

> and sculptors, many of them priests and monks, was dedicated to 'the glory of God' and for the purpose of representing the gospel story in the precincts of monastery and church, and sometimes the market square (de Gruchy, 2006: 194).

As a direct and independent topic of study, creativity received little attention until the nineteenth century with the increased interest in individual differences inspired by the arrival of Darwinism. In 1927, Alfred North Whitehead gave the Gifford Lectures at the University of Edinburgh. He is credited with having coined the term 'creativity' to serve as the ultimate category of his metaphysical scheme.

As creativity became more closely associated with man rather than God, there were many who regarded creativity in man as impious or even demonic. This was because such creativity seemed to usurp what God reserved for himself. John de Gruchy writes:

> I have searched, largely in vain, in the Bible for references to what might be regarded as the gift or *charisma* of creativity; I have also looked in many classic texts on Christian spirituality with the same result... Traditionally the Church has frowned on creativity, for it suggests going beyond the boundaries of the orthodox and acceptable, trying to emulate God, the one and only creator of all that exists. What is esteemed is faithfulness, not creativity. The danger of creativity is that of hubris or human pride, the glorification of humanity at the expense of the creator (de Gruchy, 2006: 194).

Yet, what if, as Irenaeus put it:

> '...the glory of God is humanity fulfilled', and what if 'being made in the image of God', who is creator, means that God

intends us to be co-creators in making this world more humane and beautiful? What if honourable human creativity is a way of honouring God who enables us to be creative? What if creativity is not something to be frowned on, but something to be encouraged as a gift of the Spirit? What if creativity has to do with… a recovery of childlike innocence... in which we find 'the world beautiful, magical, wild beyond dreams, dancing its complex patterns of truth, weaving its multi-coloured threads of discourse so that all things can be true and we can once more be ravished by the beauty of God?' (de Gruchy, 2006: 195).

The creative process

Creativity is a crucial aspect of the human condition but its understanding remains elusive to psychologists. There are a number of schools of thought but each holds a sharply different view on the nature of the human condition which reflects in very different explanations of creativity, its nature, source and purpose. For some it is a negative thing; for others it is overwhelmingly positive.

Freud saw the whole creative process as pathological and described a similarity between neurosis and creativity. He felt that both arose from biological drives and from wish fulfilment. Jung is much more positive. In *The Development of Personality*, with reference to those theories which associate creativity with neurosis, he writes:

> …the wholeness and healthiness of the creative function is seen in the murky light of neurosis. In this way creativity becomes indistinguishable from morbidity, and the creative individual immediately suspects himself of some kind of illness… Disease has never yet fostered creative work; on the contrary, it is the most formidable obstacle to creation (Jung, 1964:115).

However, it is Abraham Malsow who is perhaps the most thorough in his positive examination of this theme. In *Towards a Psychology of Being* he explains that he is less concerned with the 'special talent of the genius type' than with 'the more widespread creativeness which is the universal heritage of every human being'. For him, 'it was obvious that some of the greatest talents of mankind were certainly not psychologically healthy people'. On the other hand, this more widespread creativeness 'seems to co-vary with psychological health' and correlated well with other aspects of the self-actualising individual. He therefore drew the distinction between 'special talent creativeness' and 'self-actualizing creativeness' (Maslow, 1999).

This latter from of creativeness 'sprang much more directly form the personality', and 'showed itself widely in the ordinary affairs of life'. It looked like a 'tendency to do *anything* creatively'. Associated with it was a 'special kind of perceptiveness that is exemplified by the child in the fable who saw that the king had no clothes on'. This kind of creativeness was like the creativeness 'of *all* happy and secure children'. 'It was spontaneous, effortless, innocent, easy, a kind of freedom from stereotypes and clichés'. He goes on:

> Almost any child can perceive more freely, without a priori expectations about what ought to be there, what must be there, or what has always been there. Almost any child can compose a song or a poem or a dance or a painting or a play or a game on the spur of the moment, without planning or previous intent (Maslow, 1999:151-159).

In *The Farther Reaches of Human Nature,* Maslow discusses in more detail the principle characteristics of creativity. It is a long list and it is only possible to convey something of its flavour in a short paragraph. Creativity is an activity that identifies with the present, and not with the past or the future. It is spontaneous, innocent and devoid of expectations. It is free of the influence of other people. It involves a loss of fear, inhibitions and self-centredness. It involves a gain in strength, courage and independence. It is positive in outlook. It integrates. Research shows there to be a close correlation between these characteristics of the creative person and, what Maslow describes as, the person 'in good psychological health' (Maslow, 1993:59-68).

For Rollo May, in *The Courage to Create,* those who present most directly and immediately the characteristics of the creative person are the artists – the dramatists, the musicians, the painters etc. This is not surprising because he is familiar with the world of the artist and is something of an artist himself. At the same time, he recognises that the creative process represents 'the highest degree of emotional health, as the expression of the normal people in the act of actualizing themselves'. He goes on:

> Creativity must be seen in the work of the scientist as well as in that of the artist, in the thinker as well as in the aesthetician; and one must not rule out the extent to which it is present in captains of modern technology as well as in a mother's normal relationship with her child (May, 1994:22).

But creativity does not just happen; it requires courage, or the capacity to move ahead despite the difficulties. For May, 'courage is not a virtue or value among other personal values like love or fidelity. It is the foundation that underlies and gives reality to all other virtues and personal values'. He goes on:

> In human beings courage is necessary to make *being* and *becoming* possible. An assertion of the self, a commitment, is essential if the self is to have any reality. A man or woman becomes fully human only by his or her choices and his or her commitment to them. People attain worth and dignity by the multitude of decisions they make from day to day. These

decisions require courage (May, 1994:13-14).

In the book, *Paul Tillich on Creativity*, the author explains that, for Tillich, there was a clear distinction between God's creativity (*creation ex nihilo* or creation out of nothing) and man's creativity (transformation out of given material). God's creativity arose out of his nature. God was not a supernatural being but was the ground of being itself and creativity was therefore innate. Man's creativity, however, arose from an openness to God's creativity and was not possible without. Any attempt to conceive of creativity without God is meaningless but creativity must not be confused with the utilitarian inventiveness demanded by our technological society (Kegley, 1989).

For Tillich and May, creativity is of the essence of what it means to be human. Others have expressed similar sentiments. I have already quoted from David Wallace-Hadrill. More recently, Karen Armstrong has written:

> We are most creative and sense other possibilities that transcend our ordinary experience when we leave ourselves behind (Armstrong, 2005:313).

On Not Being Able to Paint

There have been many attempts to understand what it means to be creative but few have had the impact of Marion Milner's account as outlined in her book, *On Not Being Able To Paint.* The publishers have written:

> Milner, who is a practising psycho-analyst, has given an account of when, dissatisfied with conventional methods of learning how to paint, she turned to free drawings – with most unexpected results. The objective study, both of the drawings and how they were made, gradually forced her to face certain facts about the nature of the creative process

(Milner, 1957).

In the Introduction, Milner writes:

> Always, ever since early childhood, I had been interested in learning how to paint. But in spite of having acquired some technical facility in representing the appearance of objects my efforts had always tended to peter out in a maze of uncertainties about what a painter is really trying to do (Milner, 1957).

In the course of this enterprise, Milner discovered that:

> ...it was possible at times to produce drawings or sketches in an entirely different way from any that I had been taught, a way of letting hand and eye do exactly what pleased them without any conscious working to a preconceived intention (Milner, 1957:xvii).

Milner discovered that to be creative in painting it was necessary to understand and deal with the constraints imposed by traditional ways of looking at the world. Action and vitality were necessary if a painting was not to be just a boring representation of the original. She also realised that this had serious implications for learning in general if so much teaching demanded that the pupil conform to preconceived methods and standards. Furthermore, she suggested that what is true for the visual arts must also be true for every other exploration into reality, including the religious.

If man's creativity is to properly channel the creativity of God then we have to be certain that what we do is neither constrained by conformity to human demands nor distorted by human failings. This is difficult to achieve because of our vulnerability to external influences on our human personality and inherent weaknesses in the human condition. However, that does not mean that it is only those specially endowed that can be creative. It is open to all of us.

But what does it mean to be creative in religious matters? It means to 'think outside the box'. And the 'box' may be an understanding of biblical authority or of church history within which we have been nurtured since childhood. It may be the church or community to which we have belonged since birth or baptism. It may simply be the consensus of family and friends. Whatever the 'box' is for us, its boundaries must be breached if we are to be creative. And if we are not creative, then we stagnate. As with most things in life, we either go forwards or backwards. We cannot stand still.

The church is in desperate need of those who are prepared to take the plunge. The institutional church is unlikely to survive in anything like its present form without fundamental change. And we need creative people with the vision and flair to initiate and manage that change.

A vision for the future

Pierre Teilhard de Chardin was one of the great visionaries of the twentieth century. He was a scientist and philosopher but also a Jesuit priest. In his book, *The Phenomenon of Man,* he writes of the need for a deeper vision of what it means to be human:

> If to see is really to become more, if vision is really fuller being, then we should look closely at man in order to increase our capacity to live. But to do this we must focus our eyes correctly… For man to discover man and take his measure, a whole series of 'senses' have been necessary, whose gradual acquisition… covers and punctuates the whole history of the struggles of the mind (Teilhard de Chardin, 1965:37).

These senses are important to quote in detail despite the difficulty of the language in which they are expressed:

> A sense of spatial immensity, in greatness and smallness, disarticulating and spacing out, within a sphere of indefinite radius, the orbits of objects which press around us; A sense of depth, pushing back laboriously through endless series and measureless distances of time, which of sluggishness of mind tends continually to condense us in a thin layer of the past; A sense of number, discovering and grasping unflinchingly the bewildering multitude of material or elements involved in the slightest change in the universe; A sense of proportion, realising as best we can difference of physical scale which separates, both in and dimension, the atom from the nebula, the infinitesimal from the immense; A sense of quality, or of novelty, enabling us to distinguish in nature certain absolute stages of perfection and growth, without upsetting the physical unity of the world; A sense of movement, capable of perceiving the irresistible developments hidden in extreme slowness – extreme agitation concealed beneath a veil of immobility – the entirely new insinuating itself into the heart of the monotonous repetition of the same things; A sense, lastly, of the organic, discovering physical links and structural unity under the superficial juxtaposition of successions and collectivities (Teilhard de Chardin, 1965: 37-38).

In commenting on these thoughts, John de Cruchy writes:

> With the awakening of these 'senses' we begin to see ourselves entirely related to the rest of humanity, to life as a whole and to the universe. We begin to appreciate the splendour and elegance, coherence and complexity that lies before and within us (de Gruchy, 2006: 193).

This 'awakening' of the senses is perhaps another way of

expressing what it means to be creative.

Creativity and Evolution

Keith Ward is a philosopher, theologian and scholar, and a priest in the Church of England. He has a particular interest in the relationship between science and religion, and is an enthusiastic advocate of theistic evolution. Theistic evolutionists claim that classical religious teachings about God are not incompatible with modern scientific understandings about biological evolution. They believe that there is a God, that God is the creator of the material universe and all life within it, and that biological evolution is simply a natural process within that creation. Evolution is God's choice of the method of creation.

In his book, *God, Chance and Necessity*, Keith Ward refutes the scientific atheism of people like Richard Dawkins and argues forcibly that 'modern scientific knowledge does not undermine belief in God, but actually points to the existence of God as the best explanation of how things are the way they are. The overwhelming appearance of design in nature is not deceptive'. Furthermore:

> …for the theist, the universe must be created with a purpose. That purpose, however, is not just the existence of some valuable final state… The purpose must lie in the process itself… The purpose is growth in creativity, sensitivity and community (Ward, 1996: 163).

Christians who reject the notion of a theistic God can still speak of the creativity of God in the evolutionary process. If creativity is of God then it is an essential part of this process.

Imagination

> Reason is the natural order of truth; but imagination is the organ of meaning.
> C. S. Lewis

'God rejects without exception all shapes and pictures...'

John McIntyre's book, *Faith Theology and Imagination,* is introduced on the flyleaf as follows, 'The association of imagination and faith have traditionally in western culture been unhappy...' He goes on to outline the shape of this unhappy relationship.

In the Authorised Version of the Bible, three different Hebrew words in the Old Testament and three different Greek words in the New Testament are translated by the single word 'imagination'. McIntyre writes:

> The interesting thing about all these references is that they are pejorative, uniformly implying that imagination is unacceptable to God in all its machinations, and therefore to be eliminated from the minds and thoughts of his servants... The universality of use of the Authorised Version throughout the English-speaking nations for over three and a half centuries, together with its immense influence not just upon everyday speech but also upon the thought of everyday people, has ensured almost universal suspicion of the concept itself (McIntyre, 1987:5).

In the Christian tradition there have also been those who have expressed themselves forcibly against the notion that 'imagination' might have a constructive role to play in God's world. In Calvin's *Institutes of the Christian Religion,* he writes:

> God rejects without exception all shapes and pictures and

> other symbols by which the superstitious imagine they can bring God near to them. These images defile and insult the majesty of God (McIntyre, 1987:6).

Calvin is not consistent in his rejection of symbols and images since clearly he could not ignore the biblical examples. But his legacy is that there were and are some Christians, most notably the Puritans, who are at best ambivalent and at worse hostile to the positive role of the imagination.

'Icons', from the Greek word for 'image' are an important part of the practice of Orthodox Christianity. Icons are symbolic and are seen as 'windows' into the divine. But there has always been a 'puritan' streak in Christianity which has condemned icons because it saw in all images a latent idolatry. There were periods in the history of the Byzantine Empire when the destruction of icons was officially sanctioned and carried out on a huge scale.

It is not altogether surprising that 'imagination' has also had a bad press from some of the most prominent thinkers of our time. It is also not surprising that some of our most eminent theologians have had reservations about too close an identification of a human capacity with a divine attribute. The concern is that:

> The admission of imagination to any analysis of revelation and our response to it amounts to an undue weighting of the human element, opening the door even to the possibility that the human mind or heart might distort the pure given-ness of revelation (McIntyre, 1987:10).

That is to take a very narrow view of revelation. It is to suggest that revelation is somehow independent of all other sources of knowledge about God and his ways.

The imagination of God

These negative views on the role of the imagination in the

Christian enterprise have seriously stifled discussion over the years and it is only in relatively recent times that the subject has been positively addressed. It was raised, perhaps for the first time, by George MacDonald in his essay *The Imagination: Its Functions and Its Culture,* written in 1867 but not published until 1907. He writes:

> The imagination is that faculty which gives form to thought – not necessarily uttered form, but form capable of being uttered in shape or in sound, or in any mode upon which the senses can lay hold. It is, therefore, that faculty in man which is likest to the prime operation of the power of God, and has, therefore, been called the 'creative' faculty... (McIntyre, 1987:13).

This may be seen to suggest that man participates in the creativity of God but, as McIntyre points out, we must take care to preserve the gulf that exists between God and Man:

> The forms which man uses in creative imagination are not themselves created by him; they are already prepared for him (e.g., the paints and canvas used by the artist; or the words and concepts used by the poet). MacDonald claims that it is a new embodiment, created out of forms already existing. The novelty is there, just as it is in God's creativity, insofar as it gives form to thought. In fact we should expect to find creative imagination in every sphere of human activity; notably, for example in the evolution of language (McIntyre, 1987:14).

McIntyre then picks up on what he considers to be the two major threads of MacDonald's argument:

> First, he comes out boldly and claims what scarcely anyone

> before him, and very few since, ever had the courage or maybe, simply the wisdom, to declare namely, that imagination is an attribute, fully worthy, because of its involvement in God's creative activity, of its place alongside the other attributes to be found in any orthodox list of God's attributes. Secondly, he locates the *imago Dei* concept in an exceptionally novel place, not in man's rationality, or his moral character, or even his sociability, but in his imagination, and firmly links it to God's own creative activity (McIntyre, 1987:14).

The Latin, *imago Dei,* refers, of course, to the 'image of God'. The notion that 'the imagination of man is made in the image of the imagination of God' is a very powerful idea and gives new status and meaning to a concept, the potential of which needs further exploration.

Biblical imagination

The World of Biblical Imagination, is the title of a chapter in Paul Avis's book *God and the Creative Imagination,* where he writes:

> My starting point is the conviction that divine revelation is given above all (though not exclusively) in modes that are addressed to the human imagination, rather than to any other faculty (such as the analytical reason or the moral conscience) (Avis, 1999:3).

He goes on, 'Let no one accuse me of reducing divine revelation to mere human religious consciousness or projection. There is admirable precedent for my claim':

> As St Augustine saw, God is a poet and speaks to the wold in metaphors, symbols and parables. William Blake said 'the whole Bible is filled with Imagination and Visions'. Austin Farrer claimed that the revelatory character of the Bible

> resided in certain dominant images which lay at the centre of the teaching of Jesus: Kingdom of God, Son of Man and so on. For Farrer, revelation was conveyed through the imagination of the Apostles and the Bible was the product of inspired imagining similar to poetic inspiration. 'Divine truth is supernaturally communicated to men in an act of inspired thinking which falls into the shape of certain images'. It is the images that lend vitality and dynamism to the Bible, and determine its form and content (Avis, 1999: 3-4).

This is, of course, not how many Christians today see the scriptures. Sadly, not only strident conservative evangelicals but many ordinary churchgoers in the pew see the scriptures as inerrant revelation, bearing divine authority, to be taken at face value and as literally as possible:

> Conservative evangelicals remain uneasy about approaches to biblical interpretation that play down the imperative of factual accuracy and dwell on the import of such figurative genres as metaphor, symbol and myth. Like the true fundamentalist, the conservative evangelical believes that the Bible makes explicit claims for itself and sets forth divine revelation accordingly in factual statements or propositions. He is uncomfortable with the notion that scripture reveals the truth of God indirectly, obliquely, through images and similitudes, and in a manner constrained by its historical and cultural context. Augustine's hint that God communicates with us in a poetic mode and Blake's tenet that Jesus and the Apostles were artists would seem to conservative evangelicals to make divine revelation rest on the shifting sands of subjective, arrogant human subjectivity (Avis, 1999:4).

Although the views of so many Christians cannot just be discarded, the claim of this book is that these views are serious distortions of what the Bible is all about. Fortunately, there is reason to think that some who espouse these views can be persuaded otherwise by further study, wider experience and the passage of time. It is no coincidence that many prominent liberal theologians came originally from a conservative evangelical background.

Perhaps nowhere in the whole Bible is the basic character of imagination as a category of biblical thought better illustrated than in the parables where Jesus presents some of his fundamental teaching in the form of metaphor, of vivid images, pictures and stories. He had good reasons for doing so:

> Jesus did not teach in parables simply because he was a first-century rabbi preaching to first-century peasants and fishermen, but because his gospel was addressed to the whole person in its depth and integrity – to the heart as well as to the head, to children to whom the kingdom of heaven belonged as well as to the intelligentsia of scribes and Pharisees, to the alienated and outcast as well as to the aristocracy of the Sadducees. It was meant to evoke a response from the whole person as it was quickened by the Holy Spirit into repentance and faith and awoke to a new world of grace. The only request that Jesus could not accede to was: 'If you are the Messiah, tell us plainly' (John 10:24) (Avis, 1999:66).

Elsewhere in the New Testament symbols are widely used to illustrate the nature of the divine. In the Johannine literature – the Fourth Gospel and the three Epistles of John – God is described in the symbols of spirit, light and love, so 'God is spirit' (John 4:24), 'God is light' (1 John 1:5), 'God is love' (1 John 4:8). Avis comments:

> Though these statements seem to have an almost metaphysical status, as apparently abstract and ethereal asser-

> tions about the nature of ultimate reality, in their biblical context they are fundamentally practical, down-to-earth symbols, inextricably connected with right Christian worship and ethical behaviour (Avis, 1999:52).

It is not difficult to find myths in the Bible, most obviously in the Old Testament. The creation stories in Genesis are a good example of the genre. But some have gone further than to just identify individual myths. Edmund Leach, the social anthropologist, has written:

> In saying that the Bible is not a history book but a mythology, I am not arguing that the events it records could not possibly have happened in real time. It is simply that spatial and chronological relations within biblical texts always have symbolic significance whether or not they happen to correspond to reality as ordinarily understood (Leach, 1989:581).

This statement is important because it asserts that the primary way in which the Bible coveys its message is through the imagination, through figurative language, through metaphor, symbol and myth. If the message has any literal or historical content then that is a secondary issue. Avis writes in a similar vein:

> My approach is to accept that the Bible contains substantial mythical components. But I go further and claim that all stories about the interaction of God and the world have the status of myth as a narrative genre (Avis, 1999:60).

He substantiates his claim by examining the work of six writers who have brought out the poetical, figurative and symbolic character of the Bible in significant ways – Augustine, Aquinas, Burke, Coleridge, Newman and Blake. A very strong field indeed!

There are, of course, those who are worried about the integrity of revelation. They are concerned that essential elements of that revelation are lost if the message strays from literal and historical foundations. Avis responds. 'I believe that they are misguided in thinking that the integrity of revelation is compromised by its mythical form' (Avis, 1999:61).

The Light of Christ

It was in rather depressing weather that we visited the Penlee House Gallery in Penzance on a recent holiday in Cornwall. We were there to see an exhibition of paintings by the Newlyn School of painters who were active in Newlyn at the end of the nineteenth century and beyond. Walter Langley arrived in Newlyn in the 1880s and was one of the most prominent of those painters. For many years he lived and worked among the poor who eked out a living from the hazards of fishing. As the years passed he painted many of the villagers and their surroundings. He captured the mood of the people as the fishing fleet left for the Arctic north. He captured their joy as the fleet returned home intact. He captured their sorrow as the fleet returned with boats and men missing. It was difficult to look at those faces of hope and despair without feeling overwhelmed with emotion. Indeed more than one person touring the gallery was shedding a tear. This ability of the artist to convey something above and beyond the surface image of the painting was truly remarkable. It gave us a glimpse into the heights and depths of reality in a way that lifted the spirit.

This ability of painters to take us on a journey to another place is part of the ability of all creative artists to take us out of ourselves. The Barbara Hepworth Gallery in St Ives contains some of the best of the work of one of Britain's most talented sculptresses and clearly conveys to many people something quite extraordinary. Musicians, poets, actors, dancers and many others have also widened our horizons and deepened our perceptions.

They can change our view of the world and our place in it. The ability to see beyond the superficial images that engulf us every day is not just the privilege of artists but is available to us all. But we do need to stop, to look and to listen. We all have senses that can be honed. We all have an imagination that can be stimulated. We all have visions that can be stirred.

Sir Sarvepalli Radhakrishnan, the Indian philosopher and statesman once wrote:

> Most of us go through life with eyes half shut and with dull minds and heavy hearts, and even the few who have had those rare moments of vision and awakening fall back into somnolence. It is good to know that the ancient thinkers required us to realise the possibilities of the soul in solitude and silence and transform the flashing and fading moments of vision into a steady light which could illuminate the long years of life (Radhakrishnan, 2013).

For Christians, that steady light is the Light of Christ.

Engaging the imagination

This chapter would be incomplete without some reference to the work of C. S. Lewis and his contribution to the works of imaginative literature.

As Alister McGrath points out in his biography, *C S Lewis: A Life*, Lewis's inner world began to take shape in his early years in Northern Ireland:

> Where other boys of his age were playing games on the streets or in the countryside around Belfast, Lewis constructed, inhabited, and explored his own private worlds. He was forced to become a loner – something that unquestionably catalysed his imaginative life (McGrath, 2013:18).

As both student and teacher at Oxford University, his imaginative life blossomed and he became absorbed with literary challenges that would dominate his intellectual life for years to come:

> At the intellectual level, Lewis was searching for a true marriage of reason and imagination – something that eluded him totally as a young man. It seemed to him then that his life of the mind was split into two disconnected hemispheres. "On the one side a many-sided sea of poetry and myth; on the other a glib and shallow rationalism". Lewis's later discovery of the Christian faith offered him a synthesis of reason and imagination which he found persuasive and authentic till the end of his life (McGrath, 2013:74).

One of those who helped Lewis make sense of these issues was his friend J. R. R. Tolkien who, together with Lewis, was a member of the Inklings, an elite Oxford discussion group. Tolkien's devout Catholic faith was a significant factor in the conversion of C. S. Lewis from atheism to Christianity:

> Tolkien helped Lewis to realise that the problem lay not in Lewis's *rational* failure to understand the theory, but in his *imaginative* failure to grasp its significance. The issue was not primarily about *truth*, but about *meaning*. When engaging the Christian narrative, Lewis was limiting himself to his reason when he ought to be opening himself to the deepest intuitions of his imagination (McGrath, 2013:149).

Lewis's conversations with Tolkien and others 'allowed him to catch a glimpse of the imaginative potential of the Christian story, illuminating questions that had troubled him for some time':

> Yet Lewis appears to have realised that argument was only

> one of a number of ways of engaging cultural anxieties about the Christian faith, or challenging its alternatives. From about 1937, Lewis seems to have appreciated that the imagination is the gatekeeper of the human soul. Having initially merely enjoyed reading works of fantasy... Lewis began to realise how fiction might allow the intellectual and imaginative appeal of worldviews to be explored. Might he try his hand at writing such works himself? (McGrath, 2013:233).

The rest, as they say, is history!

The Chronicles of Narnia is a series of seven fantasy novels and is considered a classic of children's literature and is Lewis's best known work. Published between 1950 and 1956, it has been adapted several times for radio, television, the stage, and film. Set in the fictional realm of Narnia, a fantasy world of magic, mythical beasts, and talking animals, the series tells the stories of children who play central roles in the unfolding history of that world. For the most part, the protagonists are all children from the real world, magically transported to Narnia, where they are called upon by the lion Aslan to protect Narnia from evil and restore the throne to its rightful place:

> Narnia is an *imaginative,* not an *imaginary* world. Lewis was quite clear that a distinction had to be drawn between these ideas. The *imaginary* is something that has been falsely imagined, having no counterpoint in reality... The *imaginative* is something produced by the human mind as it tries to respond to something greater than itself, struggling to find images adequate to the reality. The more imaginative a mythology, the greater its ability to communicate more reality to us. For Lewis, the imaginative is to be seen as a legitimate and positive use of the human imagination, challenging the limits of reason and opening the door to a deeper apprehension of reality (McGrath, 2013:263).

The Chronicles of Narnia enables profound reflection on the human condition, 'about how human beings understand themselves, face up to their weaknesses, and try to become the people they are meant to be':

> They are about a quest for meaning and virtue, not simply the quest for explanation and understanding. That is perhaps one reason why *The Chronicles of Narnia* have proved to have such a powerful appeal: they speak of choices to be made, of right and wrong, and of challenges that must be faced. Yet this vision of goodness and greatness is not set forth as a logical or reasoned argument, but is affirmed and explored through the telling of a story – a story that captures the imagination (McGrath, 2013:268).

Finally, as McGrath puts succinctly, 'Lewis opened up the intellectual and imaginative depths of the Christian faith like nobody else' (McGrath, 2013:369).

Freedom

> Freedom in Christ is not freedom to do what I like, but freedom to be what I am meant to be.
> George Appleton, *Journey for a Soul.*

'Thou shalt not...'

It is not immediately obvious that God is freedom. It is still ingrained in us that somehow our faith imposes boundaries which set limitations on what we can do. We instinctively feel that any freedom we have is circumscribed by rules. 'Thou shalt not...' is also seen by many outside the faith as the distinctive approach of the Christian tradition. This means that people feel alienated from a way of life which seems so at odds with contemporary culture which places so much emphasis on the freedom of the individual. This need not be so for the Christian faith is essentially about what we can and not what we cannot do. We may find that some things do not sit comfortably with our faith but that is a secondary issue. The primary issue is what our faith enables us to be and do.

For Paul, 'freedom' is a word that encapsulates the gospel and there are many references to it in his letters. In *Galatians* he writes of 'the freedom we have in Christ' (2:4). In the same letter he writes of the freedom that we have *from* the constraints of the old law (5:1-12) and of the freedom we have *to* be slaves to one another under the new law, which 'is summed up in a single commandment, 'You shall love your neighbour as yourself' (5:13-15). In all these words Paul expresses the sense of liberation which he feels following conversion from his previous life within Judaism and wants others to experience it for themselves in contrast to their previous 'slavery' (5:1). In *Romans*, Paul devotes much of chapter eight to this theme. But what does this 'freedom' mean?

Christian Freedom

In his book *Perfect Freedom*, Brian Mountford seeks answers to the question, 'How does Christianity make us free?' His first answer is that Christianity meets the need for 'a power greater than ourselves'. He goes on:

> Belief in God helps us see ourselves in perspective within the vast expanse of the universe… God is like an infinitely elastic quality of relationship stretching beyond and around the limits of human experience and knowledge acting as a force of integration and unity, binding matter and meaning together… This idea of being freely supported and sustained by God is immensely liberating (Mountford, 2005:94).

But we do not live in isolation and we need to be constantly reminded that Christianity 'is a communal religion based on friendship and relationship, not a private hobby'. Neither is Christianity 'a private club' to which only members can belong. It is about 'breaking down barriers and bringing people together' whatever their class, wealth, ability or race:

> Relationship is one of the principal sources of meaning in our lives and most of our problems arise from messing up in the relationship department, both at the personal and political levels. Good relationships bring freedom because they release us to be ourselves… Christianity meets the need for relationship both by showing us how to accept and cherish one another at the personal level… and by assuring us that we are loved by God at the universal level (Mountford, 2005:94).

Christianity also helps us make sense of the world and gives our lives purpose and direction. 'God helps people shape their priorities and answer the teasing questions about what ultimately matters and what is worth living for'. The Bible is an important foundation and the life of Jesus provides a story that is hugely liberating. It communicates and oozes a sense of freedom, but never defines what it is – because stories don't define. His *bon mot* to the Pharisees, after being accused of breaking the Sabbath, is the nearest we get to definition, 'The Sabbath was made for man, not man for the Sabbath'. But:

> Jesus' freedom is not restricted to what he says, but is evident in his actions: he abandoned his family to lead a peripatetic life, mixing with social outcastes, with women and children, and performing signs that break the social mould: healing lepers and madmen, and taking the ultimate risk of returning to the political/religious cauldron of Jerusalem to face the wrath of his opponents (Mountford, 2005:96).

And the life of Jesus had a huge impact on history. Despite many blots on the landscape of its history, Christianity is a religion of liberation and liberty. Christians campaigned for the abolition of slavery, for civil rights in America and for an end to apartheid in South Africa. They fought against fascist and communist oppression. They fight for education and welfare of the poor.

Masters and Slaves

'Slaves, obey your earthly masters in everything, not only while being watched and in order to please them, but wholeheartedly, fearing the Lord' (Col 3:22).

It outrages many readers of the New Testament that so evil an institution as slavery is not condemned but tolerated in this letter to the Colossians – a book which, if not by Paul himself, certainly expresses Pauline theology. But we must remember the circumstances of the time. Slavery was built into the culture of first-century Palestine and its practice was taken for granted. There were almost certainly Christians who had reservations. But they would have found it very difficult to make any impact. Perhaps some might have resorted to direct action or peaceful demonstration to make their point. But that would have been quickly and violently quashed by the authorities. Perhaps others might have sought ways of influencing the authorities by force of argument and debate. But since they had no vote or political voice, little notice would have been taken of them. What they could do, however, was to let the gospel speak through them in the way they treated each other. By encouraging a new understanding of men and women they could encourage new relationships between master and slave. Relations such that the principle of one man owning and disposing of another would then became more and more unthinkable and obsolete. And eventually slavery would die out. That is, of course, what will eventually happen but, as we know, it is taking a very long time.

But let us for the moment go back to the Bible and to the shortest book in the New Testament – Philemon. Philemon was probably a Colossian Christian owing his conversion to Paul. His slave, Onesimus, had run away, possibly with stolen goods, and had somehow reached Paul in prison. Paul's letter to Philemon was written to support Onesimus as he bravely returned to his master. In Paul's time, any slave who ran away was pursued as a common criminal and, when caught, was disciplined severely, perhaps with corporal punishment, often by branding and sometimes by death. The status of a slave in relation to his master was governed by law. Slaves were treated as impersonal possessions and any suggestion of a relationship between master and slave would have been considered scandalous. In his letter to Philemon, however, Paul seeks to persuade Philemon to accept Onesimus back into his household and to treat him '...no longer as a slave but (as) more than a slave, (as) a beloved brother'. Paul believed that changes in the practice of slavery would not come from attempts to overthrow the slavery from without, but that change would only come from a change of attitudes from within; within the hearts and minds of individual believers. In other words, the consequence of applying the gospel of love to the individual relationships between master and slave would inevitably undermine the institution itself because it would be seen to be incompatible with that gospel.

It is taking a very long time to rid the world of slavery. A recent television programme described the work of Baroness Cox in the Sudan. Arab traders regularly take women and children from the villages in the south and sell them to others in the north of the country as slave labourers. Other traders are prepared to buy them back and return them to the village if someone is prepared to pay them for their trouble. In the film, we see Baroness Cox bartering with these people for the release of hundreds of women and children back into their families. They eventually negotiated a price of about £60 per person and something like 300 were released. Their stories were harrowing but their release was a joy to see. There are those who are critical of Baroness Cox and they accuse her of negotiating with the devil. But the slaves would not otherwise have been freed! I am sure that had she been able to find a better way then she would have used it. Those who renewed the campaigned for the abolition of slavery in the eighteenth century in Britain used a variety of means to get their message across. They were ultimately successful when the slave trade was made illegal in 1808. But it was not until 1833 that slavery was finally suppressed in the British Empire. In the USA, slavery was only finally prohibited by law in 1865, but it lived on in other forms well into the twentieth century. It lives on today in the form of human trafficking throughout the western world.

There is clearly a place for direct action in the face of evil of this kind. There is also a place for speaking out and campaigning. But ultimately success will never be secured without a change in the hearts and minds of those who perpetuate this evil. And only the gospel of love can make that change. But the gospel of love does not just transform relationships between master and slave. It changes the relationships between men and women, between parent and child and wherever there is the possibility of tension between one person or one group and another. As Paul writes in Galations: 'There is no longer Jew or Greek, there is no longer slave or free, there is no longer male and female; for all of you are one in Christ Jesus'.

Prisoners and Freemen

The story of the imprisonment of Paul and Silas is one of most vivid stories in Acts. Paul and Silas are in Philippi. They encounter a slave girl on the streets. She follows them round calling out to them, and displaying all the signs of possession. Paul gets annoyed with this constant irritation, and exorcises the evil spirits within her. Seeing that their hope of making money from her has gone, her owners haul Paul and Silas before the authorities. The charge against them is of propagating alien customs, but in reality it is an appeal to the prejudice that Romans often had for the Jews. They are convicted by the magistrates, stripped and beaten and placed in the innermost gaol with their feet in the stocks. The climactic scene is vivid. There is an earthquake. The foundations shake, the doors spring open and all chains become unfastened. The jailer assumes they have escaped and is prepared to commit suicide. But Paul and Silas are still there, and appear to have persuaded the others to remain, to save the jailer the shame of or the blame for their escape. They reassure him that all the prisoners are safe.

I have no experience of prisons but I imagine that they are awful places, even at the best of times. In recent years we have all heard and seen evidence of what can happen in prisons during the worst of times. We have seen pictures of the abuse of prisoners held in Iraqi gaols under the control of coalition forces. We have recoiled in horror that anyone from what we call the 'civilised' world could treat prisoners in this way. We have asked ourselves how and why these events occurred and we have found few answers. People have spoken about weaknesses in the chain of command and breakdowns in discipline. There seems to have been a good deal of 'passing the buck'. We shall probably never know just how much senior politicians and the military actually knew.

What we do know is that those who find themselves in prison, as captors or captives, are in unnatural surroundings and can behave unpredictably. If they respond to the worst that is in them then things deteriorate quickly. If they respond to the best that is in them then much is possible. It all depends on the strength of their beliefs and values. If we do not identify with a tradition that affirms the dignity of every human being, then the line between the oppressor and oppressed can become very fine indeed. And that line may disappear altogether as we have seen in Iraq.

Paul and Silas behaved differently because they did identify with a strong faith tradition. They believed in the power of God to change hearts and minds. Their captors were overwhelmed, not so much by how a violent earthquake freed the chains and opened the doors of the prison, but by the desire of those imprisoned to cause their captors no harm. The witness of Paul and Silas went on to change the lives of their jailer and his family for ever. This story reveals not only the magnitude of change that is possible in human life, but the extent of our responsibility to work for that change.

As Christians, we are called to a ministry of reconciliation, transformation and renewal. Our own behaviour and our own willingness to effect that change arises from our relationship to Jesus Christ. The capacity to be different and to act differently should be one of the characteristics of our lives as Christians. Our commitment to recognising and appreciating the best in others reflects the best of what it means to be human.

But as Christians, we also find ourselves captive and imprisoned by many things that separate us from Christ and from one another. We are imprisoned by fears, prejudices, anger and a multitude of other feelings that swell up during times of stress. At times like this, when we are unable to cope, we need spiritual support to help us deal with those areas of life for which we find ourselves ill-equipped, uniformed or unprepared.

Contracts and Covenants

'Covenant' is a word that we find frequently in both the Old and the New Testaments. In the Old Testament we find references to covenants between God and Noah, Abraham, Isaac and Jacob, and between God and the Israelites under Moses. We can think of these early covenants as God's first attempts to establish a relationship with his people. These early covenants were very crude but they provided a basic framework. As the generations passed, and as the relationship between God and his people slowly changed, so the covenant changed. It became more of a relationship in which the character and actions of the people were being formed even transformed by it. When we reach the New Testament, that change reaches a climax in the life, death and resurrection of Jesus Christ.

One of the most important characteristics of these covenants as they developed was the freedom which God allowed both himself and his people in establishing them. On the one hand, because the people had freedom to respond to God in whatever way they chose, they were vulnerable to the weaknesses of themselves and those around them. On the other hand, in giving them that freedom, God was also vulnerable to disobedience and rejection. These were no tightly worded contracts in which neither side had freedom to manoeuvre. They were open-ended covenants which both sides were completely free to accept or reject. On the face of it, such arrangements are very risky. Yet this must be so because God's gift of freedom is an act of love. Love is not love if it is not vulnerable or risky.

For many years people have looked at ways in which the

insights gained from a study of biblical covenants between God and his people can be used to illuminate the nature of our relationships with each other today. Clearly, one is not the same as the other. However, one can set the pattern for the other. By way of illustration consider one area of our national life in which relationships sometimes seem to be dominated by the contract model – the world of employment and business.

One of the first things we do when we start a new job is to sign a contract. Contracts are the most fundamental of relationships in the workplace. They describe formally and explicitly the obligations that both employer and employee have towards each other. They are written documents and have the force of law. Their strengths lie in the basic framework that they provide for relationships at work. Their weakness lies in the fact that they are only frameworks and cannot deal with the less tangible aspects of life at work. For example, a contract can deal with details of a disciplinary procedure but it cannot say anything about the ethos within which such formal disciplinary procedures can be avoided.

Most would agree that contract does not adequately describe the best relationships between employers and employees. The cement that holds companies together is not just contracts, it is something much more. Some observers have suggested that the word covenant might be appropriate. Until fairly recently, many business transactions were sealed by verbal undertakings only. Such agreements were understood to be binding and obligatory on each party, although nothing was written down. 'My word is my bond' was not just a slogan, it actually meant something. Such agreements had a lot in common with covenants because something wider than the immediate arrangement was understood to have taken place. This was an agreement in which mutual respect and loyalty were an essential part. The emphasis was more on the relationship than on the obligations.

Unfortunately, verbal agreements are no longer considered

adequate in business transactions but in the best of businesses the ethos remains. The idea of covenants seems to go some way towards understanding those aspects of business activity that go beyond the merely contractual. After the turmoil of recent years it may be time to revive those aspects of business ethics which give as much weight to the unwritten covenant as to the written contract. 'My word is my bond' is not a bad place to start.

In all our relationships there is a bond. It may be the basic bond of casual acquaintance. It may be the profound bond of marriage. It is probably unwritten. It may be unsaid. But it is there. Let us understand all our relationships for what they are. For whether we like it or not they are bonds and the best of them are covenants.

'I have a dream...'

Martin Luther King Jr did more than most to advance the cause of Civil Rights in America in the mid-twentieth century. He was dedicated to non-violent opposition to the discrimination that was endemic in American society at that time. He led many marches of protest and gave many inspirational speeches. He was also imprisoned.

The *Letter from Birmingham Jail*, to which I have referred in an earlier chapter, was written by Martin Luther King in April 1963. He was writing to a group of clergymen who had questioned his policy of direct action. In part of the letter King speaks of the 'yearning for freedom':

> Oppressed people cannot remain oppressed forever. The yearning for freedom eventually manifests itself, and that is what has happened to the American Negro. Something within has reminded him of his birthright of freedom, and something without has reminded him that it can be gained... If one recognises this vital urge that has engulfed the Negro community, one should readily understand why public

> demonstrations are taking place. The Negro has many pent up resentments and latent frustrations, and he must release them. So let him march; let him make prayer pilgrimages to the city hall; let him go on freedom rides – and try to understand why he must do so. If his repressed emotions are not released in nonviolent ways, they will seek expression through violence; this is not a threat but a fact of history (King, 1963b).

The *March on Washington for Jobs and Freedom,* as it was called, was one of the largest political rallies in United States history and called for civil and economic rights for African Americans. It took place in Washington DC on August 27th 1963. The following day Martin Luther King, standing in front of the Lincoln Memorial, delivered his historic 'I Have a Dream' speech in which he called for an end to racism. This is part of that speech:

> I have a dream that one day on the red hills of Georgia the sons of former slaves and the sons of former slave-owners will be able to sit down together at the table of brotherhood. I have a dream that one day even the state of Mississippi, a state sweltering with the heat of oppression, will be transformed into an oasis of freedom and justice. I have a dream that my four little children one day will live in a nation where they will not be judged by the colour of their skin, but by the content of their character. I have a dream that one day every valley shall be exalted, every hill and mountain shall be made low. The rough places will be made plain, and the crooked places will be made straight.

He ends with these words:

> When we allow freedom to ring from every town and every

> hamlet, from every state and from every city, we will be able to speed up that day when all of God's children, black men and white men, Jews and Gentiles, Protestants and Catholics, will be able to join hands and sing in the words of the old Negro spiritual, Free at last! Free at last! Great God Almighty, we are free at last (King, 1963a).

This was the greatest speech of King's life and it has become one of the most compelling declarations of Christian hope in our century. Sadly, a good deal of blood was to be shed before things changed and King himself was assassinated in 1968. It was my privilege to have heard King speak at a student conference in Amsterdam in the same year in which that speech was made, and I still have a tape recording of his Sunday morning address.

Martin Luther King was a visionary and some will call him a saint. In March 1968 he went to Memphis in support of local black workers who had been unfairly treated. On 3rd April he gave another inspirational speech. The following day he was assassinated on the balcony of his motel.

The 'Arab Spring'

What we have witnessed in the Middle East in recent years has been remarkable. We have seen how individual demonstrations of courage have quickly grown into huge movements for change. We have seen dictators fall and governments pushed aside. We have seen politicians change their allegiances. We have seen military units change sides. Much of the protest has been non-violent. Sadly, some of the response has been very violent indeed. And there is undoubtedly much more to come.

What we are witnessing is a demand from ordinary people for freedom; a demand for social democracy and self-determination. So many people in these regions are poor and living in squalor; so many are sick or unemployed. So many are marginalised and disenfranchised. So many crave justice and equality; so many seek compassion. This is something we cannot ignore even if we have only limited ability to make a practical contribution. They like us are part of the human family.

The people of Tunisia, Egypt, Libya and the rest certainly seek food, clothing and shelter and the basic necessities of life. But above all they seek recognition. They seek self-respect. They seek human dignity. They want to be treated as human beings. And it is the humanity that has been so lacking in the experience of so many of these people that ought to draw us towards them.

In the sixth chapter of the gospel according to Matthew, Jesus is speaking to the people of first-century Palestine. He reminds them of where their priorities should lie. 'Do not worry about your life, what you will eat or what you will drink, or about your body, what you will wear. Is not life more than food, and the body more than clothing?' 'Strive first for the kingdom of God and his righteousness, and all these things will be given to you as well'. His message was very clear to those who were listening in that distant time and place.

But this message of Jesus speaks equally clearly to us in our very different time and place. It reminds us of where our priorities should lie. 'Strive first for the Kingdom of God'. Attend to the basic needs of those who suffer. Stand with those whose humanity is threatened. Do what is right and true and loving. That is what it means to strive for the Kingdom of God. The Kingdom of God is not some celestial city of the future. It is a tangible reality right now. And it will be achieved not by religious exhortation but by a willingness to give selflessly to other members of the human family.

The people of the Middle East want to be in a position where they will not have to worry about the basic necessities of life, what they will eat, what they will drink. They want to be in a position where they can enjoy those things which really make life worth living. Yet they are denied that opportunity. We cannot be sure that these revolutions will turn out to be more successful than others have been. But we can be sure of one thing. The priorities of those who seek change accord with those of Jesus.

John Shelby Spong, former Bishop of New Jersey, is one of the most challenging speakers of our time. In an address some time ago he summed up his understanding of what it meant to be a disciple of Christ:

> Those of us who want to be disciples of this Jesus have a single responsibility and that is to try and build a world in which every person in that world has a fuller opportunity to live fully and love wastefully and be all that they can be in the infinite variety of our humanity. And when the church finally learns that that's our message, our very human message, and we begin to be faithful to that message, then there will come forth from the disciples of Jesus such a mighty reformation that the whole world will begin to look again and find in the body of Christ, life and love and wholeness. For folks, that is what God is all about and that is what you and I as disciples of Jesus must also be all about (From an unknown source).

Generosity

> Every time I take a step in the direction of generosity, I know that I am moving from fear to love.
> Henri J M Nouwen.

The final themes

The final three themes – Generosity, Compassion and Transformation – bring us back to three aspects of human flourishing which seem to capture some of the essence of what it means to be a Christian. Other words could have been chosen but in a sense the words themselves do not matter. What matters is to say something in response to the wider vision of God that this book attempts to convey. Love is, of course, the single response that matters, but it needs 'unpacking' and that is what these three themes aim to do.

The meaning of 'generosity'

There are many definitions of the word 'generosity', but one of the clearest appears on the website of *The Science of Generosity* initiative at the University of Notre Dame in the USA.

This initiative grew out of the book, *Passing the Plate: Why American Christians Don't Give Away More Money* (Smith, Emerson, & Snell, 2008), and is now being extended and developed by a group conducting interviews around the country in order to understand why some people practice generosity and others don't:

> The modern English word 'generosity' derives from the Latin word *generōsus*, which means 'of noble birth,' which itself was passed down to English through the old French word *genereux*. During the 17th Century, however, the meaning and use of the word began to change. Generosity came increasingly to identify not literal family heritage but a nobility of

> spirit thought to be associated with high birth—that is, with various admirable qualities that could now vary from person to person, depending not on family history but on whether a person actually possessed the qualities. Then, during the 18th Century, the meaning of 'generosity' continued to evolve in directions denoting the more specific, contemporary meaning of munificence, open-handedness, and liberality in the giving of money and possessions to others (http://generosityre-search.nd.edu).

The work of *The Science of Generosity* initiative is essentially about a retrieval of core themes in the Western tradition rather than a fundamentally new departure. Generosity is endangered in today's world, a world dominated by business contracts and economic exchange. Such contracts are strictly conditional. True generosity is, of course, unconditional.

The Generosity Path

The Generosity Path is the title of a book by Mark Ewert which is subtitled, *Finding the Richness in Giving.* In his book, Ewert traces the path taken by particular individuals who have been generous, and reflects on the richness of their giving. Although the book is primarily about financial giving, it is not exclusively so. In his Introduction, the author expands on basic etymological definitions:

> Generosity's rich meaning can inspire us. It implies giving *freely,* so the giver holds choice and control. It is about giving *more than necessary,* so it is not limited by being required or indispensable. It is *more than expected,* so it goes beyond the obligation to give or what is anticipated by the recipient. Finally, generosity *ennobles* us. Compare this to words such as *charity, alms,* and *aid,* which label the recipient as poor; *donation and contribution,* which are cold, technical terms; and

> *grant*, which is formal legalese. *Philanthropy* is a wonderful word in its Greek origins – loving human-kind – yet it has come to imply a rare few who have the wealth and power to be philanthropists (Ewert, 2014:1).

There is no suggestion that this latter group of words are somehow inadequate, for they certainly have their place, but that they lack an important set of ingredients that give the word *generosity* the richness that it deserves. The generosity of treasure, time and talents is important but there is more, and it is perhaps this less tangible generosity that distinguishes real generosity from mere giving. Elsewhere in the book, Ewert writes:

> Be generous with your eyes and your touch; welcome people and signal to them that you accept them as they are. Be generous with your skills and intelligence; work toward making this world a better place. Be generous with your heart; grow your personal relationships. Be generous with your muscle; help people when they need you to add your strength to theirs (Ewert, 2014:53).

We must allow for the balance between different forms of generosity to change. Someone working in an investment bank in the city may be financially generous but may be less able to be generous with his time. If that same person is made redundant, then the balance may shift so that he is now less able to be financially generous but can now offer more time.

Generosity is a learning process in which we grow in maturity of giving, particularly if we are supported by a parent, minister or mentor to guide us. As a child we respond to a direct instruction to give some of our 'pocket money' to good causes. As we grew older we perhaps imitate the example of people we respect by giving a proportion of our income to charity. As adults we understand giving as an expression of our identity and our relationship to the world and we respond accordingly. Part of this growth in maturity is about increased discernment – how much to give, to whom, in what form, and to what end.

The concept of generosity does, of course, include both giving and receiving, and the generosity of the one fuels the generosity of the other. So generous giving can be a response to the generous gift. For the Christian, generous giving is a response to a generous gift from God – something which we call 'grace'.

Ewert finishes his book with a short reflection on a possible relationship between money and grace:

> I am inspired by the wisdom of Arturo Paoli, an Italian missionary priest who lived and worked, until his very old age, among the poorest people of Venezuela. He has come to understand money as having the ability to join us together in community, and to distribute justice. Rather than money being symbolic of privilege and power, Paoli believes money can be a symbol of life and of justice. He has even reportedly expressed that money can be like grace, used as a means for individuals to exchange goodness (Ewert, 2014:196).

The notion that money, and perhaps other gifts, can be used 'to exchange goodness' is a powerful idea.

'Giving in Grace'

'Grace' is at the heart of Christian theology and although it means 'generosity', it is generosity of a very special kind. Traditionally it refers to that which God has freely given to humanity without which it could not survive and flourish. It goes beyond the gift of human life and consists of God giving himself to men and women, so that they may know him and love him, and enter into a relationship with him which exceeds the relationship of creature to creator. In this way, humanity participates in divinity and is transformed in the process. The generosity of man is always going to be a poor substitute for the grace of God but the claim of this book is that by exploring human generosity we may get a glimpse of divine generosity, for the generosity within us is of God.

Giving in Grace is a treasure trove of internet resources which are designed to support churches in their stewardship campaigns. Its aim is threefold – to help churches to increase giving by church members, to encourage 'planned giving' so that realistic budgets can be set, and to instil a 'culture of giving' to secure the future. It uses sermons, work in small groups and visits to individuals in their homes to 'hammer home' the message. A Bible Study based on Paul's campaign for generosity towards the Jerusalem Church is introduced in the following way:

> An important part of Paul's ministry was organising a financial offering from the Gentile churches for the poor in Jerusalem. Paul's extended teaching in giving is found in his second letter to the Corinthians. As Paul wrote this letter he was very concerned for the financial needs of the church in Jerusalem. Originally the church in Corinth had been enthusiastic to help, but their energy had flagged. For Paul the very real need in Jerusalem matters. But Paul also wants the Corinthians to know that their giving is a response to the overflowing grace of God, an act of obedience to Paul's apostolic authority and a concrete expression of the mutual sharing between Jewish and Gentile churches.

The authors comment that 'it is amazing that he (Paul) begins, not with a demand for money, but a discussion on grace. He doesn't even use the word, 'money' at all in the entire two chapters. Instead he uses different words, such as fellowship, service and most importantly, grace' (www.givingingrace.org).

But, the message of this, as in every stewardship campaign, is that generosity with treasure (money) is only one aspect of giving, and that generosity of time and talents are equally important and stem from the same source. Each of us, without exception, has abilities and skills that can be used in the service of each other and of the church. In the same way, each of us, however busy we are, can be generous with our time. It is not uncommon for churches to compile a list of gifts, skills and activity which individual members of the church are prepared to offer each other.

Learning to feed each other

Two men in Hell were presented with plates of food but only with very long chopsticks. They starved because they could not feed themselves. Two other men in Heaven were given similar long chopsticks. They flourished because they learnt to feed each other.

In the fourteenth chapter of the gospel according to Matthew we read the story of the feeding of the five thousand. It is a familiar story and similar accounts occur in all four gospels. It is difficult for us to know exactly what happened. Each gospel writer is telling the story in their own particular way some time after the event. But it is more important for us to glimpse something of the truth which Jesus was attempting to convey by his action. This was much more than a solution to the problem of crowds of hungry people at the end of a long hot day.

We call this event a miracle; but that means different things to different people. For some, it is simply about the multiplication of loaves and fishes. For them, Jesus demonstrates his power to overcome the hunger of the people by providing food as God did for the Israelites in the wilderness so many years before. For them, Jesus miraculously multiplied the food available. For others, this event is about people sharing what little they have with others. Jesus shares his food with the disciples and the people follow his example. It is about generosity.

Whichever way we look at this event, it is important that we understand it not as something which happened but something which happens. This is not an isolated event in history but an example of the continuous action of God in the world throughout history. We can take this miracle at face value, and wonder at the multiplication of the loaves and fishes. But this is difficult for us to understand and would be something which happened once and was possibly never repeated. If, on the other hand, we look a little closer and if we delve a little deeper we can perhaps discern something more profound; something which has a more direct bearing on our lives two thousand years later.

Picture the scene. It is the end of the day and the people are tired and hungry. It is more than likely that some would have food with them. But they would be reluctant to eat in case they felt obliged to share with others. Jesus could have suggested that they travel to the nearest village for food. Instead he chose to use the occasion to demonstrate something to them. He took the lead and he and the disciples shared their food. Others followed and shared their food with those who had brought nothing with them until all were fed. It is possible that in the event there was enough food and to spare.

If this is what happened then the miracle is not quite what it seems. The miracle is then not the simple multiplication of loaves and fishes as the event appears to be when reading the story at face value. The miracle is the change that Jesus wrought in the hearts and minds of those present by turning them from selfishness into generosity willing to share their food with others. It is a simple act but it demonstrates a profound change. At a deeper level it is the miracle of the birth of love in their hearts. In a very real sense Christ fed those people with himself.

But what has this story to say to us today two thousand years later. In a world where many people's only concern seems to be with themselves. In a world where people seem more preoccupied with their rights rather than with their responsibilities. We desperately need the message of giving, of generosity and of love. In the story of the feeding of the five thousand, Jesus demonstrates that he is able and willing to feed us with himself and to enable us to feed others.

But what does generosity mean in practice, in the routine of everyday life and in the circumstances of particular times and places.

Generosity in the workplace

In the last few years we have heard a good deal about wealthy footballers, overpaid bankers and greedy politicians. We also hear about underpaid workers, exploited immigrants and families on the edge of poverty. We have seen the income of some soar. We have seen the income of others squeezed until 'the pips squeak'. Some earn high salaries for very little work. Others earn very little for dedicated toil. The gap between rich and poor increases. Where is the justice?

In the twentieth chapter of the gospel according to Matthew we have a parable firmly grounded in the everyday experience of those to whom it was directed. Note that Jesus' parables are never about church. Not one parable is about candles, canticles or choirs. Not one of his parables is about preaching, pews, or processionals. Jesus' parables are from everyday life. They are from the market place, the farm, the family. This parable is about salaries, wages, and a fair day's pay for a fair day's work. And people always get tense, anxious and nervous when you talk about money. But what is the point of this parable which on the face of it appears to support a very unjust approach to the payment for work done.

The dominant farm crop in first-century Palestine was grapes. So Jesus tells a story about harvesting grapes. The story goes like this: There was a man who owned a vineyard and he needed workers to harvest his grapes. He went to the village square at six o'clock in the morning and hired workers who went out and worked all day until six at night. But as the day wore on more workers were needed. Some were hired at nine o'clock in the morning and they worked for nine hours. Those who came at noon worked for six hours; those at three o'clock for three hours; and those who came at five o'clock worked one hour. And surprise, surprise, they all received the same wage. And all hell broke loose.

And indignation might well have been our reaction too. But this is a parable so we should expect it to have a meaning that goes beyond its immediate context. Those who were given a full days wage for just one hour's work were surprised and elated. They had waited all day in the hope of honest work and now they were rewarded. Their full day's wage was undeserved and unearned. It was a generous gift from the owner of the vineyard. And there are many Christians who feel like that. God's gifts to them are unearned and undeserved. They are wonderful and generous. For such Christians, life is not about fair rewards but about generous gifts. It is what we call grace.

But, there were others who were there at six o'clock in the morning and worked all day long. They were paid the agreed wage and were initially satisfied because they had deserved it. But they were then livid that others who had also been paid the full wage had not deserved it. There are some Christians who think like this about life. They are born into the faith; they are baptized at birth; they sing in the church choir and come to church every Sunday. And they believe that God owes them something. If anyone deserves to be blessed by God, they do for they have been faithful to God and his church all of their lives. For these Christians, life is about a fair reward. But is that actually God's way?

There is an old rabbinic parable about a farmer who had two sons. As soon as they were old enough to walk, he took them to the fields and he taught them everything he knew about growing crops and raising animals. When he got too old to work, the two boys took over the chores of the farm. When the father died, they had found their working together was so successful that they decided to keep in partnership. So each brother contributed what he could and during every harvest season, they would divide equally what they had produced together. Across the years the elder brother never married, and stayed as a bachelor. The younger brother did marry and had eight wonderful children.

Some years later when they were having a wonderful harvest, the bachelor brother thought to himself one night, "My brother has ten mouths to feed. I only have one. He really needs more of his harvest than I do, but I know he is much too fair to renegotiate. I know what I'll do. In the dead of the night when he is already asleep, I'll take some of what I have put in my barn and I'll slip it over into his barn to help him feed his children."

At the very time he was thinking along those lines, the younger brother was thinking to himself, "God has given me these wonderful children. My brother hasn't been so fortunate. He really needs more of this harvest for his old age than I do, but I know him. He's much too fair. He'll never renegotiate. I know what I'll do. In the dead of the night when he's asleep, I'll take some of what I've put in my barn and slip it over into his barn."

And so one night when the moon was full those two brothers came face to face, each on a mission of generosity. The old rabbi said that there wasn't a cloud in the sky; a gentle rain began to fall. You know what it was? God weeping for joy because two of his children had got the point. Two of his children had come to realise that generosity is the deepest characteristic of the holy and because we are made in God's image, our being generous is the secret of our joy as well.

The quest for justice is an important issue for our time and should be pursued with vigour in the interests of all. It is surely God's will that we should seek justice particularly for those who lack the basic necessities of life and the conditions to enjoy them.

But it is well to remember that the quest for justice is only a step on the way. The quest for generosity is a higher quest. And it is generosity that is ultimately God's way.

Seeing with the eyes of the heart

In his book, *God has a Dream*, Desmond Tutu explains that he learnt generosity from his parents. They taught him that:

> ...generosity comes from seeing that everything we have and everything we accomplish comes from God's grace and God's love for us. In the African understanding of *ubuntu*, our humility and generosity also come from realising that we could not be alive, nor could we accomplish anything, without the support, love, and generosity of all the people who have helped us to become the people we are today. Certainly it is from experiencing this generosity of God and the generosity of those in our life that we learn gratitude and to be generous to others (Tutu, 2004:86).

Tutu explains that in Africa, 'recognition of our interdependence is called *ubuntu* in Nguni languages which is difficult to translate into English'. He goes on:

> It is the essence of being human. It speaks of the fact that my humanity is caught up and inextricably bound up in yours. I am human because I belong. It speaks about wholeness; it speaks about compassion. A person with *ubuntu* is welcoming, hospitable, warm and generous, willing to share. Such people are open and available to others, willing to be vulnerable, affirming of others, do not feel threatened that others are able and good, for they have a proper self-assurance that comes from knowing that they belong to a greater whole (Tutu, 2004:25-26).

It is perhaps not surprising that words in other languages sometimes convey things that are almost impossible to convey in our own language because of a richness of meaning. This should remind us that words can have great power. They are also, of course, subject to severe limitations as we have noted elsewhere.

Trevor Huddleston was clearly a person with *ubuntu*. Desmond Tutu recalls the time when he was sick with tuberculosis as a boy. He tells how Trevor Huddleston visited him every week for the twenty months he was in hospital:

> Who was I that he should visit me? I was just another poor black boy, but you would never have known it. He was a white man who made you feel you mattered. He was full of laughter and caring, and he made everyone feel special... Our generosity is conveyed in time as much as in money (Tutu, 2004:87).

How to change the world

In October 2013, in the fourth in the series of debates at St Paul's Cathedral entitled, *How to change the world*, David Lammy MP and Lucy Winkett, Rector of St James Piccadily, tackled the subject of 'Generosity'.

David Lammy spoke of the experience of his father arriving from the West Indies as part of the 'Windrush generation' in the 1950s. Despite disillusionment of expectations and widespread racial prejudice he successfully made his mark in Britain not least because of the small acts of generosity that he encountered. Lucy Winkett argued that although individual acts of generosity were important, a change in culture was necessary if generosity was not to remain as the exception rather than the rule:

> Generosity could save the world. There is enough food and money for everyone on the planet if we took only what we need and gave the rest to those who have too little. But can we

> actually change our hearts, minds and politics enough to do that? And is there more to generosity than giving things away? The original meaning was nobility of spirit, and what would it mean – and take – for generosity of spirit to inform our politics, our religion, our personal lives, our encounters with strangers? (www.stpauls.co.uk/forum).

During her address, Lucy Winkett recalled the words of Martin Luther King. In reference to the traveller who was attacked and robbed in the parable of the Good Samaritan, he notes that in similar circumstances, too many people would ask the question "What will happen to me if I help this man?" when the question ought to be "What will happen to him if I don't?"

Compassion

> Christ has no body now on earth but yours, no hands but yours, no feet but yours.
> St Teresa of Avila

Love and Compassion

Love and compassion are closely related, but are not the same. Compassion is often an expression of love, but they have different roots. In the Preface to her book, *Twelve Steps to a Compassionate Life,* Karen Armstrong explains:

> 'Com*passion*' derives in part from the Latin *patiri* and the Greek *pathein,* meaning 'to suffer, undergo or experience'. So '*com*passion' means 'to endure (something) with another person', to put ourselves in somebody else's shoes, to feel her pain as though it were our own, and to enter generously into her point of view. That is why compassion is aptly summed up in the Golden Rule, which asks us to look into our own hearts, discover what gives us pain, and then refuse, under any circumstances whatsoever, to inflict that pain on anybody else. Compassion can be defined, therefore, as an attitude of principled, consistent altruism (Armstrong, 2011:6).

Compassion Has a Face

One of the most compelling accounts of compassion occurs in the Parable of the Good Samaritan recorded in the gospel according to Luke. At the end of the story, Jesus asks the lawyer who had posed the question, "Who is my neighbour?", "Which of these three (passers-by) was a neighbour to the man who fell into the hands of robbers?" He said, "The one who showed him mercy" Jesus said to him, "Go and do likewise" (Luke 10 36, 37).

In the chapter entitled, *Compassion Has a Face,* in David Cruz's book, *The Human Face of God,* the author reminds us that the face of Jesus was in many of those whose courageous actions saved lives on September 11th, 2001 when terrorists attacked the USA. Their stories can be illustrated by the dedication of Mychal Judge:

> A Chaplain for the New York Fire Department, Fr. Mychal followed the fireman and women responding to the explosion in the World Trade Center Towers into the smoke and chaos that engulfed New York's tallest structures when they were struck by two passenger planes hijacked by terrorists. As a result of his desire to serve those he loved, he placed himself in harm's way and lost his life while discharging his priestly duties. When urged to leave the building as it began to collapse all around him he was heard to say through the smoke, "I am not finished here" (Cruz, 2007:48).

The other chapters in Cruz's book have similar titles – Trust has a face, Mercy has a face – Forgiveness, Courage, Hope have faces. By the end of the book the reader realises that all of us are invited to become human faces of God in our lives and in the lives of others.

'Thanks for this brother...'

In an anthology by Victor Gollancz called *A Year of Grace,* Turgenev, the Russian author, tells the following story:

> I was walking along the street... I was stopped by a decrepit old beggar. Bloodshot, tearful eyes, blue lips, coarse rags, festering wounds... Oh, how hideously poverty had eaten into this miserable creature! He held out to me a red swollen, filthy hand. He groaned, he mumbled of help. I began feeling in all my pockets... No purse, no watch, not even a handkerchief... I had taken nothing with me. And the beggar was still waiting... and his outstretched hand feebly shook and

> trembled. Confused, abashed, I warmly clasped the filthy, shaking hand... "Don't be angry, brother; I have nothing, brother." The beggar stared at me with his bloodshot eyes; his blue lips smiled; and he in his turn grasped my chilly fingers. "What of it brother?" he mumbled; "thanks for this. This is a gift too brother." I knew then that I too had received a gift from my brother (Gollancz, 1964:200).

We live in an age and in a society in which we sometimes pay only lip service to those qualities that make for true humanity. We live in a world in which spin and presentation seem to have the upper hand and in which integrity and substance receive little attention. We live in a world in which impersonal institutions increasingly dominate our lives and in which the interests of the individual takes second place. We live in a world in which those with power too often misuse it and those without power are too often trampled underfoot. The financial crisis arose in part because of that culture. And as a result, thousands of people have lost their businesses, their jobs and their homes. Retired people have lost their life savings. Charities have lost their financial support. People have been driven to the depths of despair often by circumstances completely beyond their control.

We also live in a complex world and there are those who would argue that it is inevitable that individuals will sometimes fall by the wayside. Yet in our increasingly sophisticated society the numbers of those who do fall by the wayside are not noticeably decreasing. The gap between rich and poor is increasing and there is no evidence that fewer people are being marginalised. We may not often see Turgenev's beggar on our streets, but in some parts of the world you certainly will. In any case, in our society the outcast is in different clothing. He or she may look prosperous and happy but deep down there is turmoil. Loneliness is just one example of the unhappiness that blights the lives of so many older people.

But in the seventh chapter of the gospel according to Mark we are presented with a very different picture. In healing a Gentile women and then a man in 'unclean' territory, Jesus breaks down conventional expectations, overturns barriers of religion and race and declares the reign of God in all times and in all places. Nobody it seems is outside God's love and concern; rich and poor, old and young, male and female, saints and sinners. All are loved by God and therefore need to be treated as possessing the worth, dignity and rights that confers. And this is precisely the point made in the second chapter of James. He is appalled by a Christian gathering in which people of different social standings are treated unequally. The well-dressed and wealthy person is given deference and attention, but there is nothing for the person who is in rags.

We live in a world in which assumptions are made continually about who matters and who does not, about whose voice should be listened to and whose ignored, about who is deserving and who not. Justice in our society, we pride ourselves on saying, is impartial. But sometimes the marginalised groups in society tell a different story and we find it difficult to hear. We are shocked and sympathetic when someone contracts AIDS from a blood transfusion, but rather less so when they do so as a result of a lifestyle of which we disapprove. We acknowledge that it is right, in theory, to lift young single mothers out of the poverty trap, but we can't help suspecting that their predicament is really their own fault and that they should put up with the consequences.

We, good church-going Christians, have our prejudices too and live with the perpetual temptation to love our own kind best. But the ministry of Jesus to the Syrophoenician woman and the man from Galilee tell of another way of loving, in which God reaches out to those considered beyond the pale. We have sometimes drawn a distinction between the sacred and the secular. We have drawn a distinction between spreading the gospel and healing the sick. The message of Jesus is that there is no distinction. That in fact they are the same thing. The gospel is all about making people whole.

The compassion of Jesus

In his gospel, Matthew records several discourses about the coming of the Kingdom of God. And in the last discourse Jesus speaks about the separation of the sheep from the goats. He distinguishes between those who are worthy citizens of his kingdom and those who are not, and concludes, 'Truly I tell you, just as you did it to one of the least of these who are members of my family, you did it to me.' So what are the qualifications for citizenship of this kingdom?

At the end of his book on the Holy Spirit, *The Go-Between God*, John Taylor, former Bishop of Winchester, tells the following story:

> A West Indian woman was told of her husband's death in a street accident. The shock of grief stunned her like a blow, she sank into a corner of the sofa and sat there rigid and unhearing. For a long time her terrible tranced look continued to embarrass the family, friends and officials who came and went. Then the schoolteacher of one of her children, an Englishwoman, called and, seeing how things were, went and sat beside her. Without a word she threw an arm around the tight shoulders, clasping them with her full strength. The white cheek was thrust hard against the brown. Then as the unrelenting pain seeped through to her the newcomer's tears began to flow, falling on their two hands linked in the woman's lap. For a long time that is all that was happening. And then at last the West Indian woman started to sob. Still not a word was spoken and after a little while the visitor got up and went… (Taylor, 1972:243).

And John Taylor comments:

> That embrace is the embrace of God, his kiss of life. And the Holy Spirit is the force in the straining muscles of an arm, the film of sweat between pressed cheeks, the mingled wetness on the backs of clasped hands. He is as close and as unobtrusive as that, and as irresistibly strong (Taylor, 1972:243).

And he might have added that the compassion of the Englishwoman was the compassion of Jesus. And the suffering of the West Indian woman was the suffering of Jesus.

When planes flew into the twin towers of the World Trade Center in September 2001, and when more than three thousand people lost their lives, many were asking, 'Where was God'? And Rowan Williams, the Archbishop of Canterbury, who was visiting New York at the time, and was himself caught up in the terror and turmoil, responded. "God was there in the midst of the devastation", he said. God was there in the response of those who cared for the victims. God was there in the suffering of the victims themselves. We in the West sometimes give the impression that God is somehow 'out there'. That he is somehow separated from the world of suffering and pain. The message of the gospels, the story of the bereaved women and in the devastation of 9/11 is that God is not 'out there' but 'in here'. God is intimately part of our suffering world. He is there in the suffering and he is there in the compassion. He is a very human God (Williams, 2002).

A Charter for Compassion

The gospel accounts tell us something fundamental about the way Jesus understood his task. They tell us about his attitude to the people who followed him in their thousands as he toured the country. They tell us that despite the fact that he and his disciples were tired and hungry, the needs of these people came first. And they tell us that his response to their needs was not the indifference and impatience of perhaps some of his disciples, but love and compassion. Compassion is at the heart of the life and teaching of Jesus and it shines through the gospel accounts of his mission. It is a word that is close to 'love' but has a more practical 'feel'. Sadly it is not a word that we hear much today even in religious devotion and discourse. We hear about love but not much about compassion.

But compassion is a theme which we do find in some contemporary writers and in particular in the work of one of our most original and respected commentators on religion. Karen Armstrong's books are read by people from a wide range of different religious traditions. She was a Roman Catholic nun in the period before the Second Vatican Council had reformed the austere regimes of monasteries and convents. Her experience as a nun was so traumatic that she had to leave the convent and initially she abandoned religion altogether. But as the years passed and she engaged in other things she was gradually drawn back to religion most especially as she met people of other faiths. And as she began to study these other traditions she began to realise that the nature of religious belief was really very different from that which she had previously understood. It was a revelation!

As she explains in her subsequent writings, the word 'belief' originally meant 'to love, to prize, to hold dear'. It did not mean 'to hold certain creedal articles of faith'. It meant 'I commit myself, I engage myself'. Religion, she writes, is about 'behaving differently':

> Instead of deciding whether or not you believe in God, first you do something. You behave in a committed way, and then you begin to understand the truths of religion. Religious doctrines are summons to action and you only understand

> them when you put them into action. Pride of place in this practice is given to compassion. And it is an arresting fact that right across the board, in every single one of the major world faiths, compassion – the ability to feel with the other – is not only the test of any true religiosity, it is also what will bring us into the presence of what Jews, Christians and Muslims call 'God' or the 'Divine'. In compassion we dethrone ourselves from the centre of our world and we put another person there. And once we get rid of ego, then we're ready to see the divine (http://charterforcompassion.org/charter-karen-armstrong).

In 2008, Karen Armstrong was awarded the TED (Technology, Entertainment, Design) prize. As it says on the website:

> The TED Prize is awarded to an extraordinary individual with a creative and bold vision to spark global change. By leveraging the TED community's resources and investing (the prize money) into a powerful idea, the TED Prize supports one wish to inspire the world (http://www.ted.com/participate/ted-prize).

In her acceptance speech, Armstrong asked TED to help her create, launch and propagate a Charter for Compassion.

This document would be based on the fundamental principles of the Golden Rule – 'Do not do to others that which you would not like them to do to you'. And it would be signed by religious leaders from around the world. It would appeal in particular to all those who believe that their religion has been hijacked by those who insist on their version of orthodoxy – 'right belief'. It would be a 'working document' with the emphasis on 'working':

> The Charter for Compassion is a document that transcends religious, ideological, and national differences. Supported by

leading thinkers from many traditions, the Charter activates the Golden Rule around the world. It is a cooperative effort to restore not only compassionate thinking but, more importantly, compassionate action to the center of religious, moral and political life. Compassion is the principled determination to put ourselves in the shoes of the other, and lies at the heart of all religious and ethical systems (http://charterforcompassion.org).

The text of the Charter for Compassion is as follows:

The principle of compassion lies at the heart of all religious, ethical and spiritual traditions, calling us always to treat all others as we wish to be treated ourselves. Compassion impels us to work tirelessly to alleviate the suffering of our fellow creatures, to dethrone ourselves from the centre of our world and put another there, and to honour the inviolable sanctity of every single human being, treating everybody, without exception, with absolute justice, equity and respect. It is also necessary in both public and private life to refrain consistently and empathically from inflicting pain. To act or speak violently out of spite, chauvinism, or self-interest, to impoverish, exploit or deny basic rights to anybody, and to incite hatred by denigrating others – even our enemies – is a denial of our common humanity. We acknowledge that we have failed to live compassionately and that some have even increased the sum of human misery in the name of religion.

We therefore call upon all men and women to restore compassion to the centre of morality and religion – to return to the ancient principle that any interpretation of scripture that breeds violence, hatred or disdain is illegitimate – to ensure that youth are given accurate and respectful information about other traditions, religions and cultures – to encourage a positive appreciation of cultural and religious

> diversity – to cultivate an informed empathy with the suffering of all human beings – even those regarded as enemies.
>
> We urgently need to make compassion a clear, luminous and dynamic force in our polarized world. Rooted in a principled determination to transcend selfishness, compassion can break down political, dogmatic, ideological and religious boundaries. Born of our deep interdependence, compassion is essential to human relationships and to a fulfilled humanity. It is the path to enlightenment, and indispensable to the creation of a just economy and a peaceful global community (http://charterforcompassion.org).

It might seem a pious hope that large numbers of individuals and groups around the world would be willing to sign the charter but that is exactly what has happened and the message is spreading fast.

Karen Armstrong's writing is part of a process of change that is taking place amongst many of those who think deeply about religion. What we are beginning to see is a new realisation that compassion really is at the heart of religious faith and is not an optional extra. And what we are beginning to see is a new realisation that compassion should be at the heart of the church's faith and practice. That certainly accords with the gospel accounts of life and teaching of Jesus. We must ask ourselves whether it accords with the life and teaching of the church today. Pope Francis has certainly made a promising start in his pontificate as he shifts the emphasis towards compassion in his reform of the Roman Catholic Church.

In Karen Armstrong's book, *Twelve Steps to a Compassionate Life,* she encourages her readers to take practical steps to be compassionate in their own lives. The book is described on the flyleaf in the following way:

> Drawing on a wide range of material – ranging from the spiritualities of the world religions to the findings of contemporary neuroscience – Karen Armstrong argues that compassion is hardwired into our brains, yet is constantly restrained by our more primitive instincts for selfishness and survival. Taking as her starting point the teachings of the great world religions, Karen Armstrong demonstrates in twelve practical steps how we can bring compassion to the forefront of our lives. These steps both reveal the inadequacies of our knowledge of ourselves and others and enable us to unlock our potential for understanding, empathy and altruism that can be translated into acts of kindness and charity (Armstrong, 2011).

Kids Company

In September 2013, Karen Armstrong shared a platform with Camila Batmanghelidjh in a debate entitled 'Compassion' at St Paul's Cathedral. This was one in a series of debates – 'Compassion', 'Freedom', 'Peace', 'Generosity' and 'Together' – under the title 'How to change the world'.

Camila Batmanghelidjh is a psychotherapist and the Founder and Director of Kids Company, which provides practical, emotional and educational support to 36,000 vulnerable children and parents in London. When she started working with what was then a very small group of damaged youngsters she was shocked by the nature and level of their violence and aggression and sought to explore the reasons for this behaviour. She commissioned research, the results of which are telling us something quite new about both the physiological and psychological aspects of the development of the human brain in children and young people. This research is also leading to new ways of dealing with the troubled youngsters in the care of Kids Company. The increased application of the neurosciences is leading to revelations in the way we understand the human condition and relationships with each other.

However, there has been a marked reluctance on the part of both psychologists and those with a religious sentiment to engage with each other in serious debate about the interaction between the two. Such engagement would undoubtedly yield to revelations about the relationship between the practice of our faith and the workings of the human brain. Neuroscientists have already discovered that love and the lack of love significantly affects its development.

The debate, under the auspices of the St Paul's Forum, was marked by a striking contrast between the two addresses which became even more prominent during questions at the end of the debate. Karen Armstrong spoke powerfully about the need for compassion and about the Charter for Compassion. Camila Batmanghelidjh, on the other hand was able to convey something of her wide experience of what it means to be compassionate in one of most challenging parts of London:

> She spoke about "the transformative power of compassion and the potency of relentless love." On her strategy of 'relentless love' with the vulnerable and traumatised children in her care she said: "Clinically, it is a very valid strategy, because in conditions of love, your brain develops a neurochemical state of resilience which protects you against reacting negatively towards stressful stimuluses and I think we're at the point of a very exciting paradigm when, for those who don't believe in it, science is fundamentally going to produce the evidence for compassionate care." Asked how to change the world, she said: "Don't think big. Compassion is somewhere right under your nose, and when you're ready, you'll find it, and then if you express it, live it through, I promise you that you're going to get one of the biggest highs you've ever come across. So try it for me (www.stpauls.co.uk/forum).

Transformation

> Life should be a giving birth to the soul, the development of a higher mode of reality. The animal must be humanised: flesh must be made spirit; physiological activity must be transmuted into intellect and conscience, into reason, justice, and generosity, as the torch is transmuted into life and warmth. The blind, greedy selfish nature of man must put on beauty and nobleness. This heavenly alchemy is what justifies our presence on the earth; it is our mission and our glory.
> Henri Frédéric Amiel, *Amiel's Journal*.

The meaning of transformation

The word 'transformation' describes 'a change in form, appearance, nature, or character'. Although it is not a theological word, it can be used theologically and is increasingly used to describe the progress that we make in our spiritual journey. To be 'transformed' is to be changed and anything which contributes to that change is said to be 'transformative'. Transformation is at the heart of what it means to be a Christian.

Transformation as 'resurrection now'

At our church at Easter we celebrate in style – lights, candles, fire, bells, organ, fireworks, champagne – and a lot of noise. In some places the celebrations are even more exuberant and have been for centuries. An eye-witness describes the scene in pre-revolutionary Moscow:

> The roaring of the bells overhead, answered by the 1,600 bells from the illuminated belfries of all the churches of Moscow, the guns bellowing from the slopes of the Kremlin over the river, and the processions in their gorgeous cloth of gold vestments and with crosses, icons, and banners, pouring forth amidst clouds of incense from all the other churches in the

> Kremlin, and slowly wending their way through the crowd, all combined to produce an effect which none who have witnessed it can ever forget (Ware, 1982).

'Christ is Risen' is the acclamation that the people of Moscow made on that Easter morning and it is the acclamation that all Christians continue to make on every Easter morning as they celebrate the resurrection. But as we encounter the resurrection afresh, we need to do more than look back to that mysterious event two thousand years ago. We need to do more than recall the accounts of resurrection appearances. We need to ask the question 'What does the resurrection mean for us today?'

We have all heard of the Big Bang that the scientists describe as the event that initiated expansion of the physical universe. Christians can claim that a similar big bang happened in the spiritual world at the resurrection of Jesus. For whatever the details of the events that took place, the disciples were transformed from a group of frightened and traumatised individuals into a confident and powerful band that spearheaded the work of the early church. Thereafter the church grew and spread so that today perhaps a quarter of the world's population is at least nominally Christian. And along the way, lives have been changed.

So, one way of understanding the resurrection for our own time is as a symbol and a sign of the human possibility of transformation. Just as the lives of the disciples were transformed two thousand years ago, our lives can be transformed now. And that transformation can be experienced at both the personal and the social level, and one can lead to another. There have been many examples of transformative resurrection at work in the world, including the long struggle for Civil Rights in America.

On 1st December, 1955 at the end of a long and tiring day a black woman got on a bus in Montgomery, Alabama in the United States. Her name was Rosa Parks and she sat down on a seat at the front of the black section of the bus. When a white man got on at a later stop she was told to give up her seat and refused. She had broken the law, a policeman was called and she was arrested. The day after Rosa Park's arrest, Martin Luther King called a meeting. A leaflet was sent out to 50,000 black people. It said 'Don't ride the bus to work, to town, to school, or any place on Monday. A Negro woman has been arrested and put in jail because she refused to give up her seat on a bus'. This was the beginning of the famous bus boycott that recharged the Civil Rights movement and changed American history. Those who took part in the boycott knew that they would have to pay for their refusal to submit any longer to harassment and humiliation. They knew that they would have to face further hatred and violence. But something had changed. Something had dropped away, some burden of fear or timidity or resignation. A whole people were transformed because one woman had the courage to refuse to go to the back of the bus.

When Rosa Parks made her decision something remarkable happened. In resurrection language, a whole people walked out of the tomb of segregation and were resurrected. For, resurrection is the refusal to be imprisoned any longer by history and tradition. Resurrection is the refusal to be contained any longer by evil and death. It is the determination to take the first steps out of the tomb and live. It may be personal circumstances that immobilise us. It may be social evils that confront us. Whatever it is, transformation is possible. And resurrection only has meaning if it leads to transformed lives. It only has meaning if it leads to transformed attitudes and transformed societies.

So resurrection is not something that just happened on that first Easter Day. It is something that is happening now. We do not know exactly what happened when Jesus was resurrected and the gospels provide conflicting accounts. What we do know is that *something* happened. What we know is that things happen now. So we can believe in *that* resurrection *then*, because we see *this* resurrection *now*. We see stones rolled away and new possibilities rising from old attitudes.

We have all been placed in the human condition. That is all we know and that is the only context within which we can act. If the appropriation of the resurrection has nothing to say about the human condition, about social justice and human dignity, then it means very little. If, on the other hand, it can transform us as human beings and enable us to be a renewed force for good in the world then it will have enduring value. And we can all identify men and women throughout history who have been transformed in this way; men and women who have been able to make their mark in the transformation of society sometimes at very great cost to themselves.

Transformation in the financial world

During the financial crisis you may have noticed that a number of words not usually associated with these markets and institutions began to appear in the financial pages of our newspapers and on the lips of those who have been commentating on events for us. Words like 'greed', 'selfishness' and 'irresponsibility' suddenly became part of the language with which we describe the actions of some of those who work in banks and elsewhere in the world of finance. These accusations may or may not be just or fair but there is certainly a perception that something is very wrong at the heart of one of our major activities as a nation.

Some have argued that the problem arises because of a lack of regulation. But by all accounts we have one of the most respected systems of regulation in the world. Clearly the problem goes deeper and is associated with the way business is done and transactions are executed. I am not an expert on the world of finance. But I know enough, as I suspect we all do, to see that we need a new framework of guidelines. It is possible that a change in the law is also required but it is certain that a change in the guidelines is long overdue. We should recall that at one time the city was an example of the very best in financial dealing. But 'my word is my bond' is not a phrase that you hear much now.

But even if the law is changed, regulations are tightened and guidelines are amended, there is a danger that the moral climate will remain much the same because it is part of a much bigger picture. With the decline in traditional religious beliefs and the collapse of traditional moral frameworks many are claiming that we can live with authenticity and integrity in a multitude of different ways. And with this has come a presumption that all ways are equally valid. This means that some will have their own individual framework of values and that others will have no framework of values at all. Therefore there is a danger that there will no longer be the consensus about basic moral values that we have enjoyed for so long.

The legacy of the financial crisis is that we are in desperate need of transformation. Transformation in the way business is transacted. Transformation in the way people behave. And we are in desperate need of people who are prepared to take a lead. There are voices out there in the wilderness encouraging a different approach. And some church people have said some powerful things; but religious 'takes' on this crisis have not exactly been banner headlines. And the moral arguments for change have not exactly been shouted from the rooftops.

It is said that no one could have predicted this financial crisis. But that is quite wrong. At least one person explained very clearly what was going wrong. But she was ridiculed for her views and her voice was not heard. Her name is Catherine Crowley. She worked for several years in a high-powered job in the city. She is now a Roman Catholic nun and university teacher of ethics – in fact she taught me. In 2006 she wrote a book called *The Value of Money: ethics and the world of finance.* She predicted pretty accurately much of what has now taken place.

This book should be required reading for all those politicians and bankers who got us into this mess. But sadly Catherine

Crowley will neither get the recognition she deserves for her insights nor will many people read her book. But the importance of her book lies, not only in what it says about the misunderstanding of risk and the misuse of money, but in the circumstances of the saying of it. Here is someone approaching one world from the perspectives of another. Here is someone approaching the secular from the perspective of the sacred. And she gets it right. The seeds of transformation are there.

Remember the three young men who were thrown into the 'burning fiery furnace' because of their refusal to worship the Babylonian gods. As they walk about in the flames they are joined by a protecting angel. Why have we been placed in the 'fiery furnace' of our world and its values? Is it then to escape from it? No! Is it finally to be consumed by it? No! Is to play our part in changing it? Yes! That is resurrection now.

The comfortable pew

The Shipping News is a popular film starring Kevin Spacey and Judi Dench. You may have seen it on one of its frequent outings on television. It tells the story of a hapless and hopeless print worker called Quoyle who returns to his former family home in a remote corner of Newfoundland. Many years have passed since the battered old house was pulled across the ice to its new resting place on an exposed cliff. There it had been tethered by thick steel cables to hold it down in the frequent storms that lashed that part of the coast. But inevitably when the big storm came, those cables snapped and the house crumpled, for the house had no foundations.

We all recall the parable of Jesus about a house without foundations. The wise man built his house on rock. 'The rain fell, the floods came, and the winds blew and beat on that house, but it did not fall, because it had been founded on rock'. The foolish man built his house on sand. 'The rain fell, and the floods came, and the winds blew and beat against that house, and it fell and great was the fall of it.' And this is the message. 'Everyone who hears these words of mine and acts on them will be like the wise man who built his house on rock'. 'And everyone who hears these words of mine and does not act on them will be like the foolish man who built his house on sand' (Matthew, 7:24-27).

Jesus is warning his friends against an easy-going discipleship. A discipleship which enjoys companionship with him but fails to take seriously the challenges of the gospel he preaches. How easy it was for them, and how easy it is for us, to be around Jesus and to enjoy his company and conversation; to share his popularity and charisma; but to be unwilling to be challenged by the content of his message. To be unwilling to make the choices about life which are demanded by his call. Easy, maybe, but as useless as trying to learn to swim while keeping one foot on the bottom for safety. We don't want to be vulnerable. We want to be safe.

Many years ago a group of Anglicans in Canada invited a prominent atheist, to write an assessment of their church from an outsider's point of view. Their aim was to open up a serious discussion about the meaning of Christian faith in a secular world. They wanted to promote dialogue and debate with anyone willing to participate. But they got rather more than they bargained for. When the book was published it caused a sensation. It prompted outrage amongst some and critical acclaim amongst others. But what did it actually say? In essence it accused the church of not engaging with the world. It accused the church of not willing to grapple with the issues facing people in the twentieth century. And what was the title of this book? *The Comfortable Pew.*

That report was written many years ago but its challenge is as relevant now as it was then. Are we too comfortable in our pews? I know some churches do not have pews but bear with me. We are happy to attend church each Sunday. We enjoy meeting friends and the atmosphere of worship. We like the beauty of the liturgy and the poignancy of the prayers. But do we engage all our faculties. Are we prepared to be challenged by the words? Are we prepared to be vulnerable to the uncertainties that they bring? Are we prepared to face the challenges of the human condition? For what Jesus was getting at in his parable about foundations was our need to dig deeper; to explore the implications of our faith and to accept what follows.

In *The Shipping News,* Quoyle loses the old family home because it had no foundations. In many ways this could be a metaphor for his old life in the city. It was shallow and insecure. It was going nowhere. When he returns to his homeland he gains a new life with new foundations. He meets new people and finds new relationships. He discovers a new dignity and new purpose. There is no doubt that this is a man whose life has been transformed.

The view from the mountain top

Many of us have experienced the exhilaration of reaching the top of a mountain after a stiff climb. I well remember reaching the top of Snowdon by the pyg track with a party of scouts many years ago. I also remember making straight for the cafe and asking for fifty cups of tea! When the lady had recovered I explained that they were not all for me. After quenching our thirst and recovering our breath we looked around and there before us lay the mountains and valleys of North Wales in the summer sunshine. A truly uplifting moment.

It was possibly to Mt. Hermon that Jesus took Peter, James and John in the account of the transfiguration. Mt. Hermon is fourteen miles from Caesarea Philippi where Jesus had been preparing the disciples for the final events of his life. And as part of this process of preparation he leads three of the disciples up the mountain. Mt. Hermon is quite high, about 9,400 feet above sea level but 11,000 feet above the Jordan valley. So this event probably happened somewhere on the higher slopes but not at the top.

It is clear that the experience was exhilarating. We are told that Jesus was transformed before the disciples in a vision. We are told that 'his clothes became dazzling white.' It's probably not helpful to speculate about what the disciples actually saw or about what physical events actually took place. It is the effect on those present that matters most. And there is no doubt that this was a high point in the revelation of Jesus to his disciples. It's a moment when he is revealed as standing in the tradition of the Law and the Prophets of the old covenant. Both Moses and Elijah appear in the vision. But it is also a moment when he is revealed in the Glory and Love of the new covenant. The disciples are witnesses of that. It is a high point indeed. But this mountain top is significant in more ways than one.

The famous archaeologist Leonard Woolley was once looking in vain for tombs in the Nile Valley and was about to give up. He had been searching long and hard for many days but without success. One evening, something prompted him to climb some nearby hills and view the site from above and with the sun low on the horizon. And there in the sand were the shadows and patterns that would later lead him to his target. Aerial photography has now become an important part of the art and science of both archaeologists and geologists. In recent years, satellite photographs have revealed much that we did not know about what is under the surface of our planet. There are times when we are just too close to things on earth and need to gain a different perspective. If that is true for the material world then it is also true of our spiritual experience. Part of our exhilaration on the mountain top is the feeling that we have left behind those things which get on top of us so that we can get on top of them.

And it was like this for Jesus. At this crucial moment he wanted both for himself and his disciples to stand back and view things in perspective. In the valley, life was on top of him with the crowds and the constant attention. On the mountain, he was apart and could think and pray quietly on his own and with those closest to him. He could prepare himself and the disciples for what was to come. But he could not stay on the mountain top for ever. What was to come meant that he would have to leave the mountain top and return to the valley. He would have to face the last journey to Jerusalem, to betrayal, to condemnation, to scourging and to death. And the disciples would also. The American evangelist Dwight Moody once heard someone testify to having been five years on the Mount of Transfiguration. 'That's too long,' said Moody. 'How many people did you help during that time?' 'I don't know' was the reply. Moody went on: 'I don't want that kind of mountain-top, when it's so high one can't reach down; there is something wrong!' When Jesus left the mountain-top he found the father of the epileptic boy waiting for him!

'Do not be conformed...'

In, *Do Not Be Conformed,* from a collection of sermons called, *The Eternal Now,* Paul Tillich reminds us of the apostle Paul's exhortation, 'Do not be conformed to this world, but be transformed by the renewing of your minds...' (Romans 12:2). He notes that it is unfortunate that the Greek word for 'aeon' is translated in our bibles as 'world' because that is not a satisfactory word to use in the context for it should have much richer connotations. Paul wants to include every aspect of 'all that is' and exhort his readers to aspire to embrace 'all that can be'. He points to 'the new heaven and the new earth' that is so prominent in the Bible (Tillich, 1963).

Tillich's sermon is not easy to follow, but in essence he argues that only those who are prepared to take risks can be truly transformed and can renew their own being and that of others. He exhorts us to resist 'making an ultimate' of our world, our culture, our church or our moral codes. He asks us to dare not to be conformed to this world, but to transform it courageously first in ourselves, then in our world – in the spirit and the power of love.

For the authors of the book, *Living the Questions*, 'the path toward transformation is different for every traveller, but the need for transformation is an integral part of the human experience':

> As we pursue the growth we're called to seek in order to reach our full potential, it may be helpful to remember what Taoism teaches its adherents: so long as bamboo is alive and growing it is pliable and flexible. Once it dies, however, it becomes brittle and is easily snapped. Creativity and transformation are principles that stave off our tendency to become hard and brittle, and open us instead to the transformative power of God's unconditional love and grace (Felton & Procter-Murphy, 2012:218).

Conclusion

In 1952, the scholar J B Phillips wrote a little book called *Your God is Too Small*. In his Introduction to the book he wrote:

> The trouble with many people today is that they have not found a God big enough for modern needs. While their experience of life has grown in a score of directions, and their mental horizons have been expanded to the point of bewilderment by world events and by scientific discoveries, their ideas of God have remained largely static (Phillips, 1969:7).

This was written more than sixty years ago and if it was true then it is even more true now in the ever increasing complexity of our world at the beginning of the twenty-first century. This present book takes seriously the charge that 'Your God is Too Small'.

What I have attempted to do in this book is to enlarge our vision of God in the hope that this will enlarge our response to that vision in love for God, our neighbours and ourselves. What I have attempted to convey is something of the breadth and depth of human experience and the extent to which it points to something beyond which we might call God. This survey of themes is not comprehensive because that would be an impossible task but the themes chosen do give a flavour of some of the qualities that we recognise as human and the depths to which they can be pursued. Other themes could have been chosen and there is no doubt that other important truths have not been explored so this survey is necessarily incomplete.

The absence of many of the traditional elements in a book about the Christian enterprise will concern many people but that is to misunderstand the nature of this book. As the foundational document of Christianity, the Bible is well represented but the emphasis is on its interpretation rather than what it conveys at face value. Theology is touched on from time to time but to pursue theological ideas any further would be to divert attention from the main purpose of this book which is to explore what it means to be human. Liturgy, prayer and the worshipping life of the church have been put on one side because they are part of a different aspect of the debate.

If the nature of the approach adopted in this book has any merit then there is scope for its aims to be pursued with greater vigour and in greater depth. Indeed the riches that can be mined from these sources are inexhaustible and the deeper we go the greater will be the reward. The human route to God has not been much explored and for historical, cultural, theological and many other reasons so that in this single-minded pursuit we are almost in virgin territory. It has already been pointed out that the insights of the human sciences – psychology, sociology and anthropology – have been woefully neglected. The physical and biological sciences – physics, chemistry and biology – also have a vital part to play.

I have already outlined the work of Camila Batmanghelidjh and have briefly described the outcomes of research into the links between the behaviour of youngsters and the development of their brains. The work of neuroscientists is transforming our knowledge of how the brain works and has the potential to revolutionise the way we understand our intellectual, emotional and volitional disposition. It also has the potential to revolutionise the way we understand the religious dimension of our lives and our spiritual disposition. We cannot ignore this work or claim that this aspect of our lives is not subject to such examination. As I said before, there is no evidence that the Holy Spirit navigates his own way through our psyche.

This research is so important that I close this book with an outline of the work of four people whose studies have major implications for our understanding of the religious sentiment.

Susan Greenfield

Susan Greenfield is a scientist, writer, broadcaster and member of the House of Lords. Specialising in the physiology of the brain, she researches the impact of twenty-first-century technologies on the mind, how the brain generates consciousness and novel approaches to neurodegenerative diseases such as Alzheimer's and Parkinson's. She has written a range of non-specialist books on issues relating to the mind and brain for the general reader.

In her book, *The Human Brain*, Susan Greenfield tells the story of a little Italian boy who is blind in one eye. I have called him Marcello in a brief summary of his story in an earlier chapter. Marcello's eye was bandaged as a baby and because the bandaged eye was not able to do its job, the brain assumed that the boy would not be using that eye for the rest of his life and failed to make the necessary neuron connections, so that when the bandage was removed, he could not see. Greenfield writes:

> As our development continues after birth, the jostling, restless neurons in the brain are very reactive as they form circuits to reflect whatever is happening in the individual outside world. Inside the brain, right up to sixteen years of age, a bloody battle is being waged between our neurons. It is a battle for establishing connections. If a new neuron does not make contact with a target neuron, or is insufficiently stimulated, then it dies… Any small change in the normal lifestyle or environment will be reflected in a change in neuronal circuitry… Thus, the degree of stimulation from the environment will determine how the cone connections between neurons are formed, and thus make you the person you are (Greenfield, 1997:115).

Susan Greenfield's contention, expressed in numerous articles and books, is that the brain's workings can be changed, often for the worse, by external influences. She is particularly concerned about the impact of modern technology and in particular the increased use of television, computers and mobile phones. This is particularly acute for youngsters whose brains are still growing and who are vulnerable to the attractions of this new world. Research has established that thousands of teenagers spend several hours each day on the internet.

Alister Hardy

Sir Alister Hardy was Professor of Zoology at the University of Oxford from 1946 to 1961. He founded the Religious Experience Unit in Oxford and was its first Director from 1969 until 1976. In 2000 it moved to the University of Wales in Lampeter. Hardy was convinced of a link between religious experience and evolutionary biology. Hardy's hypothesis can be stated as follows:

> Religious awareness is biologically natural to the human species and has evolved through the process of natural selection because it has survival value for the individual (Hay, 1994:2).

He wrote a number of books including *The Spiritual Nature of Man* published in 1979. In the first chapter of this book, Hardy writes:

> It had always seemed to me that man was religious by nature, but that modern man's craving for a spiritual philosophy had become frustrated, making him restless and uncertain. I had felt for a long time that these unappeased religious desires could only be satisfied with a spiritual philosophy which could be seen to be based upon a systematic study of recorded experience and which was not incompatible with modern biological theory (Hardy, 1980:3).

Hardy explains that, apart from work done by social anthropologists, there was for many years a dearth of scientific interest in man's spiritual awareness. He attributes this to the uneasy relationship between science and religion, and to the reductionism so prevalent in some sections of the scientific community. Increasing numbers of people seemed to believe that anything worthy of scientific study could ultimately be reduced to physical and chemical processes.

Hardy was a convinced Darwinian, but did not believe that such an understanding of the physical processes at work gave a complete account of the evolutionary process. He writes:

> Is it not possible that there are other things in the universe that are just as real and remarkable as the replicating molecules, the genes, upon which the evolution of these physico-chemical machines – the bodies of plants, animals, and man – depend? (Hardy, 1980: 14)

One of the characteristics of Hardy's research was the way in which he collected his data. He encouraged members of the public to send in accounts of their experience. He used newspapers appeals, special pamphlets and eventually questionnaires, and with considerable success.

Hardy concludes his book with these words:

> The spiritual nature of man is, I believe, being shown to be a reality. We now need a biological philosophy which will recognise both this and the need to study consciousness as a fundamental attribute of life. I hope this book will encourage this quest (Hardy, 1980:142).

David Hay was a collaborator of Hardy in this research. In his essay *The Biology of God: What is the Current Status of Hardy's Hypothesis?* written in 1994, Hay concludes that research has 'strengthened the plausibility of Hardy's hypotheses while not supporting the rival explanations.' He adds that 'there is reason to investigate Hardy's hypothesis more extensively' (Hay, 1994).

Leslie Francis

Since 2007 The Rev Canon Professor Leslie Francis has been Professor of Religions and Education in the University of Warwick. He is Honorary Director of the St Mary's Centre, and Canon Theologian of Bangor Cathedral, Wales. The St Mary's Centre coordinates the Network for Psychological Type and Christian Faith. The Network was established in 2000 as a forum for those employing Psychological Type theory in a variety of ways within the Christian churches. Psychological Type Theory arises from the Myers-Briggs Type Indicator.

The Myers-Briggs Type Indicator (MBTI) assessment is a questionnaire designed to measure psychological preferences in how people perceive the world and make decisions about it. These preferences are extrapolated from the theories proposed by Carl Jung and first published in his 1921 book, *Psychological Types*. Jung argued that there are four principal psychological functions by which we experience the world: sensation, intuition, feeling, and thinking. He claimed that one or other of these four functions is dominant most of the time. The original developers of the personality test were Katharine Cook Briggs and her daughter, Isabel Briggs Myers. They studied extensively the work of Jung, and turned their interest in human behaviour into developing the theory of psychological types for practical use.

In his book, *Personality Type and Scripture: Exploring Mark's Gospel*, Leslie J. Francis applies personality type theory to the way we study the Bible. Why, when two people are asked what they find important in a biblical text, are they likely to come up with different answers? Why, when a sermon speaks strongly to someone, do others find it incomprehensible? The book is introduced on the back cover as follows:

In recent years, both inside and outside the Christian community, the Myers-Briggs Type Indicator (MBTI) has been extensively used as an aid to spiritual growth, self-knowledge and community building. Type theory has become an invaluable resource in the spheres of education, management and pastoral care. Here, Leslie J. Frances suggests that in learning to understand our own preferred pattern of spirituality we do not only deepen our understanding of the gospels but also increase our sensitivity to the approaches of others. *Personality Type and Scripture* brings together the texts from St Mark's gospel which are included in Year B of the Revised Common Lectionary, and uses the insights of MBTI theory to explore the range of possible responses to them (Francis, 1997).

Carl Gustav Jung (1875 – 1961)

In 1959 John Freeman conducted a famous interview with Carl Jung. At one point he asked Jung if he believed in God. There was a short pause and then Jung replied "I don't need to believe, I know".

Personality has always been of interest to psychologists but they have rarely given much credence to that aspect of the personality that we call 'religious'. They have striven to maintain scientific credibility for their work and so many have been sceptical of any suggestion that there might be non-scientific factors involved. This has been part of a wider tension between 'science' and 'religion' which is touched on elsewhere.

Carl Jung, however, was a psychologist who took a very different line. Unlike Sigmund Freud and his followers, Jungians tend to treat religious beliefs and behaviour in a positive light. That the Jungian interpretation of religion has been, and continues to be, of interest to psychologists, theologians and the public is attested by the large number of books and articles published on the subject.

In his book, *Psychology of Religion* David Wulff summarises Jung's approach to what he calls the 'tasks of psychology'. According to Wulff, Jung 'wished to communicate an attitude and a challenge':

> The attitude is one of openness, especially to the non-rational and the mysterious, to what lies beyond the logic of the philosopher and the instruments of the scientists. It is a recognition of the infinity that stretches far beyond our understanding, of the powers that lie outside our comprehension and control. It is, then, also an attitude of humility and of awe. The challenge Jung throws out to us is ultimately an impossible one to fulfil: the challenge of becoming whole… The task of psychology is therefore an urgent one. Man can make no progress with himself unless he becomes very much better acquainted with his own nature. According to Jung, that knowledge will grow only when psychologists and other students of human nature take into account the full range of human experience, including the experience of God. God, Jung emphasised repeatedly, is not a matter of belief but of indisputable and valuable experience (Wulff, 1997:470).

In his work, *Psychology and Religion*, Jung writes:

> No matter what the world thinks about religious experience, the one who has it possesses a great treasure, a thing that has become for him a source of life, meaning, and beauty, and that has given a new splendour to the world and to mankind. He has *pistis* and peace. Where is the criterion by which you could say that such a life is not legitimate, that such an experience is not valid, and that such *pistis* is mere illusion? Is there, as a matter of fact, any better truth about the ultimate things than the one that helps you to live?... No one can know what the ultimate things are. We must therefore take them as we

> experience them. And if such experience helps to make life healthier, more beautiful, more complete and more satisfactory to yourself and to those you love, you may safely say: "This was the grace of God" (Jung, 1964:105).

Carl Jung has been deeply influential. In an article headed, *Jung Among the Christians,* Angela Tilby writes that:

> ...the idea that life is a pilgrimage towards wholeness in God is deeply informed by Jung. Jung's theory of psychological types has become an important tool in guiding individuals in vocation and prayer. Marriage preparation and counselling look to Jung's notion of the bi-sexuality of the self. Even the practice of religious celibacy has been strengthened by Jung's notion of the inner marriage as a mark of individuation (Tilby, 1990).

The idea that life is a pilgrimage towards wholeness in God also expresses a truth about this book.

References and Bibliography

Allport, G. W. (1969). *The Individual and His Religion*. London: The Macmillan Company.

Alves, R. (1971). *A Theology of Human Hope*. New York: Corpus Books.

Amnesty International. (2012). About Us. Retrieved from www.amnesty.org.uk

Anderson, D. (1971). *Simone Weil*. London. SCM Press.

Armstrong, K. (2005). *A Short History of Myth*. Edinburgh: Canongate Books.

Armstrong, K. (2009). *The Case for God*. London: The Bodley Head.

Armstrong, K. (2011). *Twelve Steps to a Compassionate Life*. London: The Bodley Head.

Avis, P. (1999). *God and the Creative Imagination*. London: Routledge.

Ball, O., & Gready, P. (2006). *The No-Nonsense Guide to Human Rights*. Oxford: New Internationalist Publications Ltd. Kindle file.

Baltes, P. B. (2004). Wisdom as Orchestration of Mind and Virtue. Retrieved from http://library.mpib-berlin.mpg.de/ft/pb/PB_Wisdom_2004.pdf

Barbour, I. G. (1974). *Myths, Models and Paradigms*. London: SCM Press.

Barclay, W. (1965). *The Gospel of John, Volume 2*. Philadelphia: Westminster Press.

Bauby, J-D. (1998). *The Diving-Bell and The Butterfly*. London: Fourth Estate.

Blackburn, S. (2006). *Truth: A Guide for the Perplexed*. London: Penguin Books.

Bonhoeffer, D. (1965). *Letters and Papers from Prison*. London: Collins.

Borg, M. (2003). *The Heart of Christianity*. New York: Harper

Collins.

Borg, M. J. (2011). *Speaking Christian*. London: SPCK.

Brady, B. V. (2003). *Christian Love.* Washington D C: Georgetown University Press.

Brown, G. (2007). *Courage: Eight Portraits*. London: Bloomsbury Publishing.

Cairns, D. (1973). *The Image of God in Man*. London: Collins.

Campbell, F. (2000). *Religious Integrity for Everyone*. New York: Writers Club Press.

Campbell, P. (2013). Wisdom story. Retrieved from http://people-forothers.loyolapress.com/?s=wisdom

Cox, D., Levine, M. P., & La Caze, M. (2003). *Integrity and the Fragile Self*. Farnham: Ashgate Publishing.

Crossan, J. D. (1991). *The Historical Jesus*. Edinburgh: T & T Clark.

Cruz, D. R. (2007). *The Human Face of God*. Enumclaw, USA: Pleasant World.

Cupitt, D. (2001). *Taking Leave of God*. London: SCM Press.

Curran, C. (1998). Absolute Moral Norms. In *Christian Ethics.* London: Continuum.

Dalai, L. (2000). *The Little Book of Wisdom*. London: Rider Publishing.

Dawkins, R. (2006). *The God Delusion*. London: Transworld Publishers.

De Gruchy, J. W. (2006). *Being Human.* London: SCM Press.

DePree, M. (1989). *Leadership is an Art*. New York: Dell Publishing.

Doctrine Commission. (2003). *Being human.* London: The Church of England.

Doyle, D. F. (2011). *The Promise of Christian Humanism*. USA: The Crossroad Publishing Company.

Eagleton, T. (2009). *Reason, Faith, and Revolution*. New Haven, USA: Yale University Press.

Eco, U. (1988). *The Aesthetics of Thomas Aquinas*. Cambridge, MA: Harvard University Press.

Eco, U. (1998). *The Name of the Rose*. London: Random House.

Eliot, T. S. (1971). *Selected Poems*. London: Faber & Faber.

Ewert, M. V. (2014). *The Generosity Path*. Boston USA: Skinner House Books.

Felton, D. M., & Procter-Murphy, J. (2012). *Living the Questions*. New York: Harper Collins.

Fisk, R. (2006). *The Great War for Civilisation:* London: Harper Perennial.

Fox, M. (1984). *Original Blessing:* Santa Fe, USA: Bear & Company

Frame, T. (2007). Living Our Lives by the Rule of Law. *Church Times*. (17 Oct).

Francis, L. J. (1997). *Personality Type and Scripture*. London: Mowbray.

Funk, R. (1993). *The Five Gospels*. London: Harper Collins.

Gardner, H. (2011). *Truth, Beauty and Goodness Reframed*. New York: Basic Books.

Gillman, H. (2003). *A Light that is Shining*. London: Quaker Books.

Gollancz, V. (1964). *A Year of Grace*. London: Victor Gollancz Limited.

Greenfield, S. (1997). *The Human Brain*. London: Weindenfeld & Nicholson.

Greenleaf, R. (1977). *Servant Leadership*. New York: Paulist Press.

Greet, K. (1967). Temperance in Use of Alcohol. In *A New Dictionary of Christian Ethics*. London: SCM Press.

Gumbel, N. (1993). *Alpha: Questions of Life*. Eastbourne: Kingsway Communications Ltd.

Gutierrez, G. (2001). *A Theology of Liberation*. London: SCM Press.

Halfon, M. (1989). *Integrity: A philosophical inquiry*. Philadelphia: Temple University Press.

Hall, S. S. (2011). *Wisdom: From Philosophy to Neuroscience*. New York: Vintage Books.

Hallett, G. (1989). *Christian Neighbor Love*. Washington DC: Georgetown University Press.

Hammarskjold, D. (2006). *Markings*. New York: Vintage Books.

Hardy, A. (1980). *The Spiritual Nature of Man*. Oxford: Clarendon Press.

Harries, R. (1996). *Art and the Beauty of God*. London: Mowbray.

Hay, D. (1994). The Biology of God. *The International Journal for the Psychology of Religion*, 4(1).

Hazelton, R. (1967). Courage. In *A New Dictionary of Christian Ethics*. London: SCM Press.

Hazelton, R. (1985). *Graceful Courage*. Philadelphia: Fortress Press.

Hebblethwaite, B. (2010). *The Christian Hope*. Oxford: Oxford University Press.

Hick, J. (1968). *Evil and the God of Love*. London: Collins.

Hitchins, C. (2007). *God is Not Great*. New York: Allen & Unwin.

Huskey, B. (2013). The Wisdom of Oz. Retrieved from http://wisdomresearch.org/forums/t/1154.aspx#sthash.lTbZpp0o.dpuf

Ignatieff, M. (2002). Is the Human Rights Era Ending? *New York Times*. (5 Feb)

Jacks, L. P. (1931). *Education for the Whole Man*. London: University of London Press.

Jenkins, D. (2003). *The Calling of a Cuckoo*. London: Continuum.

John Paul 11. (1995). Address in General Assembly of United Nations. Retrieved from www.vatican.va/holy_father/john_paul_ii/speeches/1995/october/documents/hf_jp-ii_spe_05101995_address-to-uno_en.html

John Paul 11. (1998). *Faith and Reason*. London: The Catholic Truth Society.

John XX111, P. (1963). Pacem in Terris. Retrieved from http://www.vatican.va/holy_father/john_xxiii/encyclicals/documents/hf_j-xxiii_enc_11041963_pacem_en.html

Johnstone, W. (1995). *Exodus*. Sheffield: Sheffield Academic Press.

Jung, C. (1964). *The Development of Personality*. London: Routledge & Kegan Paul.

Kee, A. (1988). *The Roots of Christian Freedom.* London: SPCK.

Keenan, J. (1998). Virtue Ethics. In *Christian Ethics: An introduction*. London: Continuum.

Kegley, J. A. K. (1989). *Paul Tillich on Creativity*. Lanham, USA: University Press of America.

Keller, T. (2010). *Generous Justice*. London: Hodder & Stoughton.

Kennedy, J. F. (2013). *Profiles in Courage*. Harper Perrenial.

King, M. L. (1957). Loving Your Enemies. Retrieved from http://www.salsa.net/peace/conv/8weekconv4-2.html

King, M. L. (1963a). I have a dream. Retrieved from http://www.archives.gov/press/exhibits/dream-speech.pdf

King, M. L. (1963b). Letter from Birmingham Jail. *Why We Can't Wait*. London: Longman.

Knox, J. (1959). *The Death of Christ*. London: Collins.

Knox, J. (1968). *The Humanity and Divinity of Christ*. Cambridge: Cambridge University Press.

Kuhn, T. (2012). *The Structure of Scientific Revolutions*. Chicago. University of Chicago Press

Kung, H. (1978). *On Being a Christian*. London: Fount Paperbacks.

Kung, H. (1988). *Theology for the Third Millennium.* New York: Doubleday.

Kung, H. (1995). *Christianity.* London: SCM Press.

Lang, D. (2008). *Saving Mandela's Children*. Milton Keynes: Authorhouse.

Langford, M. (2010). *Unblind Faith*. Tonbridge Wells, Kent: Parapress.

Leach, E. (1989). Fishing for men on the edge of the wilderness. In *The Lierary Guide to the Bible*. Fontana.

Lebacqz, K. (2007). *Justice in an Unjust World*. Minneapolis USA: Fortress Press.

Lewin, A. (1997). *Candles and Kingfishers*. Horsham: Foundry Press.

Lewis, C. S. (1965). *The Four Loves*. London: Fontana Books.

Liddell, E. (1981). You came to see a race today. Retrieved from

http://www.imdb.com/character/ch0016125/quotes
MacCulloch, D. (2009). *A History of Christianity.* London: Penguin Books.
MacIntyre, A. (1999). *After Virtue*. London: Duckworth.
Macmurray, J. (1957). *The Self as Agent*. London: Faber and Faber.
Macmurray, J. (1995). *Persons in Relation*. London: Faber and Faber.
Mandela, N. (2009). *Long Walk to Freedom*. London: Abacus.
Marshall, E., & Hample, S. (1980). *Children's Letters to God*. London: Fontana.
Maslow, A. (1993). *The Farther Reaches of Human Nature*. New York: Penguin Compass.
Maslow, A. (1999). *Towards A Psychology of Being*. New York: John Wiley & Sons.
May, R. (1994). *The Courage to Create*. New York: W W Norton & Co.
McGrath, A. (1997). *Christian Theology.* Oxford: Blackwell.
McGrath, A. (2013). *C S Lewis: A Life*. London: Hodder & Stoughton.
McIntyre, J. (1987). *Faith Theology and Imagination*. Edinburgh: The Handsel Press.
Meilaender, G. (2009). *Neither Beast Nor God.* New York: Encounter Books.
Messer, N. (2006). *Christian Ethics*. London: SCM Press.
Mickens, R. (2014). UN condemns Holy See over sex abuse. *The Tablet*, (8 February).
Miller, A. (2008). The Crucible. Retrieved from http://www.studymode.com/essays/The-Crucible-166136.html
Milner, M. (1957). *On Not Being Able to Paint*. London: Heinmann.
Morris, R. (2000). *Cheshire: The Biography of Leonard Cheshire*. London: Viking.
Mountford, B. (2005). *Perfect Freedom*. Ropley, Hants: O Books.
Muggeridge, M. (1971). *Something Beautiful for God*. London: Collins.

Murdoch, I. (2001). *The Sovereignty of Good*. London: Routledge Classics.

Norwich, J. (1973). *The Revelations of Divine Love*. Wheathampstead: Anthony Clarke Books.

O'Donohue, J. (2003). *Divine Beauty*. London: Bantam Press.

O'Leary, D. (2012). Grace and Radiance. *The Tablet*, (24 November).

Obama, B. (2007). *The Audacity of Hope*. London: Canongate.

Oppenheimer, H. (1974). *The Character of Christian Morality*. Leighton Buzzard, Beds: The Faith Press.

Otto, R. (1968). *The Idea of the Holy*. Oxford: Oxford University Press.

Pearce, F. (2007). But here's what they didn't tell us. *New Scientist*. (Feb)

Phillips, J. B. (1969). *Your God is Too Small*. London: The Epworth Press.

Pieper, J. (2007). *The Four Cardinal Virtues*. Indiana, USA: University of Notre Dame Press.

Pierce, G. A. (1878). *The Dickins Dictionary*. London: Chapman & Hall.

Pomeroy, R. (2002). *Paul Tillich: A Theology for the 21st Century*. USA: iUniverse.

Radhakrishnan, S. (2013). *Indian Philosophy Vol II*. India: Bane389.

Reid, M. (2013). Hope Springs Eternal. *The Times*. (7 Sep).

Robinson, J. (1963). *Honest to God*. London: SCM Press.

Robinson, J. (1973). *The Human Face of God*. London: SCM Press.

Russell, B. (2009). *The Basic Writings of Bertrand Russsell*. London: Routledge Classics.

Sacks, J. (2009). Credo. *The Times*. Retrieved from www.thetimes .co.uk/tto/faith/article2100091.ece

Schweitzer, A. (2000). *The Quest of the Historical Jesus*. London: SCM Press.

Scruton, R. (2011). *Beauty: A Very Short Introduction*. Oxford: Oxford University Press.

Smith, C., Emerson, M. O., & Snell, P. (2008). *Passing the Plate.* Oxford: Oxford University Press.

Sobrino, J. (2008). *The Eye of the Needle.* London: Darton, Longman & Todd.

Solzhenitsyn, A. (1978). *A World Split Apart.* New York: Harper & Row.

Spong, J. S. (2002). *A New Christianity for a New World.* San Fransisco: Harper Collins.

Spong, J. S. (2013). *The Fourth Gospel: Tales of a Jewish Mystic.* New York: Harper Collins.

Stackhouse, M. (1997). Humanism after Tillich. *First Things,* (April).

Sykes, W. (1992). *Visions of Love.* London: Bible Reading Fellowship.

Sykes, W. (2002). *The Eternal Vision.* Norwich: Canterbury Press.

Taylor, J. (1972). *The Go-Between God.* London: SCM Press.

Teasdale, W. (2001). *The Mystic Heart.* Novato CA: New World Library.

Teilhard de Chardin, P. (1965). *The Phenomenon of Man.* London: Fontana Books.

Thompson, D. P. (1971). *Eric H Liddell.* Crieff, Scotland: The Research Unit.

Tilby, A. (1990). Jung Among the Christians. *The Way, Supplement* (Autumn 1990).

Tillich, P. (1971). *Love, Power, and Justice.* London: Oxford University Press.

Tillich, P. (2001). *Dynamics of Faith.* New York: Harper & Row.

Tillich, P. (1963). *The Eternal Now.* London: SCM Press.

Tillich, P. (1964). *The Shaking of the Foundations.* London: Penguin Books.

Tillich, P. (1965). The Right to Hope. Retrieved from http://www.religion-online.org/showarticle.asp?title=62

Tillich, P. (2000). *The Courage to Be.* New York: Yale University Press.

Tutu, D. (1984). *Hope and Suffering*. London: Collins.

Tutu, D. (2004). *God has a Dream*. London: Ebury Publishing.

Tutu, D., & Tutu, M. (2010). *Made for Goodness*. London: Ebury Publishing.

Underhill, E. (2009). *Mysticism*. Digireads.com. Kindle file.

United Nations. (1948). Universal Declaration of Human Rights. Retrieved from http://www.un.org/en/documents/udhr/

Vallely, P. (2013). *Pope Francis: Untying the Knots*. London: Bloosbury Publishing.

Vardy, P., & Grosch, P. (2002). *The Puzzle of Ethics*. London: Fount.

Wallace-Hadrill, D. (1990). *No Title*. Unpublished manuscript.

Walsh, K. (1973). *Sometimes I Weep*. London. SCM Press.

Ward, K. (1996). *God, Chance and Necessity*. Oxford: Oneworld Publications.

Ware, T. (1982). *The Orthodox Church*. London: Penguin Books.

Weil, S. (1959). *Waiting on God*. London: Fontana Books.

Williams, R. (2002). *Writing in the Dust*. London: Hodder & Stoughton.

Williams, R. (2006). *The importance of trust*. Retrieved from www.churchtimes.co.uk/articles/2004/2-january/news/the-importance-of-trust

Winterson, J. (2006a). Summer Solstice. *The Times*. (24 Jun)

Winterson, J. (2006b). *Weight:* Edinburgh: Canongate Books.

Wright, J. (2004). *The Jesuits*. London: Harper Perennial.

Wright, T. (2012). *Twelve Months of Sundays*. London: SPCK.

Wulff, D. M. (1997). *Psychology of Religion*. New York: John Wiley & Sons.

CHRISTIAN
ALTERNATIVE

Throughout the two thousand years of Christian tradition there have been, and still are, groups and individuals that exist in the margins and upon the edge of faith. But in Christianity's contrapuntal history it has often been these outcasts and pioneers that have forged contemporary orthodoxy out of former radicalism as belief evolves to engage with and encompass the ever-changing social and scientific realities. Real faith lies not in the comfortable certainties of the Orthodox, but somewhere in a half-glimpsed hinterland on the dirt track to Emmaus, where the Death of God meets the Resurrection, where the supernatural Christ meets the historical Jesus, and where the revolution liberates both the oppressed and the oppressors.

Welcome to Christian Alternative... a space at the edge where the light shines through.